Taunton's COMPLETE ILLUSTRATED *Guide to*

Woodworking

Taunton's COMPLETE ILLUSTRATED *Guide to*

Woodworking

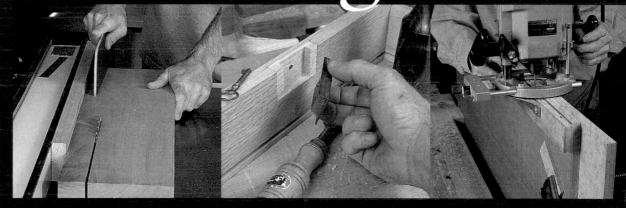

LONNIE BIRD
JEFF JEWITT
THOMAS LIE-NIELSEN
ANDY RAE
GARY ROGOWSKI

The Taunton Press

The Taunton Press
Inspiration for hands-on living®

The Taunton Press, Inc., 63 South Main Street, PO Box 5506, Newtown, CT 06470-5506
e-mail: tp@taunton.com

Taunton's Complete Illustrated Guide to Woodworking was originally published in 2005 in hardcover by The Taunton Press, Inc.

EDITOR: Helen Albert
DESIGN: Lori Wendin
LAYOUT: Cathy Cassidy

ILLUSTRATOR: Mario Perro

PHOTOGRAPHERS: Lonnie Bird, Andy Rae, Gary Rogowski, Scott Gibson, Susn Lawson Jewitt,
David L. Minick, Vincent Laurence

LIBRARY OF CONGRESS CATALOGING-IN-PUBLICATION DATA:

Taunton's complete illustrated guide to woodworking / Lonnie Bird ... [et al.].
    p. cm.
  Includes index.
  ISBN-13: 978-1-56158-769-8 hardcover
  ISBN-10: 1-56158-769-9 hardcover
  ISBN-13: 978-1-60085-302-9 paperback
  ISBN-10: 1-60085-302-1 paperback
  1. Woodwork. 2. Woodworking tools. I. Title: Complete illustrated guide to woodworking. II. Bird, Lonnie. III. Taunton Press.
  TT180.T28 2005
  684'.082--dc22
  2004028678

Printed in the United States
10 9 8 7 6 5 4 3 2 1

The following manufacturers/names appearing in *Taunton's Complete Illustrated Guide to Woodworking* are trademarks: Bessey®, Biesemeyer®,
Festool®, Lufkin®, Omnijig®, Space Balls®, Stanley®, Starrett®, Tormek®, Veritas®, X-Acto®

About Your Safety: Working with wood is inherently dangerous. Using hand or power tools improperly or ignoring safety practices can lead to permanent injury or even death. Don't try to perform operations you learn about here (or elsewhere) unless you're certain they are safe for you. If something about an operation doesn't feel right, don't do it. Look for another way. We want you to enjoy the craft, so please keep safety foremost in your mind whenever you're in the shop.

To Tage Frid (1915-2004), whose teaching and writing helped generations of woodworkers learn the craft.

Acknowledgments

B ack in 1998 our publisher suggested that we consider revising *Tage Frid Teaches Woodworking.* On second look, we discovered just how pertinent both the information and the format remain. Ultimately, we decided that Frid's classic reference should be allowed to endure "as is."

Instead, we started afresh and began to create *The Complete Illustrated Guides* series. Lonnie Bird, Andy Rae, and Gary Rogowski had more than seventy-five years of experience among them as professional woodworkers, teachers and authors, but they hardly knew what they were getting into when we met together in Newtown, Connecticut, in January of 1999. Not only did they write over 1,000 pages for *Joinery, Shaping Wood,* and *Furniture and Cabinet Construction,* they took over 3,000 photographs and contributed hundreds of drawings to illustrate the first three books.

Next, we turned to toolmaker Thomas Lie-Nielsen to author *Sharpening,* and chose finishing and refinishing expert Jeff Jewitt to write *Finishing.* Jeff's wife, Susan Lawson Jewitt, contributed the photographs for his book. Scott Gibson ably edited and took the photography for *Sharpening.* Tony O'Malley edited Lonnie Bird's *Using Woodworking Tools,* while Paul Anthony served as developmental editor for *Finishing* and Andy Rae's *Working Wood.*

Meanwhile, at The Taunton Press, Paula Schlosser and Jennifer Renjilian worked with me to develop the visual concept and finding devices in the books. Rosalind Wanke managed the design and layout of thousands of pages. Jenny Peters coordinated acres of manuscript and, with Wendy Mijal, scores of photo CDs and cartons of 35 mm slides.

It's been a real privilege to work with so many knowledgeable and creative individuals in publishing *The Complete Illustrated Guides.* Special thanks to publisher Jim Childs for being willing to take on the risk of this enormous project and to our finance manager, Kathy Worth, who bluntly told me that I was crazy, but that it was a good idea anyway.

Contents

> **SECTION 1** **The Workshop** 6

> **SECTION 2** **Outfitting the Shop** 10

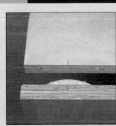

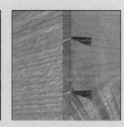

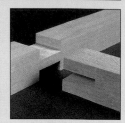

Introduction

PART OF THE APPEAL OF WOOD-WORKING is the wide range of tasks that go into making even a simple piece of furniture. We begin by milling wood square and then dimension it to make parts. To make a piece that will endure the stresses of seasonal wood movement, we cut joints to hold the parts together. To add interest to a piece, we can shape wood by adding curves, moldings, and edge treatments. Along the way we set up, use, and sharpen tools. Finally, we apply a finish to protect the wood and bring out its beauty.

Woodworking is a craft that has evolved over millennia, resulting in a multitude of methods to accomplish all these tasks, from the low tech approach of hand tools to the speed and efficiency of sophisticated machines. Choosing the right method for you depends on many factors, including your skill level, the tools in your shop, and whether you need to work quickly or can take the time to savor the process. And for many of us, the process is the purpose. It's the pleasure and satisfaction of working wood, whatever technique you choose.

This book collects in one volume the essential information that every woodworker needs to know, no matter their skill level. It's taken from the subject-specific books in *The Complete Illustrated Guides* series: *Joinery, Furniture and Cabinet Construction, Shaping Wood, Finishing, Sharpening, Using Woodworking Tools,* and *Working Wood.* The selections included here are my own, based on teaching woodworking classes and editing woodworking books for the last dozen years. If you don't find your pet technique, please accept my apologies. A single concise shop reference must have, by definition, limits.

If you own the volumes that comprise *The Complete Illustrated Guides,* this book is a manual you can leave in the shop as a basic reference. If you're just starting out in woodworking, it can be your guide to the skills and techniques you'll need to master to become a woodworker. Wherever you are in your woodworking path, I hope *The Complete Guide to Woodworking* gives you a taste of the rich variety of ways to work wood and keeps you coming back to the shop to learn more.

—Helen Albert,
Executive Editor
Taunton Books

How to Use This Book

FIRST OF ALL, this book is meant to be used, not put on a shelf to gather dust. It's meant to be pulled out and opened on your bench when you need to do a new or unfamiliar technique. So the first way to use this book is to make sure it's near where you do woodworking.

In the pages that follow you'll find a wide variety of methods that cover many of the important processes of woodworking. Just as in other practical areas, in woodworking there are often many ways to get to the same result. Why you choose one method over another depends on several factors:

Time. Are you in a hurry or do you have the leisure to enjoy the quiet that comes with hand tools?

Your tooling. Do you have the kind of shop that's the envy of every woodworker or a modest collection of the usual hand and power tools?

Your skill level. Do you prefer simpler methods because you're starting out or are you always looking to challenge yourself and expand your skills?

The project. Is the piece you're making utilitarian or an opportunity to show off your best work?

In this book, we've included a wide variety of techniques to fit these needs.

To find your way around the book, you first need to ask yourself two questions: What result am I trying to achieve? What tools do I want to use to accomplish it?

In some cases, there are many ways and many tools that will accomplish the same result. In others, there are only one or two sensible ways to do it. In all cases, however, we've taken a practical approach; so you may not find your favorite exotic method for doing a particular process. We have included every reasonable method and then a few just to flex your woodworking muscles.

To organize the material, we've broken the subject down to two levels. "Parts" are major divisions of this class of techniques. "Sections" contain related techniques. Within sections, techniques and procedures that create a similar result are grouped together, usually organized from the most common way to do it to methods requiring specialized tools or a larger degree of skill. In some cases, the progression starts with the method requiring the most basic technology and then moves on to alternative methods using other common shop tools and finally to specialized tools.

The first thing you'll see in a part is a group of photos keyed to a page number. Think of this as an illustrated table of contents. Here you'll see a photo representing each section in that part, along with the page on which each section starts.

Each section begins with a similar "visual map," with photos that represent major groupings of techniques or individual techniques. Under each grouping is a list of the step-by-step essays that explain how to do the methods, including the pages on which they can be found.

Sections begin with an "overview," or brief introduction, to the methods described therein. Here's where you'll find important general information on this group of techniques, including any safety issues. You'll also read about specific tools needed for the operations that follow and how to build jigs or fixtures needed for them.

The step-by-step essays are the heart of this book. Here a group of photos represents the key steps in the process. The accompanying text describes the process and guides you through it, referring you back to the photos. Depending on how you learn best, either read the text first or look at the photos and drawings; but remember, they are meant to work together. In cases where there is an

The "VISUAL MAP" tells you where to locate the essay that details the operation you wish to do.

A "SECTION" groups related processes together.

The "OVERVIEW" gives you important general information about the group of techniques, tells you how to build jigs and fixtures, and provides advice on tooling and safety.

alternative step, it's called out in the text and the visual material as a "variation."

For efficiency, we've cross-referenced redundant processes or steps described in another related process. You'll see yellow "cross-references" called out frequently in the overviews and step-by-step essays.

When you see this symbol ⚠, make sure you read what follows. The importance of these safety warnings cannot be overemphasized. Always work safely and use safety devices, including eye and hearing protection. If you feel uncomfortable with a technique, don't do it, try another way.

At the back of the book is an index to help you find what you're looking for in a pinch. There's also list of further reading to help you brush up on how to use tools and keep them sharp, as well as some general references on design.

Finally, remember to use this book whenever you need to refresh your memory or to learn something new. It's been designed to be an essential reference to help you become a better woodworker. The only way it can do this is if you make it as familiar a workshop tool as your favorite bench chisels.

–The editors

"STEP-BY-STEP ESSAYS" contain photos, drawings, and instructions on how to do the technique.

"CROSS-REFERENCES" tell you where to find a related process or the detailed description of a process in another essay.

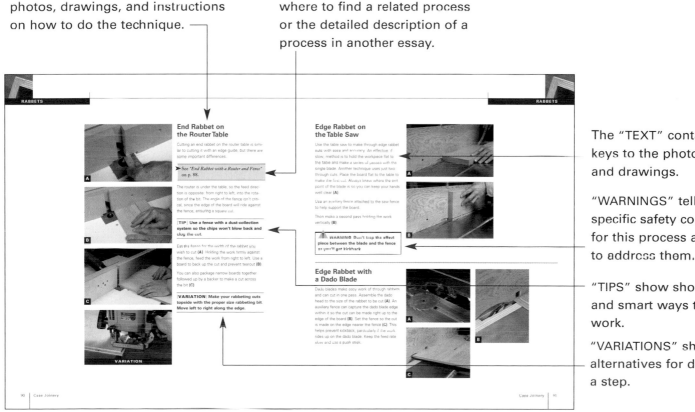

The "TEXT" contains keys to the photos and drawings.

"WARNINGS" tell you specific safety concerns for this process and how to address them.

"TIPS" show shortcuts and smart ways to work.

"VARIATIONS" show alternatives for doing a step.

The Workshop

BUILDING FURNITURE AND CABINETS brings immense satisfaction. But frustration often blocks our aims. I remember the aggravation I encountered starting out, working in a cramped studio space with very few tools. My first attempts at building furniture were clouded with problems. Attempts at making an accurate cut often ended up in less-than-satisfactory results, due to a combination of poor light, confined space, and tools pushed far beyond their capacities. Looking back, I think there's a better way.

The following paragraphs are written with the intention of steering you clear of the frustrations I faced as a fledgling furniture maker. I'll talk about some essential gear you'll need for years of satisfying woodworking. But by no means should you consider these items sacred. I mention them as a guide only. Some gear I consider essential for constructing cabinets and furniture, such as a table saw and good light. Other "necessities" are handy to have, but you can always make do with less.

The fact is, almost all the woodworking operations and techniques that I describe in this book can be accomplished with a variety of tools, not just the ones I show. If you don't own a jointer, try jointing with a handplane. Or use a handsaw if you can't get to a motorized version. The point is to make do with what you have. We all start woodworking this way. As you learn the craft, you'll build up not only your tool collection but your hard-won skills.

Shop Space and Fixtures

Certain items for the woodworking shop are necessary, and for the most part they're easy to come by. Good light is essential. If you can't get natural light, use a combination of incandescent and fluorescent. Incandescent clamp-on spotlights, or task lights, are cheap and allow you to position the light right where you need it. Overhead fluorescent fixtures can brighten a room considerably.

[TIP] You can buy lamps with magnets on their bases from many woodworking suppliers. The magnet clamps to any ferrous metal surface, making it possible to position a light on a woodworking machine, such as a bandsaw, for a better view of the cutting action.

When laying out your work space, make sure you allocate enough room for assembly. Cabinets, with their multitude of parts and pieces, can quickly overcome a small room. One answer is to make your machines and fixtures moveable, so your can clear a space when necessary.

► See *"Mobilize Your Workshop"* on p. 9.

Another is to group core machines together in a central hub, such as the table saw, jointer, and planer. And don't overlook heating your work space. Not only will you and your hands be comfortable but most finishes and glues can't survive temperatures below 65°F.

For me, the workbench is the heart of my shop, where some of the most important action takes place. Scrimp on or skip this tool at your own peril. A workbench should be solid, sturdy, and stout. The top should be flat, so you can reference your work on it, and the top and base should be heavy, to resist the pounding, pushing, and pulling that takes place on it.

Plywood clamped to sawhorses can make a bench, but it won't compare to the sheer mass and work-holding capacity of a European-style joiner's bench. Its broad, heavy top is ideal for joinery and layout tasks. This style of bench has a tail vise and a series of angled holes in the vise and along the top of the bench into which you place a pair of

bench dogs made from wood or metal. By placing a workpiece between two dogs and tightening the vise, you can pull the work flat to the benchtop. This is useful for carving and cutting operations and is especially well suited for handplaning.

Another effective means of clamping work tight to your benchtop is to drill a hole right through the top, and pound a holdfast over your workpiece. Be sure to use some scrap stock to prevent the holdfast from marring your work. I had a metal-working friend make my holdfast, but they're commonly available from woodworking catalogs.

At the far end of the bench, the shoulder vise is ideal for holding long boards on edge or for grasping tapered or irregular work-

Pinching the workpiece between bench dogs helps pull it flat to the benchtop, especially useful when handplaning.

A holdfast uses a wedging action through the bench-top to keep a piece in position for handwork, especially for carving or chopping tasks.

The open jaws of a shoulder vise allow larger workpieces to pass right through for easy clamping. The vise has a swiveling jaw to provide even pressure onto tapered workpieces.

A low work table for assembly, clamping, and sanding will help save your back.

ASSEMBLY TABLE

Plywood or MDF, 1 in. thick, edged with hardwood

40 in.

60 in.

³/₄-in. plywood spine

Wooden runners guide bins.

This side open for storing large items.

Plastic bin for screws.

25 in.

3 in.

3 in.

³/₄-in. plywood

Make rails from 2-in.-thick hardwood.

pieces, since the jaw pivots to accommodate angles. Best of all, there are no obstructions or hardware between the jaws, so long work can pass right through the vise. You can build your own bench, as I did and as many other woodworkers do (see *The Workbench Book*, by Scott Landis, The Taunton Press), or buy a commercial bench from a wood-working catalog or store.

An assembly table does well to comple-ment the workbench, as shown at left. Its low working surface lets you work on large assemblies with good control and comfort. And it works overtime as a glue-up table or a platform for applying finishes. You can also make good use of the space below for storing screws, hardware, clamping devices, and other tools.

Keeping your tools organized will make them accessible; a tool cabinet serves this purpose, especially if you keep it near your workbench. I recommend building your own so you can lay out the interior to fit specific tools. It's a good idea to construct lots of shallow drawers and cubbyholes or to hang tools from box-type doors, dedicating specific spots for their storage. This way, you can get to a tool in an instant—and see when it's missing. (For more ideas and information on building your own toolbox, see *The Toolbox Book*, Jim Tolpin, The Taunton Press.)

As you read through this book, you'll notice plenty of smaller jigs and fixtures. Shopmade jigs complement a tool or a pro-cedure, making construction easier or more accurate—or a combination of the two. The more furniture you build, the more jigs you'll acquire. You'll even—I hope—devise a few jigs yourself for some of the woodworking procedures shown in this book. Write notes

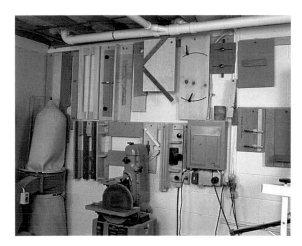

Running cleats along an open wall provides room to store your collection of jigs and fixtures.

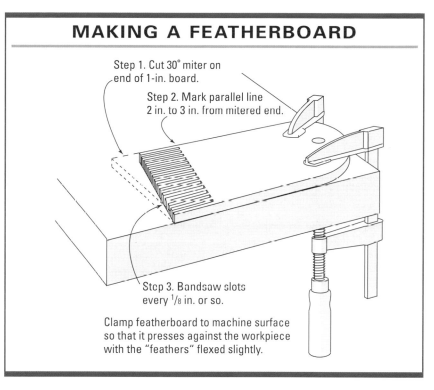

MAKING A FEATHERBOARD

Step 1. Cut 30° miter on end of 1-in. board.

Step 2. Mark parallel line 2 in. to 3 in. from mitered end.

Step 3. Bandsaw slots every $\frac{1}{8}$ in. or so.

Clamp featherboard to machine surface so that it presses against the workpiece with the "feathers" flexed slightly.

directly on your jigs; then the next time you use them, you'll have all the set-up information at your fingertips.

Keep some basic materials on hand for making jigs. Medium-density fiberboard (MDF) and Baltic birch (multi-ply) plywood are great; and pneumatic (air-driven) staples or brads and glue afford a quick way of putting jigs together. Build them fast, but make sure they're accurately constructed, so they work with precision. Don't fuss too much over a jig's aesthetics. Remember that jigs are only aids to the more important stuff, the actual furniture you make. When your shop starts to overflow with jigs and fixtures, keep them organized where you can get at them. A wall is handy spot.

Mobilize Your Workshop

One of the most efficient moves I ever made in outfitting my shop was to put wheels on almost all of my major machines and fixtures. Mobilizing your tools makes it easy to reorganize areas when needed.

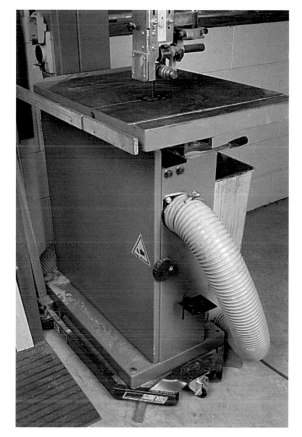

A mobile base allows you to move heavy machines and equipment easily. Make sure power runs through extra-long wires.

Outfitting
the Shop

Before spending a lot of money on tools and equipment, consider the area of woodworking you would like to pursue. For example, if you're primarily interested in constructing kitchen cabinets and built-ins, you'll probably need more power tools and the space to operate them. However, if you enjoy carving, the bandsaw and a lathe are perhaps the only machines you'll need.

No matter what, you should obtain a sturdy workbench, along with a vise and clamps for holding work. When considering hand tools for purchase, buy the best you can afford; cheap hand tools are no bargain and tend to lead only to frustration. In the following section, I'll guide you through many of the tools and machines that you should consider for your shop.

Holding the Work

While sawing, planing, chiseling, and routing, you'll need a sturdy workbench to hold the work. Your workbench need not be fancy, but it should be strong and heavy to resist pounding and racking. Additionally, the best workbench is one that fits you, so I would avoid purchasing this essential tool unless you can modify the height to suit your height and needs. Consider buying the materials and making it yourself to fit your height and the space available in your shop. To hold the workpiece, you'll need to outfit your bench with a vise. Purchase the largest vise you can afford and mount it on one corner of your bench so you'll have the greatest access to the workpiece.

Good lighting is important, too. Locate your bench near a window to take advantage of the natural light. And use plenty of electrical lighting as well; fluorescent lights work well overhead while incandescent fixtures provide close-up lighting.

A solid workbench is an essential tool for any woodworking shop.

Handscrews apply broad clamping pressure, even on nonparallel surfaces.

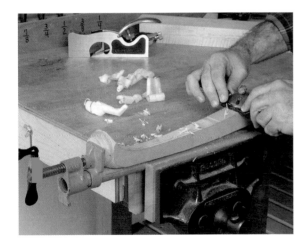

A strong vise completes the workbench. A pipe clamp locked in a vise is a great way to hold irregular work, such as this cabriole leg.

Clamps play an important role in any shop; they hold glued-up assemblies while the glue sets, and they secure work to the benchtop. The old favorites, such as pipe clamps and handscrew clamps, are versatile performers and a great choice for your first clamp purchases. Later on, as your woodworking skills and shop expand, you can purchase more clamps as the specific need arises.

Pipe clamps are inexpensive and useful for a wide array of assembly tasks.

A modest tool kit consists of a few planes, a couple of chisels, and a dove-tail saw.

Chisels are available in a variety of shapes and sizes to suit the job at hand.

Carving chisels and gouges let you create fine details that can only be done with handwork.

Edge Tools

Edge tools include chisels, planes, handsaws, scrapers, and gouges for turning and carving. This collection of hand tools shapes, cuts, smoothes, and otherwise creates the details in the furniture that machines simply cannot.

Chisels are available in various shapes, widths, and lengths. The most common, bench chisels, are used to cut joinery and fit hinges and other hardware. Carving and turning gouges create shapes for adding decorative embellishments to your work. For the greatest control with any chisel or gouge, it is important to keep it sharp.

Planes are the workhorses among hand tools and are used for smoothing, shaping, and fitting joints. A finely tuned bench plane will create a smoother surface than any sander. Bench planes can also be used for flattening and squaring stock that is too large for your jointer. For one-handed trimming and fitting, especially of small parts, include a block plane in your tool kit; low-angle block planes are ideal for trimming end grain. Shoulder planes are finely tuned

A bench plane, shoulder plane, and block plane form the foundation of a versatile plane kit.

The block plane excels at light trimming.

Molding planes create profiles with a hand-made look.

precision tools designed for careful fitting of joints. They feature precisely ground soles and irons for removing feathery-thin shavings.

Wooden molding planes feature a profiled sole and matching iron that create a contoured surface. Many molding planes, such as hollows and rounds, were once produced in mass quantity and are still available today. These beautiful old planes are still useful for shaping large moldings beyond the capabilities of your router table.

➤ HOW EDGE TOOLS CUT

You'll be able to sharpen, tune, and use your edge tools most effectively, and you'll get more enjoyment from them, if you understand the dynamics of the cutting edge.

An edge is formed by two surfaces that intersect; the angle and sharpness of the intersection directly affects how well the edge cuts. A sharply honed edge will slice the wood and create a thin, delicate shaving while a dull edge works more like a thick wedge to splinter the wood.

A low-bevel angle, 20 degrees, for example, will slice more cleanly and with less resistance than a higher angle of 30 degrees. Of course, there are trade-offs, too. A lower angle weakens the edge, which makes it prone to fracturing. (This is why you should avoid striking paring chisels with a mallet.) Also, a lower-bevel angle is not as effective at breaking and curling the shaving, which can lead to tearout in difficult grain (such as curly maple).

A higher-bevel angle, such as 30 degrees, is stronger (which is why it works well for mortising chisels) but also has a greater cutting resistance. An angle of 25 degrees is a compromise that works well for most chisels and plane irons.

A plane is essentially a souped-up chisel. As the cutting edge lifts the shaving, the sole holds it down while the cap iron breaks and curls it. This is why it is essential to set the cap iron close to the edge of the blade and close the mouth of the plane as tightly as possible.

The spokeshave is a small plane ideal for smoothing curves.

All backsaws have a thickened back edge, which stiffens the blade for cutting fine joinery.

A rip-tooth saw works best for dovetails.

A bench hook is a companion to the backsaw; it cradles the workpiece perfectly as the cut is made.

When smoothing bandsawn surfaces, I reach for a spokeshave. This small plane has a short sole and handles on each side, which makes it the ideal tool for smoothing curved stock.

Handsaws are for cutting fine joinery and cutting away large portions of stock before planes refine the surface. Dovetail joinery, for example, is cut with a small backsaw, known as a dovetail saw. Backsaws work best for joinery because they cut a fine kerf, and the back is reinforced with a brass or steel spine. Coping saws have a narrow blade designed for cutting curves and scrollwork.

Saws are designated by the teeth, either rip or crosscut. Rip teeth are designed for cutting parallel to the grain, while crosscut teeth are shaped like tiny knives to cleanly sever the wood when cutting across the grain.

Western saws cut on the push stroke while Japanese saws cut on the pull stroke. Their smooth yet aggressive cutting has

Scratch stock are quiet tools for scraping simple profiles.

The cabinet scraper will smooth even the most difficult woods.

made Japanese saws a favorite among many woodworkers.

You can cut your sanding time more than in half by using a scraper. This tool smoothes wood with a small burr, and when sharp, it produces shavings like a plane yet it doesn't tear the wood like a plane sometimes can. A scratch stock is a profiled scraper used for shaping small moldings. This is another tool that will shape profiles that are difficult or impossible to shape with a router.

Measuring and Marking Tools

The old adage "measure twice, cut once" is still good advice. Most every woodworking project begins with careful measuring and marking, otherwise known as layout. Layout tools consist of rules, tapes, squares, dividers, and marking knives, to name a few.

The 6-ft.-folding-wood rule is still my favorite tool for measuring. This vintage-style rule folds compactly to slip easily into a pocket. Steel tapes quickly retract onto a spool for storage and are useful for measuring long lengths of rough lumber.

Accurate layout work begins with an assortment of essential layout tools.

The folding rule, though less common than the measuring tape, is still an accurate and convenient measuring tool.

A machinist-quality combination square should be among the first layout tool purchases.

The bevel gauge is used to lay out, copy, and transfer angles.

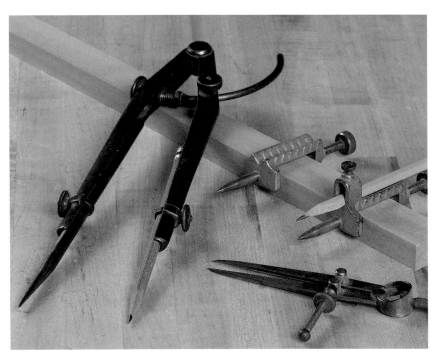

Trammel points, the compass, and dividers are useful for layout of circles and arcs.

A reliable square is a tool that no shop should be without. My favorite is a 12-in. combination square. This multipurpose tool serves as an inside square, outside square, 45-degree square, depth gauge, and straight-edge. Get the machinist-quality square; those sold at home centers lack the quality and accuracy for fine work.

The sliding-bevel gauge is used for laying out and checking angles other than 90 degrees. The steel blade pivots and locks in place at virtually any angle.

Dividers, trammel points, and compasses all mark a space between two points. Dividers are used to transfer measurements and step off linear dimensions. The compass is similar to a divider, except a pencil is substituted for one of the points. The compass is the tool of choice for drawing small arcs and circles. Trammels are used for drawing large circles, such as a tabletop, that are beyond the reach

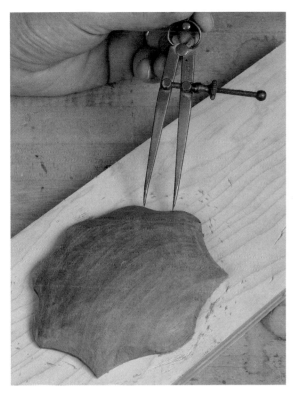

Dividers measure and allow you to transfer points on irregular shapes, such as carvings.

Trammels are used to lay out circles and ellipses.

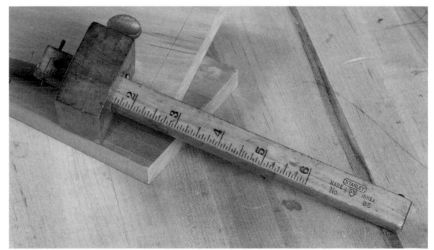

A marking gauge inscribes the wood with a tiny knife.

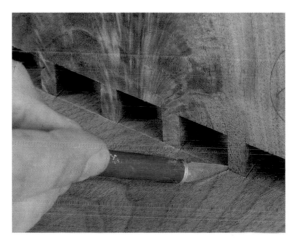

A marking knife is an essential layout tool.

of a compass. Trammels come in a pair and clamp to a stick of any length. By adding a third trammel to the stick, you can draw an ellipse.

A marking gauge and layout knife belong in every tool kit. These tools incise the wood, unlike a pencil, and create a sharp guideline for chiseling and sawing. The best marking gauges have a graduated beam that makes it easier to set the tool for a precise measurement. Although you can purchase expensive layout knives with rosewood handles, an X-Acto® knife is inexpensive, and the thin blade reaches into areas that are inaccessible to larger knives. And when the blade dulls, you can toss it out and replace it with a new one.

No shop should be without an assortment of hammers and mallets.

A dead-blow mallet (far right) provides a controlled, non-marring impact for assembly.

Hammers and Striking Tools

Hammers, mallets, and other striking tools are used to deliver a precise impact. Hammers are used to drive nails and brads and feature a crowned, or convex, face that helps prevent marring of the wood surface.

Dead-blow mallets feature a shot-filled head that eliminates bouncing upon impact. For assembling joints and casework, a dead-blow mallet is used for gently tapping parts into alignment.

Carving mallets are used to direct controlled force to a chisel or carving gouge. Some are made of dense tropical hardwood, while others feature a urethane head fitted to a wood handle. When selecting hammers and mallets for woodworking, choose the lighter ones, typically those that weigh under a pound. Greater force just simply isn't needed for most woodworking, and heavy mallets are both tiring and awkward to use.

After you've acquired a solid mix of hand tools, keep them organized and within easy reach. Small tools, such as chisels, squares, and files, store easily in a rack. The rack can be wall-mounted or attached to the back of your bench.

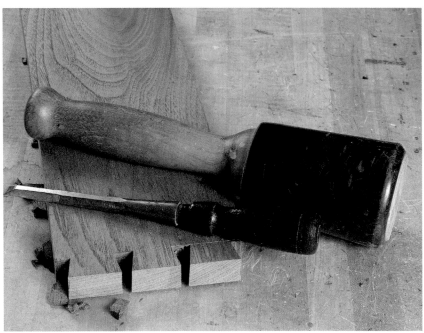

Carving mallets come in a variety of sizes for delivering a precise blow to gouges and chisels.

▶ THE ESSENTIAL PLANE KIT

If you are new to woodworking and have not begun to acquire planes, you may be wondering where to start. A bench plane is a good first choice. Once you learn to use this essential tool, you'll reach for it often for smoothing panels, fitting drawers, and leveling joints at assemblies.

Woodworkers disagree on the optimum size for a smooth plane; no doubt that's why there have always been a number of different sizes from which to choose. I feel that the No. 4 is the best choice for the first smoother. The plane has enough weight to give it power through the stroke, yet it has excellent balance and maneuverability. Close cousins to the No. 4, the No. 3 is just slightly too small and light, and the No. 4½ is a bit heavy.

The bench, block, and shoulder planes (right to left) are essential for any furniture craftsman.

Later on, consider adding a No. 6 or No. 7 to your tool kit. Either of these bench planes will allow you to flatten wide boards that exceed the width of your jointer. They're also useful for fine-tuning the edges of stock before glue-up.

The second plane on my list of essential hand tools would be a block plane. This small, one-handed plane can be used for a number of light tasks, from smoothing the end grain of a small tabletop to fitting small drawers to light chamfering and shaping. Look for a low-angle plane with an adjustable mouth.

The third and final plane on my essentials list would be a shoulder plane. Unlike the previous two planes on the list, this tool has open sides at the mouth so it can trim into corners. Shoulder planes are the best tools for trimming and fitting tenons to their mortises. Although I prefer a large shoulder plane, one of the fine-quality smaller planes is a good choice.

Determining what to add to your list of planes will become easier once you've mastered using these three. As your woodworking knowledge and skills increase, you'll develop your own working style, and you can add planes as the need for them arises.

A storage cabinet will organize and protect your hand tools.

A storage rack keeps chisels and gouges sharp and close at hand.

THE IMPORTANCE OF SHARP TOOLS

Sharp tools are a pleasure to use, as they slice thin shavings and leave the surface of the wood glistening. Sharpness gives you much better control of the tool and enables you to do your finest, most precise work. Sharp tools slice and shear the wood cleanly while dull tools crush and tear.

When I'm teaching woodworking classes, two things often surprise students—how quickly an edge dulls and yet how quickly it can be brought back to sharpness. Sure, stopping to sharpen a tool interrupts the work flow. But once you've learned the steps you'll soon be back to planing, dovetailing, and carving. You'll also have mastery of the tool, and your work will dramatically improve.

For larger tools, such as planes and saws, a cabinet works well for storage. I avoid storing tools in drawers, especially those tools I use often. Drawers easily become cluttered, and they hide their contents from view. So finding the tool you need can turn into a busy search. In contrast, cabinets and racks keep tools organized, sharp, and close at hand.

Sharpening Equipment

Although it's best to send router bits and circular saw blades out for sharpening, you'll want to sharpen your own hand tools. The steel in hand tools dulls quickly compared to the carbide on bits and saw blades, and so it isn't practical to send these tools out for sharpening. To keep your edge tools in top performance, you'll need a grinder and a set

To keep edge tools sharp, you'll need a set of sharpening stones.

Portable planers are affordable alternatives to a stationary machine.

of benchstones. Grinders feature a coarse stone wheel and rests or supports to hold the tool at the proper angle. Grinders are powerful tools that you can use to quickly restore the bevel of a chisel or plane iron. Afterwards, benchstones are used to hone the edge, which sharpens it further.

Portable Power Tools

Portable power tools allow you to take the tool to the workpiece. Sometimes the work is too heavy or awkward to maneuver through a stationary power tool. That's when portable tools, such as drills and jigsaws, take over. Some portable power tools, such as routers and miter saws, can be mounted to a table or stand and used as stationary equipment. Yet they cost much less and take up less space in your shop than large, heavy, stationary equipment.

These days, many portable power tools are cordless. They use powerful batteries that can be quickly recharged. This allows you to work without dragging an extension cord around the room.

The cordless drill has quickly become a shop favorite.

A jigsaw will cut curves on work too large to maneuver at the bandsaw.

The plate joiner cuts fast joints for simple cabinet construction.

With their narrow reciprocating blade, jigsaws excel at cutting curves. Although it won't replace the bandsaw for resawing, the jigsaw is a good option for cutting interior cuts or cutting curves on a workpiece too large to handle at the bandsaw.

Although biscuit joiners and sanders are not typically used for the finest work, these tools are great for quickly joining and sanding shop and kitchen cabinets and other less demanding jobs. Biscuit joiners use a small-diameter saw blade to cut a circular slot. The slot is cut in two mating pieces and joined with a compressed-wood plate, or "biscuit."

Portable sanders can efficiently level joints and smooth surfaces. However, these tools cut very aggressively and are not known for creating flat surfaces, so their best use is on inexpensive cabinetry. To smooth your finest work, reach for your bench plane and scraper.

Power sanders don't leave the surfaces flat, so avoid using them on your finest work.

The router is one of the most useful tools you can own.

The router table has replaced the shaper in many small shops.

Over the past few years, routers have dramatically changed woodworking. Once tools for shaping the edge of a tabletop or a small molding, routers can now cut joints, mortise for hinges and locks, and even shape the edges of raised panels. The transformation is due to the large selection of router bits, jigs, tables, and accessories that have been developed for this universal tool.

Although technically portable tools, routers often get the most use mounted in a table. This in effect creates a mini-shaper. Like shapers, router tables have fences and miter gauges to support and guide the workpiece. Best of all, mounting your router in a

table allows you to use large bits that would be unsafe otherwise.

Fixed-base routers feature a motor that mounts in the router base and locks in place. Plunge routers are designed so that the motor and bit can be lowered into the workpiece while running. Plunge routers are most useful for cutting mortises and other types of joinery, using a jig to guide the cut.

Miter Saw

The popularity of the electric miter saw (sometimes called a chopsaw) has almost led to the extinction of the radial-arm saw. It's a portable tool, found on just about any job

➤ USING A MITER SAW

Undoubtedly the most useful purpose of a miter saw is for cutting miters on moldings and trim. Equipped with a sharp crosscut blade, most miter saws will cut an extremely smooth miter that needs no further handwork before assembly.

When attaching molding to a cabinet, such as the small, dovetailed box in these photos, I begin by planing the joints flush at the intersections. Position the plane at a 45-degree angle to avoid tearing out either of the joining pieces (A). Also, check the surfaces for trueness (B). As you can imagine, it's much easier to apply molding to a straight surface.

Miter one end of the front molding first (C). Then position the molding on the cabinet (D) and mark the miter at the opposite end (E). Now attach the front molding first (F). Then apply glue (G) and attach the side returns (H).

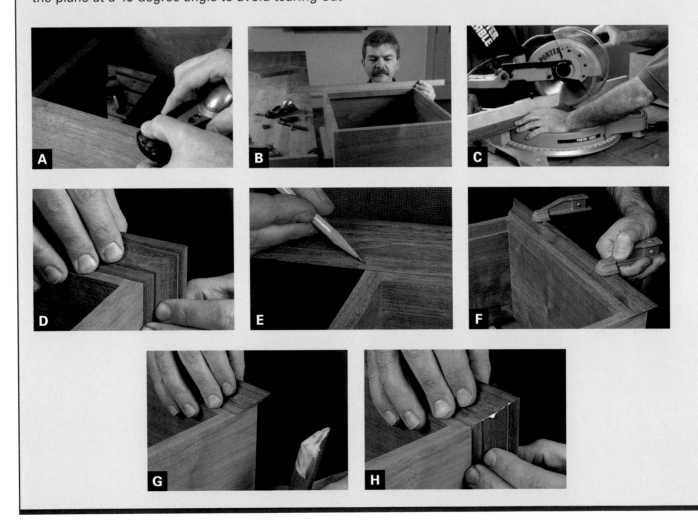

site where clean crosscuts or miters are needed. Mounted on a stand and upgraded with a high-quality blade, the miter saw functions more like a stationary power tool in most woodworking shops. It excels at making accurate, repetitive crosscuts and is far more convenient than the table saw for crosscutting long stock like moldings. The head of a sliding miter saw is mounted on rails that allow it to slide outward and cut wide stock beyond the capacity of standard miter saws. The head of a compound miter saw tilts for cutting crown molding and other work with compound angles.

When shopping for a miter saw, stick to the 10-in. models. Twelve-in.-diameter blades don't cut as accurately because the teeth are further from the support of the arbor. Besides, a 10-in.-diameter saw is large enough for most work.

Stationary Machines

Large machines have the heft and weight to dampen vibration. Generally speaking, they hold settings longer and produce smoother cuts.

Table Saw

Most people start out woodworking with a table saw. This universal machine can rip and crosscut stock to size; cut tenons, grooves and rabbets, among other joints; and even shape coves for moldings.

The cabinet-model table saw weighs in at a quarter-ton and features a cast-iron top supported by a heavy-gauge steel cabinet. The less expensive contractor-style saws reduce cost by using less iron and more sheet metal as well as an open stand. Either way, equip your saw with a guard and splitter and a high-quality saw blade.

A table saw is usually the first power-tool purchase. In addition to doing ripping and crosscutting, it's used for finished joinery and even shaping operations.

The jointer will true the faces and edges of stock.

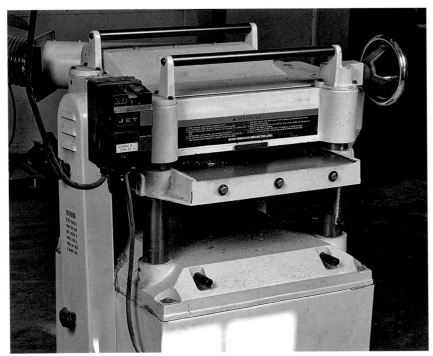

The planer is a workhorse that mills stock to size.

Jointers and Planers

Jointers and planers work as a team to flatten and square rough stock and plane it to thickness. Fortunately, as the popularity of woodworking has risen, the price of these expensive machines has come down. If you can, avoid the 6-in. jointers and purchase an 8-in. or even a 12-in. machine. To create fine work, you'll want to flatten boards on the jointer before planing them to thickness. A 6-in. jointer is simply too small, and you'll often be reaching for a bench plane to flatten rough stock.

After the jointer flattens a face of the board, the planer mills stock to final thickness. Twelve-in. to 15-in. planers have become quite affordable, and this size is ideal for most small shops.

► COMBINE MACHINES AND HAND TOOLS TO BEST ADVANTAGE

Hand tools are a pleasure to use, but I don't want to ever handplane a whole pile of lumber for a large project. A power jointer and planer are the best tools for that job. For smaller jobs, and if you don't have a jointer yet, you might flatten the first face of all your stock with a handplane, but power plane the second face with a relatively affordable portable planer. I use hand tools for creating the fine details that machines can't create.

For example, you can flatten boards with a long bench plane and winding sticks. However, you may soon become weary of this labor-intensive chore.

Instead, consider purchasing a larger jointer. A 12-in. machine will handle 90 percent of the lumber that comes through your shop. After flattening the face on the jointer to remove cup or twist, use the power planer to smooth the opposite face.

The bottom line is this: Savvy woodworkers use both power tools and hand tools. Power tools can efficiently handle the labor-intensive chores. This will give you more time to enjoy using hand tools to cut dovetails, fit drawers, and carve, as well as creating other fine details that can't be produced with machines.

The Bandsaw

Like the table saw, the bandsaw is another universal machine that will surprise you with its versatility. The bandsaw is the tool of choice for sawing curves—all types of curves from broad and sweeping to tight and scrolling. And the bandsaw is also the only machine that will resaw, or rip, a thick board into thinner ones. Resawing is a great way to save money when making small projects that require thin boards. This technique can also be used to saw your own veneer from a figured plank. But that's not all. The bandsaw will also cut surprisingly accurate joinery, such as dovetails and tenons.

The 14-in. bandsaw is a widely popular size and will handle most any sawing task, especially when equipped with a riser block, which increases the resaw capacity from 6 in. to 12 in.

In addition to cutting curves, a good bandsaw can resaw boards and rip stock to rough width more safely than the table saw.

A drill press has far more power and precision than any hand drill.

A hollow-chisel mortising machine creates precise mortises quickly and accurately.

Drill Press and Mortiser

The drill press will do what's nearly impossible with a portable drill—cut perfectly perpendicular holes. When I need a large-diameter, accurately bored hole, I turn to the drill press. Drill presses are inexpensive, and you can stretch your budget (and shop space) further with a benchtop model. If you build a dedicated stand for it, you can optimize the storage space that's wasted on a floor-model drill press.

Mortise machines are beefy little specialized drill presses. The mortise machine uses a drill enclosed within a square, hollow chisel to cut mortises. These machines will cut deep, accurate mortises quickly and efficiently. Benchtop models are inexpensive and easily stowed away inside a cabinet or in a corner when the job is finished.

The Shaper

The shaper is a powerful workhorse for shaping a kitchen full of paneled doors or miles of moldings. A shaper functions like a table-mounted router but with greater accuracy and lots more horsepower. However, this is a machine that you can postpone purchasing for a while. Later on, after you've gained plenty of experience with a router table, you'll be able to better determine whether you need a shaper.

The Lathe

The lathe spins stock while it is shaped with special gouges and chisels. You can use a lathe to turn a bowl or a decorative table leg.

Lathes vary tremendously in their size. The most common size is a 12-in. lathe with 36 in. between the head and tailstock. Before purchasing this specialized machine,

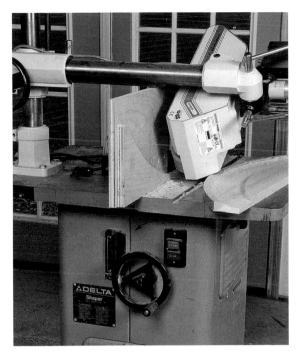

The shaper is a powerful machine that requires skill to operate effectively. Here it's shown with a power-feed attachment that ensures both accuracy and safety.

► HORSEPOWER

Consider motor horsepower when shopping for machinery. When you're making a heavy cut or during extended periods of use, motors can overheat and temporarily shut down. This can sometimes be avoided by keeping blades and cutters sharp and using a slower feed rate. But underpowered machines are no bargain. Skimping on horsepower can limit the potential use for a machine. It's important to compare horsepower when shopping for machines. Also keep in mind that when the cutter size increases (for example, from a 6-in. to an 8-in. jointer), the motor horsepower should increase as well. As you acquire woodworking machines, you may find it necessary to hire a licensed electrician to add designated electrical outlets to your shop—or perhaps even a larger service panel.

you may want to take a short course in turning to gain a few skills and determine your level of interest.

Combination Machines

As the name implies, combination machines combine the features of several machines on one piece of equipment. Most have a table saw, jointer, and planer, and perhaps a shaper. When you turn knobs and release levers, the machine makes a quick metamorphosis from one tool to another.

Although you may find it tedious to continually adapt the machine from one function to another, combination machines can be a great option for some woodworkers—specially those with limited shop space.

Acquiring Tools

If you're new to woodworking, you may find the process of purchasing so many tools exciting or overwhelming. Oftentimes woodworking catalogs promote almost every tool within the pages as one that you "must have." Also, too often jigs and gadgets are promoted as a way to avoid acquiring the skills needed for using basic tools. Just be aware that some of the finest furniture and woodwork ever produced was crafted before the age of power tools and dovetail jigs. It's tough to measure the enjoyment and satisfaction that come with using basic hand tools.

If you're excited about woodworking but are unsure of where to begin, a good place to start is with a few essential hand tools. A couple of planes, a few layout tools, a dovetail saw, and a set of bench chisels are a great foundation for any collection of tools.

Buying Machines

Fortunately, there are a number of companies producing affordable woodworking machines for the small shop. However, there are still some to avoid. It's best to visit a woodworking store or tool show and examine a machine before making a purchase. Fit, finish, and balance of moving parts have the most importance. It's difficult to do accurate work on a machine that vibrates excessively. Bandsaws are especially prone to vibration and require precise balancing of pulleys, wheels, and even the motor.

Blades, Bits, and Cutters

The cutting tool is the heart of any machine. A great blade will significantly boost the performance of an average saw, yet the finest machine will disappoint you when equipped with poor-quality tooling. High-quality blades, bits, and cutters are well machined and balanced, which insures smooth cutting.

Every power tool will perform better with quality bits, blades, and cutters.

The best carbide tips are thick, which allows for repeated sharpening, and made from fine-grain carbide.

The edges of blades and bits can be carbon steel, high-speed steel, or carbide. Many bandsaw blades are made from carbon steel, the same type found on edge tools, such as plane irons and chisels. Although carbon steel takes a fine edge, it isn't as heat resistant as high-speed steel and carbide.

High-speed steel can be sharpened to a keen edge and is heat resistant—good qualities for tooling. In fact, many turning gouges are made from high-speed steel. However, high-speed steel will not wear as long as carbide. And high-speed-steel dulls quickly when used on man-made sheet stock, such as particleboard.

Carbide is a hard powder metal that is bonded and brazed to the tip of blades and cutters. Because of the extreme hardness of carbide, it is extremely long-wearing.

Be aware that many of the factors that are involved in producing high-quality tooling are difficult or impossible to physically examine. The quality is in the cut. One way to evaluate tooling is to read the reviews and comparisons in magazines.

Dust Collection

You can dramatically improve the working conditions in your shop by adding dust collection. Fortunately, the cost of dust-collection units has come down as the popularity of woodworking has increased. A portable unit on casters can easily be rolled around the shop and used where needed. As you add equipment, you may want to consider using a central dust collector. A central unit is powerful and convenient, and you'll

➤ WORKING SAFELY

Woodworking is inherently dangerous. Using tools improperly can lead to a serious injury or perhaps even death. Don't attempt to try the techniques in this book until you are sure that they are safe for you in your own shop.

Here's an additional set of guidelines that I follow in my own shop:

- Always read and follow the manufacturer's safety guidelines that come with any tool.

- Use guards that come with machines.

- Keep blades, bits, and cutters sharp.

- Use safety devices, such as push sticks and push blocks, to distance your hands from the cutters.

- Always wear eye and hearing protection.

- Don't force tools; if the tool isn't working properly, STOP!

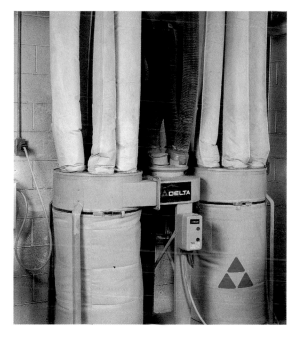

This compact, two-stage dust collector will handle almost any machine in your shop.

A large, central dust collector can handle several machines at once.

no longer have to push the portable unit around to each machine.

No dust collector traps 100 percent of the dust at the source. Here's where the ambient air cleaner takes over. Using a fan and a furnace-type filter, an ambient air cleaner traps the extremely fine dust that normally remains suspended in the air for several hours (giving you plenty of time to inhale it). Most ambient air cleaners have three speeds,

a timer for automatic shut-off, and a remote control. With an ambient air cleaner mounted against the ceiling, your shop will stay cleaner—and you'll breathe less dust, too.

[TIP] To help remove sanding dust from your shop, use an ambient air cleaner. They're available in ceiling-mounted or portable models.

Working Wood

A VITAL ASPECT OF MAKING quality furniture is having an intimate relationship with your material. What material to use, how and where to purchase it, and how it will behave from birth as rough stock to the ripe age of a 100-year-old piece of furniture are important pieces of information that will improve your woodworking, even before you pick up a chisel. And knowing your material will help you work wood safely, probably the most important skill in the craft. The following information should help you get started. For a more in-depth look at the technical aspects of wood and its properties, including plywoods and other man-made boards, read *Understanding Wood,* by R. Bruce Hoadley (The Taunton Press).

Working Wood Safely

The first and most important technique to learn and master in woodworking is to work safely. You can fix a woodworking mistake, but you can't take back a woodworking accident. Our shops are full of any number of sharp tools that can cause serious or permanent damage to your body. The good news is that safety won't cost you much. The biggest investment you'll make is in your mind. Or, more precisely, in your attitude. Although there is certainly plenty of safety gear that you should own, I believe that safe woodworking is primarily a mind-set you adopt every time you're in the shop. Be attentive to your energy level; if you're tired, don't fire up a machine. And listen to your

tools. Yes, with your ears. Any audible feedback—a change in pitch or tone—can warn you that danger is fast approaching and tell you to stop and re-evaluate what you're doing. If a procedure feels risky, find another way to do it. There is *always* another method that will work, and you should *always* feel safe and confident in the doing of it.

Safety gear is vital, too. Protect your ears with sound-deadening ear plugs or ear-muffs, particularly when using high-decibel universal motors such as routers, miter saws, and benchtop planers. Keep your eyes safe from chips and dust whenever you're cutting material, swinging a hammer, or using compressed-air tools. Wear eye protection in the form of safety glasses, goggles, or shields.

Watch out that your lungs don't gather dust. Sweet-smelling shavings may highlight the romance of woodworking, but they often come cloaked as fine dust that floats languidly in the air for hours. These micron-size particles are known as some of the worst offenders when it comes to respiratory and other illnesses. Use a nuisance mask when possible and wear a powered air-purifying respirator when the dust is really bad. To overcome big chips and some dust, hook up major machines to dust vacuums or install a central dust-collection system. An air-filtration box, hung from the ceiling, is another way to capture really fine dust.

Like it or not, even the cleanest wood-working shop collects dust. And dry woodworking dust is a fire hazard. To keep things safe, clean and sweep your shop and regularly blow out electrical panels and outlets using compressed air. Always keep a charged fire extinguisher on hand, just in case.

During finishing, you'll want to protect your lungs, skin, and clothes from harsh chemicals. Latex gloves, similar to those used by the medical profession, are inexpensive and keep your hands clean. An organic cartridge-type respirator worn over your mouth and nose will prevent fumes and other noxious vapors from reaching your lungs. And a shop apron helps preserve your favorite T-shirt or pants.

Even more important than safety gear is reading about and understanding the finishes you use. Learn more by asking for a material safety data sheet (MSDS) from the manufacturer or supplier of the products you use. Remember that oil-based finishes generate heat as they dry and can burst into flames (spontaneous combustion)—so be sure to dispose of wet or damp rags in a sealed, metal container or spread them out on a bench outdoors until they're dry.

When it comes to moving wood past sharp steel and carbide, keep your fingers out of harm's way by using push sticks, push blocks, and featherboards. You can make them from scrap wood or buy them. Either way, use them whenever possible, instead of your hands.

[TIP] **Working safely on a woodworking machine involves total attentiveness to the task at hand. Advise your family, friends, and colleagues never to approach you from behind while you're working at a machine. A sudden interruption can break your concentration.**

Last, and certainly not least, are the safety guards and shields on your machines. They protect fingers and flesh, and they shouldn't be overlooked or taken for granted. Check to see that your guards are properly installed and use them. If possible, use a splitter, or riving knife, to reduce the likelihood of kickback on the table saw. If you find that a guard is inconvenient—table saws are the worst offenders—then look into replacement safety devices. There are plenty of good designs available from woodworking catalogs and stores.

Buying and Preparing Solid Wood

If you buy dimensioned wood at the lumberyard, save it for small projects—jewelry boxes and the like. Use rough lumber for furniture. Buying rough lumber lets you to take control of the dimensioning process, resulting in stock that's flatter, more stable, more consistent in color and texture, and prettier. All because you took the time to study your rough boards throughout the milling process.

For furniture making, it's vital that you work with dry wood. How dry? A good rule of thumb is 6 percent to 8 percent moisture content, which will keep the material in equilibrium with its intended surroundings indoors. You can buy kiln-dried wood, but don't overlook air-dried lumber. It's relatively easy to dry lumber yourself and save some money in the process, and there are many good articles and books on the subject.

The main thing to keep in mind, regardless of whether you use air-dried or kiln-dried lumber, is to make sure it's stored in an environment with a relative humidity of

Cut several inches from the end of a board to get an accurate reading of the moisture content from the interior.

Press both pins firmly into the end grain to take a moisture-content reading.

When laying out boards, it's a good idea to figure in about 4 in. on each end for planer snipe caused by the shift in pressure of the rollers as the board exits the machine.

and scientific supply catalogs, but a cheaper version works accurately if you keep it clean (hang it under a shelf to prevent dust buildup), mount it in an area with good air circulation, and check its calibration regularly. Monitor your hygrometer during the year to find out how much your shop's relative humidity level changes.

Once you become familiar with your shop's humidity level, use a moisture meter to check the actual moisture level in your lumber. For an accurate reading, cut the end of a board to read the stock's core and use the meter on the center of the end grain. The moisture meter shown at middle left has a digital readout, which lights up when a pair of steel pins are pressed into the wood. Use the meter to check your wood when you first bring it into the shop. Then check it regularly over the course of a couple of weeks. When your readings are consistent, the wood has equalized with the shop's environment and is ready for working.

[TIP] Buy or gather your lumber and store it in the shop well in advance of building a project. Stack and sticker the boards in a well-ventilated area and plan on waiting a few weeks for the wood to equalize with your shop's environment before working it.

With your stock at rest with your shop's atmosphere and at the correct moisture content, you'll want to lay out your boards and inspect them for defects before you begin the milling process. Look for stray hardware, such as staples or nails, and remove it with pliers. Mark around splits and unwanted knots. Then divide long boards into smaller lengths to make the milling process easier.

around 40 percent and that you store it in that location for a couple weeks before using it. Most woodshops have this ideal setting, which you can check by keeping an inexpensive hygrometer in your shop. You can buy expensive hygrometers from woodworking

TYPES OF WARP

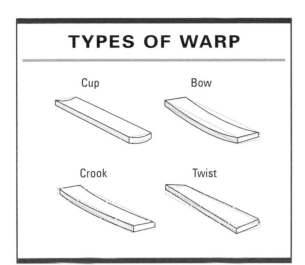

Cup

Bow

Crook

Twist

When face jointing a board, place the cupped side down and use rubber-coated push blocks so you can safely control the work.

Plan on losing about 4 in. on each end of a board owing to checking or from planer snipe. It's convenient to mark your cuts with regular chalkboard chalk. I like the "dustless" variety. White chalk shows up well on rough boards and, if you need to make a change, you can easily erase a mark by swiping the chalk with a damp sponge.

Now, if all went well, your lumber will be warped. Relax. This is a natural part of the drying process and *now* is the time to deal with it—not after you've built your furniture. There are essentially four types of warp, and you can easily train your eyes to spot each type in a board (see the drawing above). Knowing which kind of curve is in your board, and where, will help you determine the best course of action when it comes to removing it and milling your boards flat and square.

Face-jointing your lumber is essential if you want to make furniture that's flat and square. Many woodworkers commonly mistake the jointer as being solely an edge-straightening tool. Although it serves this purpose wonderfully, the best use of a jointer

is to flatten the face of a board before planing it to thickness. However, if you don't have access to a wide jointer, you can hand-plane one side flat instead.

►See *"Flattening a Board by Hand"* on p. 37.

Before jointing, sight along the board, looking for a cup or bow. Then place the cupped or bowed face down on the bed of the jointer. Set the knives for a light cut, about 1/32 in., and be sure to use push blocks to control the work and to prevent your hands from contacting the knives.

With one face flat, you can thickness plane the stock to even thickness. Start with the jointed face down on the bed of the planer, orienting the stock so you plane with the grain to avoid tearout.

►See *"Working with the Grain"* on p. 38.

To minimize further warping caused by internal stresses in the wood, always take an even amount of wood from both sides of the

To avoid tearout on the thickness planer, always plane with the grain. Flip the board over after each pass to plane an equal amount from each side.

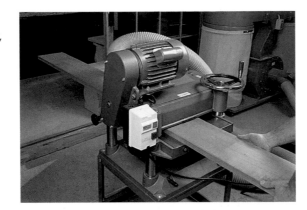

To ensure a square edge, press down and against the fence. Edge jointing cuts should be limited to about 1/16 in. maximum.

Align the grain where you want it, such as parallel to an edge, by drawing a straight line. A single bandsaw cut along the line establishes the new orientation.

To prevent long boards from wandering, sight along the rip fence rather than the sawblade as you push the board through.

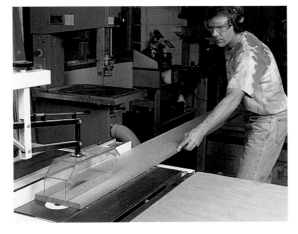

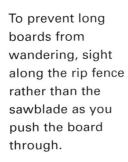

board. This means flipping the board over and end for end—to orient the grain direction—after every pass.

After planing, joint one edge of the stock. Pay attention to keeping the board snug to the fence, because this keeps the jointed edge square. For narrow edges, you can take off a little more than when face jointing. A depth of cut of about 1/16 in. is fine.

Once you've milled your lumber flat and to thickness, but before you cut out parts, it pays to get better acquainted with your wood. By studying your boards for grain pattern, color, and texture, you can learn to be a composer of wood grain in your work. Mark like-colored parts so they balance each other. For example, the two stiles on a door frame should come from similar areas of a board. And don't be ruled by straight edges; instead, follow nature's lines. Lay out your furniture parts, by studying the grain patterns, then draw straight lines in chalk, parallel with the pattern you want. Cut to your lines on the bandsaw; then clean up the sawn edges on the jointer and rip the opposite edges on the table saw. Now you have a board with the grain going where *you* want it.

When cutting out individual parts from a solid-wood board, it's best to rip pieces about 1/4 in. over final width, placing a jointed edge against the rip fence. Use leverage when ripping long boards and focus your attention and pressure at the rip fence, not at the blade. Then go back to the jointer and re-joint an edge to remove any bowing caused by tensions released in the ripping process. (Look for cupping on the face, too. You may have to face joint the ripped stock and then thickness plane it once more.)

Then go back to the table saw to rip to final width, again referencing the jointed edge against the fence.

Finish up by crosscutting the boards to length on the table saw, using the miter gauge or a crosscutting jig.

► See *"Crosscutting with a Table-Saw Sled"* on p. 73.

Another alternative is to use the miter saw for cutting to length. A stop block lets you cut multiple parts to exactly the same length without having to measure and mark each board.

Flattening a Board by Hand

If you don't own a jointer, or your jointer is too narrow for your stock, you can still work wide planks into beautifully flat surfaces with some initial prep work from a handplane. Don't worry. This is not the sweat-drenching work our woodworking forebears carried out when they worked without power tools. Instead, it involves a sharp plane and your thickness planer.

At the bench, clamp the plank that you want to flatten cupped-side up, tapping wedges under the board at key points to prevent rocking. Use a long plane set for a fairly heavy cut and plane the high spots on the cupped face. Work the plane diagonally across the face. As you plane, use a straight-edge and a pair of winding sticks to check your progress, reading the face for cup and twist. Don't try to plane the entire surface; just make sure the perimeter, or outer edge, is flat.

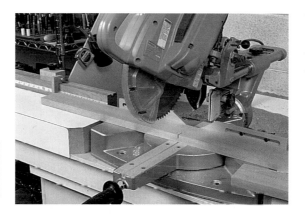

The flip-up stop block (to the left of the saw) allows you to easily cut multiple pieces to the same length.

Wedges keep the workpiece from rocking as you plane the perimeter of a cupped board. Once the outside edges are flush, you can finish the job with a thickness planer.

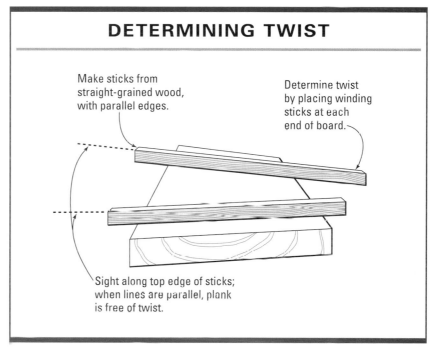

DETERMINING TWIST

Make sticks from straight-grained wood, with parallel edges.

Determine twist by placing winding sticks at each end of board.

Sight along top edge of sticks; when lines are parallel, plank is free of twist.

After handplaning, turn the planed side down on the bed of the thickness planer and flatten the top side.

Now flip the board over and send it through the thickness planer to flatten the opposite, unplaned face. A few passes is all it should take. When you've established a broad, flat surface on the second face, continue planing both faces evenly until you reach the desired thickness.

Working with the Grain

Working with solid wood demands that you pay attention to the direction of the wood's fibers, or grain. When you cut *with the grain*, such as when routing, planing, or even sanding, you'll produce smoother surfaces. Cutting *against the grain* pulls and lifts the wood fibers up, resulting in tearout, or a rough surface. Take the time to study the grain patterns in your boards to determine which direction to orient them for cutting. Most of the time, you can see the grain rising or falling by looking at the edge of a board. But certain woods can fool you. Sometimes you can pass your fingers along the long-grain surface in both directions and feel which direction is smoother. The technique is very much like stroking the fur of a cat. The final test is to cut the wood itself. If it tears, cut from the opposite direction.

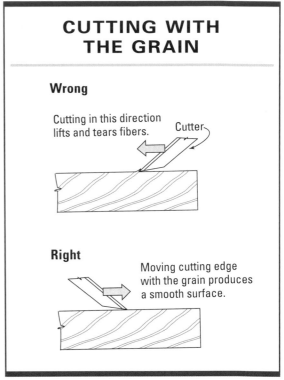

CUTTING WITH THE GRAIN

Wrong

Cutting in this direction lifts and tears fibers.

Cutter

Right

Moving cutting edge with the grain produces a smooth surface.

Smoothing with Edge Tools

Boards straight from the thickness planer or jointer (or the lumberyard) aren't smooth enough for furniture. Small millmarks—usually tiny ridges and hollows left by the rotation of a cutterhead's knives—will be glaringly apparent when you apply a finish. You can sand out these marks with a belt sander or a random-orbit sander, but it's dusty work and, worse, you risk leaving a surface that's far from flat. To remove marks and smooth any imperfections, a handplane is fast and efficient and leaves a flat, gleaming surface unsurpassed by any other tool.

If you're working with a flat surface, such as a long, wide board, clamp it to a flat surface such as your benchtop. If you try to plane on an out-of-flat surface, the plane will skip and skitter over small humps and valleys. Assuming your work has been accurately thickness planed, use a no. 4 or no. 5 plane for the initial smoothing. Make sure your plane iron is razor sharp and set the depth for a fine cut.

Body English is all-important when planing. To gain leverage, spread your feet apart, hold the plane directly in line with your wrist and shoulder, and use your legs to power the stroke. Plane in one smooth, decisive movement, letting your upper body pivot over the work as you push the plane. You should be able to plane a board about 5 ft. long without taking a step or moving your feet—and without huffing to catch your breath. Proper handplaning is a fluid, enjoyable action. For longer boards, take several passes by landing and taking off the plane from the surface, just like an airplane. This technique helps avoid stop and start marks.

From time to time, check your progress with a straightedge to ensure the surface is flat. If you detect a small hollow that the plane has skipped over, try skewing the plane to the direction of the cut to effectively reduce the length of the sole. If the wood is difficult and starts to tear, plane in the opposite direction. Sometimes it's quicker simply to reverse the plane and pull it rather than to reposition the board.

[TIP] You can reduce friction and make handplaning easier by regularly oiling or waxing the sole of your plane. Light oil or paraffin (candle) wax works well, or rub some paste wax on the plane and buff it off with a clean cloth.

For working difficult woods, when a handplane tears the grain—not uncommon

Lifting the plane off the work before ending a stroke prevents choppy plane marks.

The frequent use of a straightedge during planing helps ensure that surface is flat.

Skewing the plane while still pushing straight ahead helps reach slight hollows.

Pulling the plane is sometimes easier than changing places as you tackle difficult grain.

Use a sharp hand scraper, rather than a handplane, when working figured woods with difficult grain.

Sandpaper wrapped around a felt block provides a sensitive touch for hand-sanding, and uses sandpaper more effectively.

A granite block wrapped with sandpaper is great for getting into corners and for leaving a crisp edge with no fuzzy transitions.

Spray adhesive, sandpaper, and a scrap piece of MDF are used to make a sanding block with different grits on each side.

on wood with swirled or highly figured grain—use a hand scraper. Tilt the scraper at an angle to the surface until it begins to cut. A properly sharpened scraper makes shavings—not dust. Many books and articles describe how to sharpen a scraper, and it's worth reading about how to tune up this indispensable hand tool.

In most cases, you'll still have to sand to remove small ridges left by planing and to ensure that all your surfaces have an identical texture for an even finish. However, the surface left by a plane or scraper is so smooth that you can start sanding with a very fine grit, reducing sanding time—and dust—considerably.

Good Sanding Techniques

Proper sanding will yield flat, swirl-free surfaces ready for a fine finish. Careless sanding can result in scratches, or—much worse, in my opinion—rounded surfaces that reflect light unevenly and look downright shoddy. Not sanding at all can leave patterned machine marks or plane track marks and lead to hard edges or inconsistent-looking surfaces when the finish is applied. Take the time to look carefully at the surface and be sure to sand through each successive grit. Final sanding is always done by hand, *with* the grain of the wood.

Whenever you're sanding a surface by hand, wrap the paper around a block. A sanding block prevents rounding or dipping into surfaces, and makes the sanding process much more efficient. On broad surfaces, use a felt block for its sensitive feel to the hand and to the surface itself.

On edges, or arris, use a hard wooden block to gently round over the sharpness where the two planes meet. The denser the block, the better. Please don't sand an edge by hand. The results will be inconsistent. My favorite back-up block is a chunk of dead-flat granite, which is great for getting into corners for a nice, even look.

By far the most-used sanding block in my shop is a piece of MDF with a sheet of sandpaper glued to both sides. I make lots of blocks in a range of grits, spraying both sides of the MDF and the back of the paper with contact cement, and then sticking the paper to the block. You can use these blocks for leveling flat surfaces or for cutting or rounding over edges. And they're useful when sanding small parts, by clamping them to the bench and moving the work over the blocks, instead of the other way around. Think recycle, too. When the sandpaper loses its effectiveness, just heat the paper with a blow dryer or a heat gun and peel it off. Then apply a fresh sheet.

To keep your sandpaper organized, consider building a cabinet dedicated to storing full sleeves of sandpaper, cut paper, and all your other associated sanding gear. Size the shelves to fit sleeves, and then organize them by grit.

Keeping Parts Flat

Once you've flattened and milled your solid stock, and perhaps even sanded it, you still have to contend with the fact that wood left lying around the shop will warp if given a chance. (Letting the wood acclimate to your shop for several weeks before milling will help minimize this but won't stop it entirely.) In an ideal world, you would dimension the stock, cut all your joints, and assemble and glue all the parts together immediately. An

Sanding blocks clamped end to end with multiple paper grits are effective for sanding small parts.

Using a heat gun, you can peel the old sandpaper from a block; then apply a fresh sheet.

Building a cabinet with adjustable shelves lets you organize sandpaper by grit.

➤ CUTTING SANDPAPER WITH A JIG

I like to keep my sandpaper in sizes that fit my jigs and tools. To cut sandpaper into thirds, a convenient size for me, I use a home-made fenced jig. You can make the jig to suit your favorite size of sand-paper. Mine is 9½ in. by 10 in. To use the jig,

A piece of plastic laminate that's one-third the size of a sandpaper sheet helps the author tear off sections.

place several sheets against the two fences, position a piece of plastic laminate on top of the stack of paper, then lift and tear individual sheets to size.

When possible, dry-assemble case pieces while working on other components to keep the parts from warping.

Stacking and weighing precut parts prevents them from warping while you're away from the shop.

Small parts can be shrink wrapped to control wood movement.

assembled piece of furniture keeps itself flat and free from warping. However, most often we work piecemeal, and joints cut today may not see glue until weeks or months have passed. To keep parts flat and to accommodate a busy schedule, there are a couple methods to follow.

After milling the stock flat, sticker and stack it as soon as possible on a dead-flat surface. Make your stickers from shop scrap

to a uniform width and thickness, typically ¾ in. by ¾ in., and stack the pile so that the stickers are in line above and below each other. After stacking, add another row of stickers on top of the stack and place weights on them. This simple routine will save you untold headaches later.

If you've cut the joints, but aren't ready for final assembly, it's a good idea to dry-

Panel Characteristics

Panel	Cost (A-2 grade)	Weight (¾ in. x 4 ft. x 8 ft.)	Flatness	Screw Holding	Rigidity
Softwood plywood	$ 20	68 lb.	Poor	Good	Good
Hardwood plywood	$ 45, birch $ 80, cherry	75 lb.	Fair	Good	Good
Solid-core plywood	$ 40, birch $ 60, cherry	80 lb.	Good	Fair	Fair
Lumbercore plywood	$100, birch $140, cherry	75 lb.	Fair	Excellent	Excellent
MDF	$ 25	100 lb.	Excellent	Fair	Fair
Particleboard	$ 20	100 lb.	Good	Poor	Fair

Information courtesy of Georgia Pacific Corporation, American Plywood Association, Hardwood Plywood and Veneer Association, and National Particleboard Association.

assemble the parts. This way, the joints themselves will hold the parts flat.

Another option that's particularly handy for smaller parts is to wrap them in plastic. I use industrial shrink wrap, which is strong and comes in wide lengths from shipping companies. Cover all surfaces—especially the end grain—and store the wrapped parts on a flat surface until you're ready to work them.

Plywood and Other Man-Made Boards

Using plywood, you can dimension all the panels for an entire kitchen in the time it would take to thickness enough solid stock for one piece of furniture. It's this ready-made width that's one of the most compelling reasons for choosing man-made boards. Another reason is the variety of panels or sheets to choose from, including the most common: hardwood plywood,

fiberboard, and particleboard. And the stability of man-made boards means you're free from the concerns of wood movement. The chart above shows some of the pros and cons of each panel type to help you decide which material has the characteristics you need for a particular job.

Plywood, available as veneer core, solid core, combination core, and lumbercore, can have softwood or hardwood face veneers. For furniture makers, hardwood plywood is the panel of choice. It is inexpensive; does a good job of holding hardware such as screws; and is relatively rigid, making it a good choice for shelving.

Newer hardwood plywood types, such as solid-core and combination core, offer inner plies of less-expensive particleboard or fiberboard and are generally flatter—an important consideration if you're building unsupported work such as floating door

A, Hardwood veneer-core plywood with walnut face; **B,** Baltic birch plywood; **C,** softwood plywood with fir face; **D,** combination-core plywood with cherry face; **E,** MDO; **F,** lumbercore with birch face; **G,** MDF; **H,** hardboard (for example, Masonite); **I,** solid core of MDF with oak face; **J,** particleboard; **K,** MCP.

panels or large tabletops. Lumbercore, as its name suggests, has a core of laminated solid wood, making it exceptionally stiff and rigid. One board, medium-density overlay (MDO), combines inner plies with a face of kraft paper impregnated with exterior glue, making it ideal for outdoor sign makers.

Keep in mind that the thin face veneers on hardwood plywood necessitates careful cutting, handling, and finishing to avoid breaking or chipping the face and exposing the inner plies. Typical hardwood plywood has random spaces or voids between the inner plies, which show up as holes along the edges of panels. The raw edges must be covered or banded to conceal the voids and the inner plies.

Three products—Baltic birch plywood, ApplePly, and Europly—are made from multiple layers of veneers and are void free. You can polish their edges for a finished

look. Also, their higher density and stability make them great for jig making.

[TIP] Use a *triple-chip* (TC) blade for clean, chip-free cuts in delicate faced panels such as hardwood plywood, melamine, and plastic laminate. A 60-tooth, negative-hook pattern reduces tearout on both the top and the bottom faces.

MDF is inexpensive and is the best choice for flat work because it's flat and stays that way. With its exceptionally smooth surface, MDF is a favorite for veneering or high-end paint work, and it's another great material for making jigs. The cons: It's heavy, making it difficult to handle in the shop; it won't hold fasteners well; it bends under heavy loads; the rough, porous edges of the panels need filling or edgebanding; and when exposed to moisture, it swells irreversibly.

Its "cousin" particleboard is made from chips—not the fine fibers used in MDF. The result is a coarser surface that's not suitable for thin or very fine veneers. It has most of the benefits of MDF—it's easy on your wallet and it's generally flat—and all of the cons. With its rough surface, particleboard is best as a substrate under thicker materials, such as plastic laminate. Melamine-coated particleboard (MCP) is, as its name implies, coated with a hard plastic, making it ideal for interior case pieces, since it provides a durable finished surface.

When buying particleboard, make sure to select the industrial, or high-density, grade; the builder's variety, called chipboard or flakeboard, is much too coarse and lacks the strength and rigidity of the denser grade.

Mixing solid wood and plywood can be an effective technique. Although the door frames, edging, and trim of this home library are made from solid mahogany, the panels are sapele plywood.

The desktop is made from sepele plywood with solid wood edging and leather.

Mixing Materials

There's no denying that the look and feel of solid wood has its advantages. But commercial hardwood veneered panels can be used in conjunction with solid wood to provide a rich feel to just about any project. For example, I made all the panel frames, door frames, edging, and trim in the home library shown in the photos above from solid mahogany. But the panels—including the desktop—are made from sapele plywood. The overall look is solid and luxurious.

Even when wood is the look you want, it's sometimes wise to mix it with other materials. A simple solution is to use prefinished panels for the insides of your utility cases and hardwood plywood for the outside. In the case shown at right, most of the inside—including the top, bottom, and dividers—is constructed from MCP. Melamine provides a hard-wearing surface, and you don't have

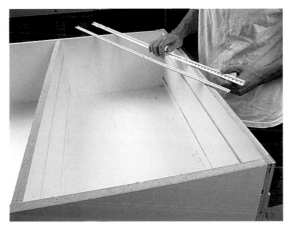

You can use melamine-coated particleboard inside a cabinet to create a durable surface.

On the outside of the same cabinet, maple plywood dresses up the public side.

The maple doors and visible exterior parts of this melamine cabinet create a natural wood look.

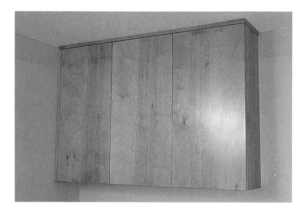

Working with a cutting list and graph paper, you can minimize waste by creating a cutting diagram for each sheet of plywood.

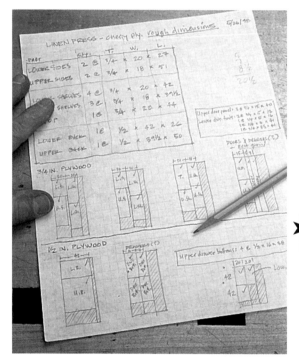

Use chalk to create the initial rough layout on a sheet of plywood.

to apply finish to the insides of the case, an often tedious task. The show sides of the case are maple plywood, and a coat of paint takes care of the interior. Once the wood doors are mounted on the outside of the completed cabinet, you see only maple in all its natural beauty (see the photo top left).

Laying Out and Cutting Plywood

While plywood affords you large, stable surfaces that need little or no prepping, the downside is handling such big sheets. That's why it's important to plan your cuts and to break up large sheets into more manageable bite-size chunks.

The first thing to do is to make a cutting list, including a sketch of each 4-ft. by 8-ft. sheet of plywood and how you plan to cut it into parts.

► See *"Using Cutting Lists"* on p. 47.

Laying out your cuts in this manner lets you create the most efficient cutting sequence. When you move from paper to panel, it helps to lay out the cuts on the actual plywood so you can more closely select grain patterns for individual parts. Using blackboard chalk lets you preview the cuts and makes it easy to change the layout; simply remove unwanted marks with a damp sponge.

Large sheets of plywood can be difficult to manage on the average table saw, even with side and outfeed support, so it's usually best to cut up the sheet into smaller parts first. The jig shown in the drawing opposite lets you cut sheets using a circular saw with very little setup. Simply clamp the jig to the

Simple jigs are often best. This circular-saw guide provides an easy way to cut up a sheet of plywood into manageable pieces.

This jig is easy to use because you place the edge directly onto the layout line; the saw is guided by the particleboard fence.

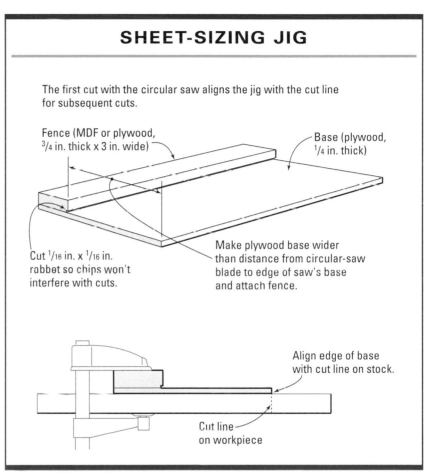

SHEET-SIZING JIG

The first cut with the circular saw aligns the jig with the cut line for subsequent cuts.

Fence (MDF or plywood, 3/4 in. thick x 3 in. wide)

Base (plywood, 1/4 in. thick)

Cut 1/16 in. x 1/16 in. rabbet so chips won't interfere with cuts.

Make plywood base wider than distance from circular-saw blade to edge of saw's base and attach fence.

Align edge of base with cut line on stock.

Cut line on workpiece

cutline and ride your saw on the base to make the cut. Once you have your sheets cut into smaller sizes, take them to the table saw to cut out the individual parts.

Using Cutting Lists

Making a cutting list is a good way to keep organized, and working from a list prevents mistakes during the building phase. For complex projects, make a list of each and every part and mark the dimensions of each piece on a single sheet of paper. Graph paper makes it simple to organize your thoughts. As you progress on the piece, check off each part as you cut it to dimension.

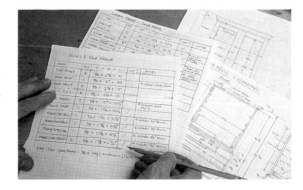

For projects with a lot of parts, a cutting list is an important tool for making sure everything gets cut to the proper size.

Making Your Mark

Like cutting lists, marking the work itself will keep you organized and reduce the time you spend looking for misplaced parts. For most work, an ordinary pencil works fine. On dark woods, consider using a white pencil, the kind sold in art-supply stores.

A marking knife is the most accurate method of transferring layout lines.

marking scheme—the actual symbols aren't important. One of my favorite techniques is to designate front and top edges with two respective marks: a line to represent the front, and a triangle—or a series of triangles—to mark a top edge and inside edge. This simple system lets me keep track of the numerous parts in the right order.

Choosing and Using Glue

When it comes time for assembly, you'll grab your trusty glue bottle. But just as you wouldn't build cabinets strictly from one type of material or wood, you shouldn't rely on one glue for all your assemblies. Having said this, about 90 percent of my furniture goes together with ordinary woodworking white glue. Technically a polyvinyl acetate (PVA) glue, this glue comes in white and yellow varieties. White glue generally offers more open time (the time you have once you've spread the glue to get all the joints together), making it useful for complex assemblies. And like all the glues for woodworking, it's plenty strong for its intended purpose.

Mark the edges of your parts with triangle symbols so you can orient the faces and edges correctly during joint cutting and assembly.

An astounding variety of wood glues is available. Glues range from traditional hide glue to modern synthetics that bond instantly.

Other glues offer other compelling characteristics, such as the ability to take the work apart when you need to by nature of its reversibility, increased moisture resistance, or even waterproofness. The chart opposite helps you select the right glue for the job.

[TIP] Many glues have a shelf life of 1 year; some less. Look for a manufacture date on the glue you buy; if there isn't one, write the date you bought the glue on the bottle. Dating your glue lets you know how fresh it is.

When you need a higher degree of accuracy, such as when marking out dovetails, the fine line left by a marking knife is best.

To keep track of parts in a project, you'll need some system of marking. I use a triangle and a straight line. You can make up your own

Once you've chosen an adhesive, you need to learn the balance between using too much and using too little, because each approach has its respective drawback. Too little glue and you risk starving the joint line, especially when the pressure from clamps spreads the glue away from the joint. The result is a joint that's likely to fail. It's better to err on the side of too much glue, but not to the point that you have a gooey mess on your hands. Excess glue that's not removed will always haunt you later when it shows up as a bland smear under any finish. So how much is enough? A good rule of thumb is use enough glue so that you see an even bead squeeze out from the assembled joint.

When applying glue, shoot for an even bead of squeeze-out after clamping.

Timely Glue Characteristics

Type	Open Time	Clamp Time	Comments
PVA (yellow and white)	3 min. to 5 min.	1 hr.	General woodworking; water cleanup
Cross-linking (type II water resistant)	3 min.	1 hr.	Good outdoors; water cleanup
Hot hide glue	Unlimited, with heat	Limited	Hammer veneer work; reversible
Cold (liquid) hide glue	30 min.	12 hr.	Reversible with heat and water
Polyurethane	20 min.	2 hr.	Moisture resistant; foams during cure
Plastic resin (resin powder/water powder)	20 min./20 min.	1 hr./12 hr.	Moisture resistant; veneer and bent laminations
Two-part epoxy (fast/slow)	1 min./1+ hr.	30 sec./24 hr.	Doesn't shrink; laminations; submersible
Cyanoacrylate glue (Super Glue)	5 sec.	5 sec.	Quick fix for small parts; filling cracks
Contact cement	30 min. to 3 hr.	Immediate bond	Plastic laminate work
Hot-melt glue	15 sec.	Temporary hold	Jig and template making

Dimensioning Wood

Jointing and Planing

Ripping

Crosscutting

Cutting Sheet Goods

IN THIS SECTION we'll look at the milling process, which involves turning rough planks into finished parts ready for joinery or assembly. In order to size stock accurately, it helps to understand how your woodworking machines work. It's equally important to become familiar with how your material reacts under different machining processes. Following the correct milling procedure allows you to take control of dimensioning boards so you get the parts you need. Dealing with large stock, such as oversize boards or full sheets of plywood, is another challenge you can successfully tackle if you approach it in a sensible manner and with a few helpful aids. And producing complex shapes, such as the flowing curve of a chair leg, requires the right tools and knowing how to use them correctly.

Milling Raw Stock

Dimensioning stock involves milling the material so that it is straight, flat, of a consistent thickness, and has square edges. Properly done, the process flattens any warped surfaces and yields pieces that are smooth enough for layout work and joinery. The milling sequence can be outlined in a general way by tracing the route of the lumber from machine to machine:

A small engineer's square is accurate for reading the edge of a board to check whether it's perpendicular to an adjacent surface.

1) At the jointer, begin by flattening one face of the board.
2) At the thickness planer, dress the board to its final thickness.
3) Back at the jointer, straighten and square one edge.
4) At the table saw, rip the board to final width.
5) At the miter saw or table saw, crosscut the board to final length.

Milling lumber in the proper sequence is necessary to ensure stock that's ready for furniture. If you try to save time by buying pre-milled stock, one of the above steps may have been overlooked or performed poorly,

producing wood that is warped or rough. Making your stock truly flat and square is a job worth doing yourself.

When milling wood, you'll need to be able to set up machines to make square cuts, such as when setting a table saw blade square to the table. You'll also need to be able to accurately check the resulting cuts, so invest in quality squares, and use the appropriate size for the surface you're reading.

During the milling process, ear and eye protection are needed to combat the roar of machinery and the flow of dust and chips. Blade guards are a must. If, like most of us, you find your stock table-saw guard clumsy, fit your table saw with one of the excellent aftermarket versions. To save fingers and place pressure against tables and fences, make sure to use push sticks, push blocks, and hold-downs when appropriate.

An often overlooked piece of safety equipment is the table-saw splitter, or riving

Blade guards and push sticks save fingers. This tall push stick clears the guard and is made from plywood so its heel won't split or break during use.

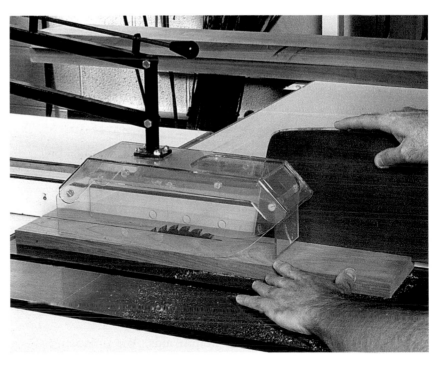

HOW WOOD PINCHES A SAW BLADE

Kerf Opens Up

Wood is forced away from fence and contacts back of blade.

Kerf Closes

Wood closes toward blade and makes contact at back.

A splitter prevents wood from moving into the blade as it's ripped, eliminating the chance of kickback. This aftermarket "snap-in" Biesemeyer® splitter is easily removed and replaced without the use of tools.

knife. This little piece of metal can be a lifesaver by preventing kickback, which is caused by the blade lifting the workpiece and hurling it towards you with great force. Kickback most commonly happens when you're ripping a board. Sawing can release internal tensions inside the board, allowing the two separated parts to warp and press against the rising rear teeth of the blade, which then lift and throw the board (see the drawing at left). A splitter doesn't allow the wood to press against the blade. Unfortunately, most stock splitters are troublesome to install and use. The answer is to buy an aftermarket splitter that can be installed or removed without tools.

Milling stock correctly also involves removing knots, splits, and other defects. Learn to carefully inspect a board after it has been cleaned up in the thickness planer but before cutting to final dimension. Most cracks and other blemishes show up easily at this stage. If a knot isn't a visual problem, you can leave it in, but be sure to tap it to make sure it's sound and won't fall out later.

➤ See *"Filling Cracks and Knots with Epoxy"* on p. 290.

One of the trickiest parts of checking for sound stock is inspecting for end checks—those cracks at the ends of boards that result from the drying process. Hairline checks can be hard to see, so it's best to cut slices off the end of the board, and then check the slices for cracks. First crosscut an inch or two from the rough end, then cut off a slice about ⅛ in. thick. Check the slice for cracks by gently bowing it with your hands. If it

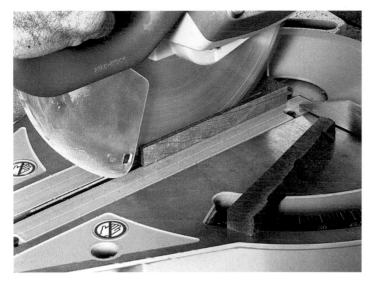

To check for hairline end checks, first crosscut a thin slice from the end of a board.

Bend the sample slice by hand. If it contains checks, it will snap easily.

bends a fair amount without breaking, the end of your board is sound. However, if it snaps easily, you'll have to keep cutting further into the board until your test slice doesn't break.

Cutting to Final Length

You can crosscut to final length using a miter saw or table saw. Final cuts sometimes involve removing just a whisker from the end of a board. Unfortunately, the hard end grain can cause blades and other cutters to deflect, misaligning the cut when you try to remove just a hair from the end of a piece. One trick to reduce this deflection is to make the cut very slowly. However, this doesn't always work, and you may need to try another approach.

A nice trick for removing just a smidgen of wood off the end of a piece is to use the side of your miter saw blade. Lower the blade, and butt the end of the workpiece against the plate (not the teeth). Gently lift the

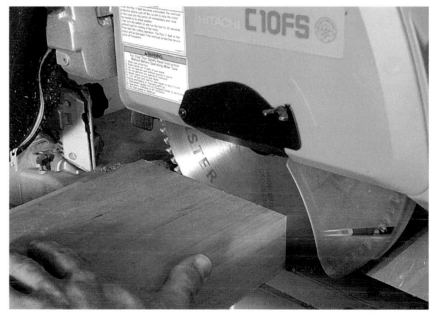

You can remove about $\frac{1}{64}$ in. by pushing the stock into the blade's plate and then lifting up the saw and cutting.

Clamp or hold the work against the trimmer's fence, and start to lever the blade across the wood.

Shaving the end of a piece with a low-angle plane offers more precision than any other method.

The miter trimmer lets you remove very thin shavings for a perfect fit, and the finished cut is glassy smooth (inset).

machine with the fence angled at 45 degrees. The tool has a massive, fixed knife that levers its way across the wood, leaving a shaved surface that's super-smooth and at a true 45-degree angle.

For super-precise cuts, try setting a low-angle plane for a very light cut and shaving the end of a piece. A handplane can take shavings so thin that they fall from the cut as dust. The nice thing about using a plane to trim work is being able to remove such an exacting amount of wood that it allows you to sneak up on a perfect fit.

stopped blade while holding the work firmly, and then make a cut. You'll remove about ¹⁄₆₄ in., or the amount of set on the blade.

One way to shave miters is to use a knife-cutting machine called a miter trimmer. After a miter has been rough-cut on a miter saw, the workpiece is clamped into the

Flattening on a Jointer

All rough wood has some degree of warp, and the best tool to use to begin straightening your stock is the jointer. As woodworker Paul Anthony demonstrates here, start by sighting along the plank to determine its curves so that you can place the cupped or bowed side down on the jointer table **(A)**.

➤ See *"Types of Warp"* on p. 35.

Make sure to joint with the grain to avoid tearout. One way to inspect a rough board's grain orientation is to take a few swipes on the edge of the plank on the jointer **(B)** to reveal the grain lines in the wood **(C)**.

Once you've noted the direction of the grain, set the infeed table for a medium cut (about ½₂ in. to ¹⁄₁₆ in.), and place the bowed side down on the table. Long planks can be maneuvered without strain if you stand away from the infeed end of the table and gently bow the board so it flexes, placing pressure on the infeed table **(D)**. Continue walking up to the jointer behind the board, keeping one hand over the infeed table while the other hand lifts the trailing end of the board slightly to make the leading end press down onto the outfeed table **(E)**.

As your hands approach the cutterhead, keep the board moving with one hand while you reach for a push block with the other **(F)**. Use the push block to place pressure over the outfeed table near the knives, and use a second push block with a heel at its end to grab the end of the board so your hands are safe while above the cutterhead **(G)**. As the board nears the end of the cut and starts to hang off the outfeed table, use your upper body weight over the push blocks to keep the stock from tipping **(H)**

(Continued on p. 56.)

A

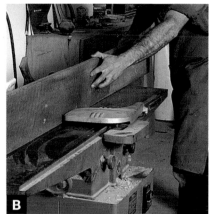
B

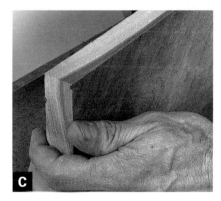
C

D

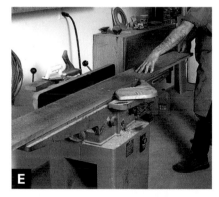
E

F

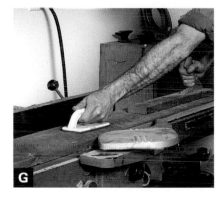
G

H

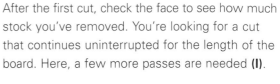

After the first cut, check the face to see how much stock you've removed. You're looking for a cut that continues uninterrupted for the length of the board. Here, a few more passes are needed **(I)**.

Boards with a bow in the middle will be flattened as material is gradually removed from each end, until the center is lying against the jointer tables. It's more efficient in this case to take several passes at a time from each end of the board, rather than running it full length each pass. When flattening the trailing end, you can swing the guard away from the fence and pull the board halfway back to take another pass **(J)**. Then simply place it onto the tables and make another pass **(K)**.

Once the freshly cut surface runs uninterrupted along the board's length, stop to eyeball the plank for straightness **(L)**. If you notice any significant curvature, take another pass. When you're done, the board should be flat over the majority of its surface, although it can still contain some uncut areas **(M)**.

Planing to Thickness

After jointing one face, you're ready to bring the board to the desired thickness using the thickness planer. Start by measuring the thickest part of the board **(A)** and adjusting the depth of cut on the planer to that dimension **(B)**.

Note the grain orientation, and be sure to feed the plank into the planer in the correct direction to avoid tearout. Make the first pass with the jointed side down on the bed, standing at the end of the board **(C)**.

[TIP] To minimize planer snipe, lift the board slightly as it enters the planer, and again as it exits.

Stay on the infeed side of the planer as you guide the stock through the machine to support the overhanging end **(D)**. Once the board is centered in the planer and well supported, move to the outfeed side and support the opposite end to keep it from tipping up and into the cutterhead **(E)**.

(Continued on p. 58.)

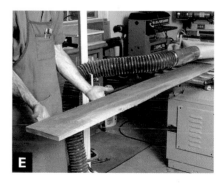

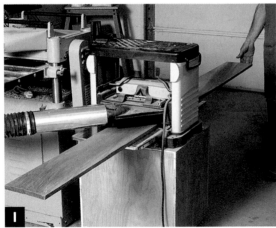

Once you've established a continuously cut surface on the first planed face, flip the board end for end and onto its opposite face **(F)** before sending it through the planer again **(G)**. This reorientation keeps the grain in the correct direction and ensures that you take equal amounts from each side to minimize warp.

> ⚠ **WARNING** Removing material from only one side of a plank will usually cause it to distort due to uneven stresses inside the wood. Be sure to cut both sides equally to keep the plank flat.

A large planer with an induction motor is a great machine for taking aggressive cuts when you're milling rough stock, although it may produce a rough, washboardlike surface. Unfortunately, when you're taking a very light cut, the serrated-metal feed rollers may leave a series of fine-line impressions in the board **(H)**. For a better final cut, some woodworkers finish up by taking a light pass with a benchtop planer, which has a higher-speed universal motor that provides more cuts per inch. These machines also have smooth rubber feed rollers that won't leave marks in the board **(I)**.

Milling Square Stock

Square stock is used often in furniture making for such items as table legs and bedposts. If you're starting with a wide plank, rip it down first on the bandsaw.

The first step in jointing is to flatten a face. Afterwards, an adjacent face is jointed straight and 90 degrees to the first face. It's easier to flatten a concave face; it has two surfaces resting on the jointer table (A) instead of just one (B). Position a push block at each end and take a light cut (C). You'll notice that the jointer will cut stock from each end of the workpiece (D). Now take one or two more passes until the workpiece is smooth and flat along the entire length (E).

Now you're ready to square an adjacent face. First, check the jointer fence for squareness to the table and adjust it if necessary (F). Next, position the workpiece on the jointer with the

(Text continues on p. 60.)

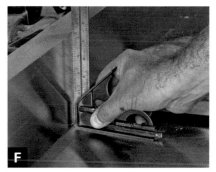

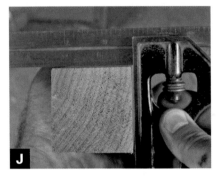

smooth, true face against the fence (**G**). It's important to view the workpiece from the end; although it may appear to be against the fence when viewed from the top, it may not be making full contact (**H**). Now joint the second face (**I**) and check the two surfaces for square (**J**).

Now you're ready to plane the stock to final thickness (**K**). Always position the jointed face down and remember to plane both the remaining two surfaces (**L**). Finally, square the end (**M**) and use a stop to cut the piece to final length (**N**).

Thicknessing a Board by Hand

To thickness a board with planes, begin by flattening one face of the board, The easiest and fastest method is to use a long bench plane, such as a No. 6, 7, or 8, and push the plane diagonally across the face of the board (**A**). It's not necessary to smooth the board with the large, coarse cutting plane, only to flatten it (**B**). Afterwards, smooth the flat face with a smoothing plane and carefully follow the grain (**C**).

Next, set a marking gauge to the dimension of the final thickness and carefully scribe all four edges of the stock (**D**). As you plane the second face, the scribe line will appear as a fine, feathery wisp of wood (**E**).

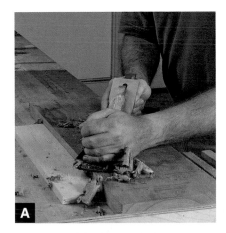

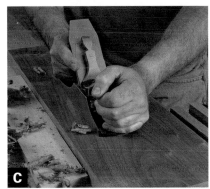

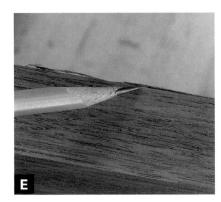

A

B

C

D

E

F

G

Flattening a Wide Board

I avoid gluing several narrow boards edge-to-edge to create a wide panel. The mismatched grain and color is just too distracting. Instead, I prefer to use one wide board for tabletops and door panels. It's best to flatten stock before planing it to thickness to remove any warp or twist. If your jointer is too small to accommodate anything beyond 6-in. or 8-in. wide, you can use a bench plane to flatten the board. A long plane, such as a No. 7 or No. 8, works best. The extra length will bridge the low areas, making it easier to flatten the board. And the extra weight of a long plane will help propel it through each cut with minimal chatter.

You'll want to use a heavy cut; remember that the purpose is to flatten the board, not to smooth it. I grind the iron convex and adjust the frog and iron for a coarse, heavy cut **(A)**. Afterwards, I use a No. 4½ bench plane to smooth the surface of the plank.

Begin by examining the board for twist with winding sticks **(B)**. A quick sight across the top of the sticks will reveal the high corners. Position stops against two adjacent edges and plane the board diagonally, from corner **(C)** to opposite corner **(D)**. After the initial planing, the highest points will be cut down.

Next, turn the plane slightly and broaden the areas cutting across the grain **(E)**. Continue planing until the two broad areas at each corner meet in the middle of the board **(F)**.

Finally, use a straightedge to find any remaining high spots and plane them away. When you're finished, the board should be flat and ready for planing to final thickness **(G)**.

Jointing an Edge by Hand

Edge jointing is the process of straightening the edge of stock prior to ripping or gluing it to another piece of stock. In the process of straightening the edge, it's also important that the edge is square to the board's face.

The sole of a plane is a great aid in truing the edge, provided that the sole is flat. However, the natural tendency is to hollow the edge of the stock when planing, or to remove more wood from the center of the cut. To compensate for this tendency, it's helpful to apply pressure at the toe of the plane when starting the cut (**A**), then to transfer the pressure to the heel of the plane toward the end of the cut (**B**). Use your thumb to apply downward pressure and your index finger to steady the plane against the stock (**C**). If necessary, a final pass with an edge-trim plane will insure that the edge is absolutely square (**D**).

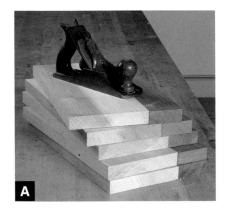

A

B

Planing Glued-Up Panels

After gluing panels edge-to-edge, I use a bench plane to flush the mating surfaces before planing the panel to thickness **(A)**. In this photo-essay, I'm planing panels created from walnut and poplar. The panels will be resawn to create dividers inside a spice cabinet. Because most of the divider will be hidden by drawers, I glued inexpensive poplar to the walnut primary wood to reduce costs.

If you're careful to match the grain direction in the mating boards, it will greatly simplify planing. Just plane in the direction of the grain **(B)**. If the grain changes direction in either board, it often works best to plane the stock diagonally **(C)** to minimize tearout **(D)**. Then finish smoothing the panel with a sharp scraper **(E)**.

[**TIP**] **Dried glue can dull a plane blade, so always remove the glue squeeze-out before planing a glue-up panel.**

C

D

E

Ripping Freehand on the Bandsaw

Ripping thick, rough stock is much safer and more efficient on the bandsaw than on the table saw. Unlike a table saw, the bandsaw can't kick back. And the thin blade of the bandsaw won't bog down in thick stock.

Begin by marking a layout line **(A)**. Select a ½-in. or wider blade and adjust the upper guide to the thickness of the stock **(B)**. As you rip the stock, you may have to adjust the angle of the work slightly to compensate for blade drift **(C)**. Position your hands on each edge of the stock for greatest control **(D)**. As you exit the stock, reduce the feed pressure, and keep your thumbs out of the blade's path **(E)**.

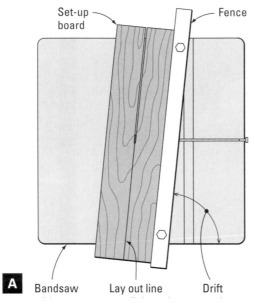

Set-up board | Fence

A | Bandsaw | Lay out line | Drift

Ripping on the Bandsaw with a Fence

The bandsaw can make surprisingly accurate rip-cuts. The key is to use a fence. However, some bandsaws don't rip in a path that is square to the table, a phenomenon called drift. The solution is to angle a wood fence to compensate for the drift **(A)**.

Start by marking a line parallel to the edge of the board **(B)**. Next, use a ½-in.-wide blade and cut freehand along the line; as you carefully follow the line, you will naturally feed the stock at an angle to compensate for the drift **(C)**. About midway down the board, stop the saw and clamp a board along the edge of the stock to serve as a fence **(D)**. As you continue to rip the stock, distance your fingers from the blade by using a push stick **(E)**.

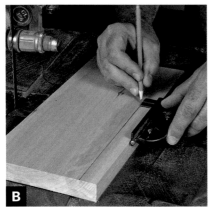

B

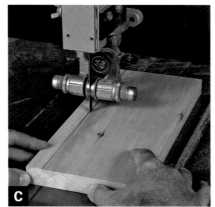

C

D

E

Resawing

Resawing is the process of ripping a thick board into thinner ones. You can use this technique for creating book-matched panels **(A)**, matching sheets of veneer, or just saving lumber when building small projects. It's a great technique that can only be done on the bandsaw. But first you'll need to select a blade for resawing. For this demonstration I'm using a ⅜-in., 3-tpi hook-tooth blade **(B)**.

[**TIP**] **If you own one of the many 14-in. bandsaws on the market, you can double the resaw capacity, from 6 in. to 12 in., with a riser block.**

To resaw accurately, it's best to use a tall fence to provide support to the entire width of the workpiece. You can attach a wide board to the rip fence on your bandsaw, or you can make a fence from plywood **(C)**. Begin the process by setting the fence at the drift angle. Mark a stick to the width that you want to resaw **(D)** and cut freehand along the line **(E)**. When you reach the halfway point along the length of the stick, stop

(Continued on p. 68.)

A

B

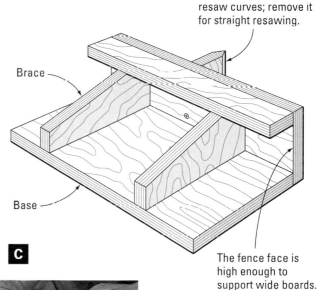

Attach the point fence to resaw curves; remove it for straight resawing.

Brace

Base

The fence face is high enough to support wide boards.

C

D

E

the saw. You will have naturally compensated for the drift angle, if any, as you follow the line. Now simply position the rip fence next to the stick and secure it to the table with clamps **(F)**. Now you're ready to begin resawing.

As you start the cut, keep the stock positioned firmly against the fence **(G)**. Feed the workpiece slowly, be aware of the sounds and vibrations of the bandsaw, and adjust your feed rate if necessary **(H)**. As you approach the end of the stock reduce the feed pressure and use a block of wood to complete the cut **(I)**.

Ripping a Wide Plank on the Table Saw

After jointing and planing your stock flat and to a consistent thickness, you're ready to saw it to width on the table saw. But first you'll have to straighten and square one edge on the jointer by standing the stock on edge with one face against the jointer's fence. At this stage, don't try to remove any defects that might be near the jointed edge (**A**).

After squaring one edge, set up the saw by adjusting the blade height for the thickness of the stock. A good rule of thumb is to raise the blade high enough so the bottom of its gullets are just above the workpiece (**B**).

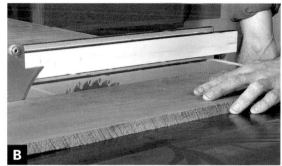

Begin by placing the jointed edge against the rip fence. When sawing a long board, stand near its trailing end to begin feeding it into the blade. Place yourself to the left of the blade (as you face it) and concentrate your attention not at the blade but at the fence, to ensure that the stock contacts it fully throughout the cut (**C**). When you're within reach of the saw table, keep your left hand stationary on the tabletop to apply pressure towards the fence, while your right hand feeds the plank (**D**).

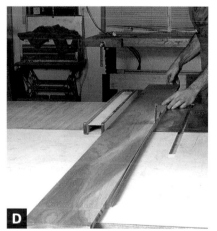

[**VARIATION**] When ripping thick boards or planks with wild grain, add a short fence to your existing rip fence, with its end aligned with the rear of the blade. Make the fence 1 in. thick so it's easier to set up cuts using your fence's cursor. Ripping in this manner is perfectly safe and creates space for the wood to spread apart towards the fence without binding on the blade.

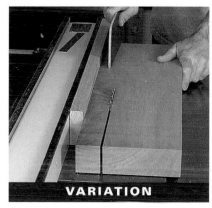

(Continued on p. 70.)

VARIATION

[**VARIATION**] When you deal with thick, heavy, hard-to-handle stock, it can help to first reduce the size and weight of the piece on the bandsaw. Thanks to its downward cutting action, the bandsaw has no potential for kickback. You can set up a fence, or simply gauge the width with a pencil, and then saw to the line freehand. After bandsawing, move back to the table saw and make a trim cut to clean up the bandsawn edge.

As you near the end of the cut, move your left hand out of the way and push the board past the blade. For safety, ride one finger along the fence to ensure that your hand stays away from the blade (**E**). At the end of the cut, the board is likely to tip over the end of the saw table due to its overhanging weight. The safest approach is to have an outfeed table behind the saw to support the work. Also, apply downward pressure to the board as you feed it past the blade (**F**).

If there were any defects near the original jointed edge, orient the sawn edge against the rip fence and adjust the fence to the desired width of cut, taking note of the defects so you remove them in this final pass (**G**).

E

F

G

Ripping Narrow Boards from a Wide Plank

Due to internal stresses in almost all boards, ripping multiple narrow sections from a wide board requires the right approach to ensure that your sawn stock remains straight. Begin by setting the rip fence for a cut about ⅛ in. wider than your desired finished width. With the jointed edge against the fence, feed the work smoothly past the blade with your left hand keeping pressure against the fence (A).

Whenever you're ripping stock that's less than about 4 in. wide, use a push stick as the end of the board nears the blade (B). As the board separates, guide the dimensioned piece with the push stick while your left hand pushes the freed section past the blade (C).

Without resetting the fence, continue ripping the remainder of the board into separate, slightly oversized pieces. To illustrate how wood moves after ripping, group the individual boards back together in the order that they were sawn. Chances are, you'll notice gaps between them, which reveals bowed edges from the sawing process (D). To re-straighten the edges, take each board back to the jointer and re-joint one edge (E). With such narrow stock, you can use the same push stick you used on the table saw to keep your hands clear of the knives (F).

After jointing each board, orient its jointed edge against the rip fence and trim the opposite edge to finished width (G). Remember to use a push stick for the last portion of the board (H).

[TIP] **For optimal cutting, keep your blade clean. Spray the blade with a citrus-based cleaner, and then use a nylon abrasive pad or a brass brush to scrub the gunk from the blade.**

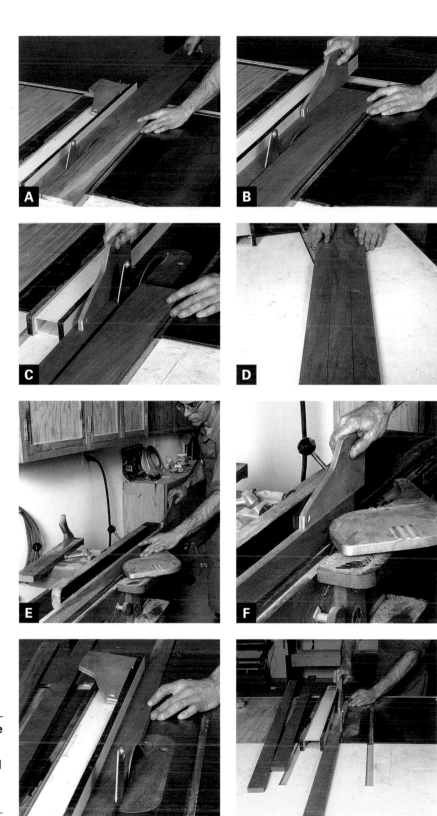

Crosscutting Using the Miter Gauge

The miter gauge lets you make excellent cross-cuts on the table saw, but you'll only use it for small work, as it can't safely support long or very wide stock. With the power off, position the stock at your cutline, holding it firmly against the gauge's fence with your left hand **(A)**. Push the stock and gauge in an even, controlled movement, using your right hand on the gauge's knob to feed the work past the blade **(B)**.

Once the cut is made, use your left hand to slide the workpiece slightly away from the blade **(C)** before pulling the work and gauge back to you **(D)**. This prevents you from splintering the sawn edge as you retract the workpiece.

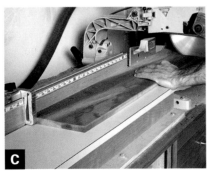

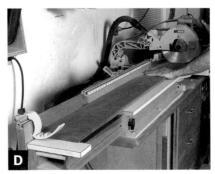

Crosscutting Using the Miter Saw

A better option for crosscutting, particularly with long or heavy stock, is to use a power miter saw, also called a chopsaw. The first step is to cross-cut one end of the workpiece perfectly square by holding the stock firmly and accurately against the saw's fence. For the best results, build a crosscutting station to house your saw so you'll have longer work tables and a longer fence against which to register the stock **(A)**. Be sure to remove enough stock from a rough end so the sawn edge is free of end checks and other defects **(B)**.

Next, flip the stock end for end, registering the previously cut end against a stop block as you cut the opposite end to finished length **(C)**. If your stock is longer than the working fence of your sawing station, you can make an extension that allows you to accurately register longer boards **(D)**.

Crosscutting with a Table-Saw Sled

Wide panels, such as case parts, are best cross-cut on the table saw. If a panel is short enough, it's a simple matter to set the rip fence and guide the work past the blade. But do this only if the edge that bears against the fence is long enough to keep the panel from veering away from the fence during travel **(A)**.

To crosscut long and wide stock, you can build and use a shop-made sled. Runners attached to the bottom of the sled ride in your saw's miter-gauge grooves, and a stout fence at the front of the sled registers the stock square to the blade for square cuts every time. The workpiece can be carried primarily to the left of the blade **(B)** or to the right, depending on how your table saw is set up **(C)**. Either way, be sure to support the over-hanging end of a long workpiece with a spacer of the same thickness as your sled's base at the far end of your saw.

For repetitive cuts in parts that are longer than your sled's fence, you can clamp an extension to the fence and then clamp a stop block to the extension **(D)**. The block will accurately register multiple parts and ensure that your final cuts are all to the same length **(E)**.

Crosscutting Short Stock

For obvious safety reasons, always cut short stock from a longer workpiece to distance your hands from the sawblade. And never use the fence as a stop; the work will bind between the blade and the fence and kick back. Instead, clamp a thick block to the fence a few inches behind the front of the blade to serve as a stop **(A)**. To make the cut, first position the workpiece against the stop block **(B)**, then make the cut **(C)**. As the pieces are cut, stop the saw occasionally and remove them from the table **(D)**.

Cutting Sheet Goods on the Table Saw

To cut a full sheet you'll need an outfeed table. It helps if you have infeed support in front, such as a table that's the same height or slightly lower than your table saw's height. Lay one end of the sheet on the infeed table, with the opposite end on the saw table, and one edge against the fence but away from the blade, and turn on the saw. Walk back to the end of the panel, stand at the far corner of the sheet to triangulate your feed pressure, and move the panel into the blade by pushing diagonally towards the rip fence (**A**).

To keep the sheet against the fence at the start of the cut, try lifting the end of the panel slightly so it bows a bit. This will increase pressure on the fence as you push the sheet into the blade (**B**).

Walk with the panel as you push it forward, staying on the far side to maintain pressure against the fence (**C**). As the sheet nears the end of the cut, move to the back of the panel and guide each divided section with one hand, again keeping your eyes on the fence (**D**). As the parts separate, lean over the saw to place downward pressure over each piece, then push the keeper piece past the blade while holding the offcut stationary (**E**).

Once you've separated the parts from the sheet, be sure to place the sawn edge of each piece against the rip fence and trim the opposite factory edge, which is typically not very straight nor particularly smooth (**F**).

Case Joinery

Butt Joints

➤ Butt Joint with
Nail Gun (p. 78)

➤ Butt Joint with
Nails (p. 79)

➤ Butt Joint with
Screws (p. 80)

➤ Butt Joint with
Pocket Screws
(p. 81)

➤ Butt Joint with
Cross Dowels
(p. 82)

Biscuit Joints

➤ Flush-Corner Biscuit
Joint (p. 83)

➤ Offset-Corner Biscuit
Joint (p. 85)

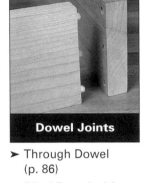

Dowel Joints

➤ Through Dowel
(p. 86)

➤ Blind Dowel with
a Doweling Jig
(p. 87)

Rabbets

➤ End Rabbet with a
Router and Fence
(p. 88)

➤ End Rabbet with a
Router and Rabbeting
Bit (p. 89)

➤ End Rabbet on the
Router Table (p. 90)

➤ Edge Rabbet on the
Table Saw (p. 91)

➤ Edge Rabbet with a
Dado Blade (p. 91)

➤ Edge Rabbet on the
Router Table (p. 92)

Grooves

➤ Through Groove on
the Table Saw (p. 93)

➤ Groove on the Router
Table (p. 94)

Finger Joints

➤ Hand-Cut Halved
Joint (p. 111)

➤ Finger Joint
on the Router Table
(p. 112)

➤ Finger Joint
on the Bandsaw
(p. 113)

➤ Finger Joint
on the Table Saw
(p. 114)

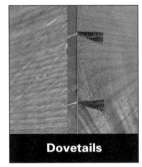

Dovetails

➤ The 5-Minute
Dovetail (p. 116)

➤ Hand-Cut Through
Dovetail (p. 117)

➤ Through Dovetail
with Mitered
Shoulder (p. 119)

➤ Hand-Cut Half-Blind
Dovetail (p. 120)

➤ Half-Blind Dovetail
with a Router and
Omnijig (p. 122)

➤ Half-Blind Dovetail
with a Generic
Jig (p. 123)

➤ Through Sliding
Dovetail (p. 124)

Dadoes

➤ Through Dado with a Router (p. 96)
➤ Through Dado on the Router Table (p. 97)
➤ Through Dado on the Table Saw (p. 98)
➤ Stopped Dado with a Router (p. 99)

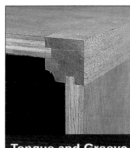

Drawer Lock Joints

➤ Drawer Lock Joint (p. 100)
➤ Rabbeted Drawer Lock Joint (p. 100)

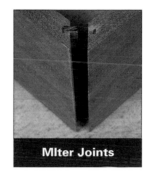

Tongue and Groove

➤ Tongue-and-Groove Joint on the Router Table (p. 101)
➤ Hand-Cut Tongue-and-Groove Joint (p. 102)
➤ Tongue-and-Groove Joint with a Router (p. 102)
➤ Making a Loose Tongue (p. 103)
➤ Tongue-and-Groove Joint on the Table Saw (p. 105)

Miter Joints

➤ Biscuit-Reinforced Miter (p. 106)
➤ Splined Miter (p. 107)
➤ Plywood Splines (p. 107)
➤ Solid-Wood Splines (p. 108)
➤ Keyed Miter on the Router Table (p. 109)
➤ Keyed Miter on the Table Saw (p. 110)

Butt Joint with Nail Gun

An air-actuated brad or nail gun works about 10 times faster than doing the job by hand but also adds that much more danger. First, mill the stock to size and make an accurate crosscut.

➤ See *"Crosscutting"* on pp. 72-74.

Preclamping and gluing the parts to be joined make it easier to keep them straight **(A)**. Either you can drive the nails straight into the work or you can slightly angle the gun. Nails driven at a slight angle have better holding power **(B)**.

A brad gun, if run with enough air pressure, will automatically bury the nails or brads below the surface of the board. It's then just a matter of filling the nail holes with putty. Water-based putties are a bit nicer to use than solvent-based materials, because they make it easier to clean up your tools. Apply just enough putty to fill the hole plus a bit more. Later, use sandpaper to smooth the putty level with the surface of the wood **(C)**.

> ⚠ **WARNING** A nail gun is aptly named: It fires a nail at a speed and pressure that can seriously injure you or someone else. Keep your fingers away from the surface you're nailing into and make sure no one is in the line of fire.

Butt Joint with Nails

Your first woodworking project was probably this simple: Butt two boards together and bang a nail in to keep them together. First, mill the stock to size and make an accurate crosscut.

➤ See *"Crosscutting"* on pp. 72-74.

Clamping and gluing the box together first helps hold the joint while you nail **(A, B)**.

When nailing by hand it's up to you to keep the nail going in straight. Sight from the side of the board you're nailing into to see how the nail is progressing and make your corrections early rather than after the nail pokes through the side piece **(C)**. Use a nail set to punch the nail heads below the surface of the project so they won't mar anything **(D)**.

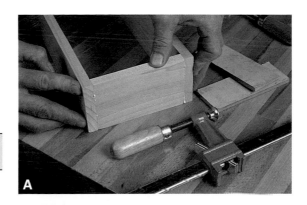

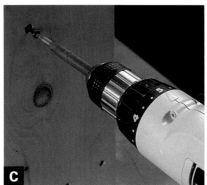

TIP

Butt Joint with Screws

Screwed butt joints are similar to nailed butt joints: Only the fastener is different. Screws, of course, provide better purchase in the wood because of their threads. First, mill your stock to size and make an accurate crosscut.

➤ See *"Crosscutting"* on pp. 72-74.

As for many joints, gluing and clamping the work holds the joint in position until you can add the fastener **(A)**. Although driving a screw may not split the wood as easily as a nail might, you still need to predrill and countersink for most applications. Otherwise, the screw head will stand proud of the surface or, as with hardwoods, may not go into the wood at all.

The quickest way to predrill is to use a portable power drill with a taper bit mounted with a countersink head and stop collar on it. If you want to hide the screw head and countersink it, continue drilling and bore out for a wood plug **(B)**. Drive the screw in straight and square to the edge being joined.

[TIP] **Grease your screw with a little bit of wax to make for easier entry.**

If the driver slips out of the screw head, check that you're using the right size driver **(C)**.

Butt Joint with Pocket Screws

Clamp the pocket screw jig tightly in place. Place some masking tape on the bit to mark the depth of the holes or set a depth stop. Make sure the depth is shallow enough to keep the screws from breaking through on the other side. Drill out the pocket (**A**).

The screws made for this application have a round Phillips head and self-tapping threads that cut into the wood for fast entry (**B**). It's still advisable to glue butt joints, like the ones on the drawer shown here (**C**), but the pocket screws eliminate the need for lots of clamps.

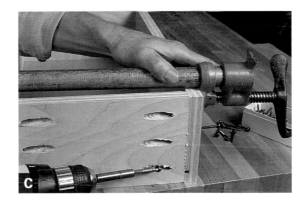

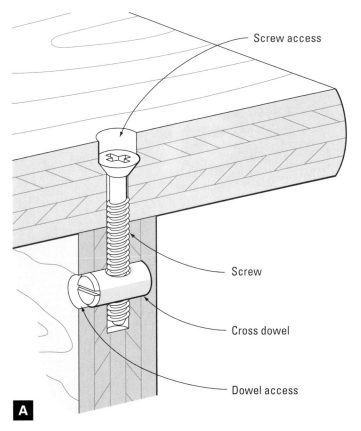

Screw access

Screw

Cross dowel

Dowel access

A

Butt Joint with Cross Dowels

Cross dowels **(A)** are round metal rods made with a threaded hole right in the center of their length. A machine screw then threads into that hole, pulling an assembly tight **(B)**.

If you want to hide the dowel, first drill a ½-in. countersink hole. Then drill a hole slightly larger than the ⅜-in. cross dowel, so the dowel enters it easily **(C)**. Also drill an access hole for the machine screw to contact the threaded part of the cross dowel. Drill deeply enough for the screw to run all the way through the dowel. Use epoxy to cement a cross dowel that will be hidden under a wood plug **(D)**, but align the dowel's screw hole before the glue sets. The dowel has a slotted end so you can turn the dowel with a screwdriver to align it **(E)**.

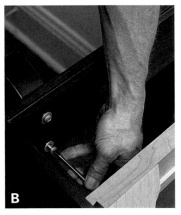

B

C

D

E

Flush-Corner Biscuit Joint

Mark the cabinet panels for the biscuit slots **(A)**. Use as many as will fit into the width of the piece, but be careful near the edges of the panel because you don't want a biscuit slot to show there. Also be sure to set the height adjustment on the biscuit joiner to center the cut in the panel. Check that the height adjustment is locked securely and have the fence locked down in the 90-degree position. Shim the joiner fence if it isn't perfectly parallel to the cutterhead. There is a centering mark for the height on the side of the biscuit joiner shown here. Line it up with the center of the panel or use the scale mounted on the joiner **(B)**.

Use a pencil to mark the position of the biscuits on the boards. You will index the cuts off the outer face of one board and the outer edge of the other **(C)**. Your biscuit joiner has a centering mark for the center of the rotation of its cutterhead. Line it up with the pencil marks to make the cuts. Clamp the workpiece down or push it tightly against a stop to hold it firmly in place.

When making the biscuit cut, push down firmly on the handle of the machine to keep the joiner flat to the workpiece **(D)**. As with any joinery cut, first make a practice cut to check the settings.

(Continued on p. 84.)

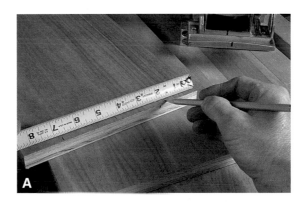

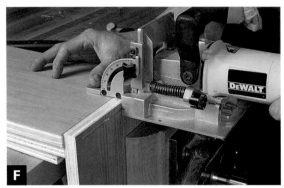

It's easy to make the cuts in the end of a panel; however, it's a bit trickier to make the cuts in the flat of the other panel. Use another carcase panel to support the biscuit joiner when you're making an end cut **(E)**. Clamp it in place flush with the top edge of the piece getting cut and keep the biscuit joiner flat on this surface when making the cuts **(F)**.

Make the cuts at a moderate feed rate. Too fast a rate only forces the tool to work unnecessarily hard, can cause the motor to stall, and can dull the blade. On the other hand, don't burn the wood by moving too slowly. Use a dust bag on the joiner or, better yet, hook up a vacuum to capture the dust.

Apply glue with a flux brush to the biscuit slot. Don't skimp here, as it's important there's enough glue to swell the biscuit. Expect some squeeze-out when you hammer the biscuit down into place. Make sure it's centered before moving onto the next biscuit **(G)**.

> **⚠ WARNING** Do not hold a small piece with your hand when making a cut with the biscuit joiner; always use clamps.

Offset-Corner Biscuit Joint

Offset panels, shelves, or dividers that stick into a carcase side anywhere but right at the corner need a different technique for biscuiting. Obviously, you can't use the fence in its locked-down position to locate the cut in the middle of a side. What you use instead is the shelf going into the side. Mark out the position of the biscuits on the shelf. Use a square as a depth guide to place the shelf on the carcase side.

Mark the top or bottom face of the shelf on the carcase side, and mark out the biscuit centers **(A)**. Then clamp the shelf down flat onto the carcase side right up against the pencil mark. This will act as a fence for the biscuit cuts. Then cut the biscuit slots on the carcase piece with the fence in place **(B)**. Use the biscuit joiner to cut into the ends of the panel as you would for a flush-corner joint.

➤ See *"Flush-Corner Biscuit Joint"* on p. 83.

Remember when gluing that the squeeze-out on an assembly like this can be difficult to clean, so be judicious with the amount of glue you use **(C)**.

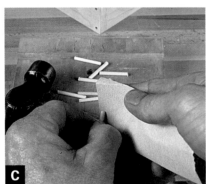

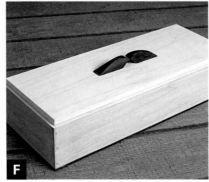

Through Dowel

Strengthen a butt-jointed box with through-dowel pins. They're very simple to drill for and to apply because you do all the work after the box has been put together.

Sight the drill from the side to line up the holes in the box side **(A)**. The dowels I used here, although very small in diameter, dried oval and fit too snugly in the holes. Since the holes were drilled so close to the end of the side, I drilled them again ⅟₆₄ in. oversize just to avoid any short-grain breakout when I hammered the dowels in. Always check the dowels against the drill bit size before pounding them in.

You can also size the dowels using a dowel pop. Use good, straight twist bits to drill a metal plate with some convenient dowel sizes. Then bang the dowels you want to use through the dowel pop to size them correctly. The metal hole will shear off any distortion that may have occurred as the dowel dried and shrunk **(B)**.

Before applying the glue, chamfer the ends of the dowel pins with a bit of sandpaper. This makes entry that much easier **(C)**. Once the glue has dried on the dowel pins, use a saw to cut them off close to the surface of the box. Place a piece of cardboard on the surface of the box to protect it and rest the saw on that. This raises the sawteeth off the wood just enough so they won't cut into the box **(D)**. Make sure your hand is on the opposite side of the sawteeth as well when it comes through that dowel.

Finally, pare the pins flush to the box surface with a sharp chisel **(E)**. The end grain of the pared dowel shows a bit darker than the surrounding wood, creating a decorative effect **(F)**.

Blind Dowel with a Doweling Jig

Use a centering doweling jig for drilling dowel holes in a carcase or box parts. Carefully lay out the dowel centers on the workpiece **(A)**. Place a few more dowels out near the edges of a board where it's more likely to cup. Use a good brad point bit for drilling the holes. The centering point on these bits helps locate the cut in end grain, which can be difficult to drill accurately.

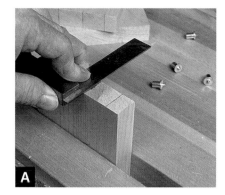

Measure the depth of the cut and mark the bit with tape while it's in the doweling jig **(B)**. Remember to figure in the length of the brad point. When the jig is too close to the end of a board, use another piece of the same thickness to support the jig. Then tighten the jig down onto both boards. This way the jig won't twist **(C)**.

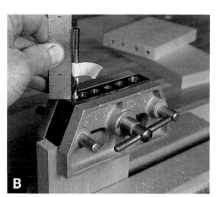

After drilling the ends of the box sides, mark out the dowel positions on the mating boards. Use dowel centers in the drilled holes to locate the mating holes; you can use a glued-up spacer to help locate offset parts in their proper positions. Line up the boards and give them a little pop with a hammer to transfer the center points **(D)**. To drill the matching holes, use a drill press for the best accuracy. Place a fence and set the bit depth so it goes just far enough without going through the face side of the board **(E)**.

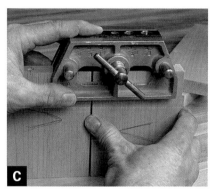

Score the dowels several times along their length with saw kerfs. This will allow glue to escape. Then insert the dowels in the ends of each board. Use a height block to tell you when you have driven the dowels in enough **(F)**. Once the dowels are in place, put the entire box together. Make sure a dead-blow hammer and some clamps are nearby and ready to go **(G)**.

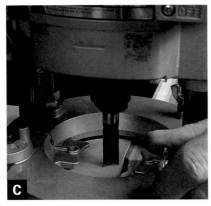

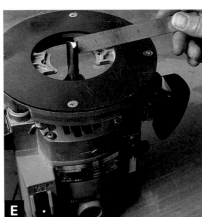

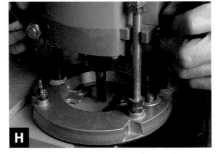

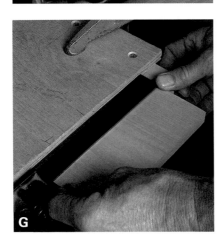

End Rabbet with a Router and Fence

Use a straight bit and fence to make end rabbet cuts topside with a router. Select a bit as large as the rabbet you wish to cut. If it's slightly undersize, first just take a trim pass on the outside edge. An auxiliary fence attached to the router fence helps guide the cut better because it gives you more bearing surface **(A)**.

Mark the depth of the rabbet on the workpiece. On a plunge router, set up the depth stop for the final depth **(B, C)**. Make a deep rabbet in a series of passes **(D)**. At the end of the cut be careful of tearout. You can stop just short of the end and run back into the cut for the last 2 in. to avoid this. This method can also be used to cut edge rabbets.

Topside cuts can also be guided with a right-angle fence clamped on. The fence is just a straight piece of stock with a jointed straightedge. Measure the distance from the end of the router base to the outer edge of the bit **(E, F)**. This is the offset, which determines the placement of the fence. Make sure the fence is square to the edge (on a right-angle jig, this should automatically be square) **(G)**.

Clamp the fence securely to the work and the bench. Double-check your bit position against the pencil mark **(H)**. To produce matching rabbets, cut a spacer to the width of the distance from the edge of the board to where the fence should be set. Glue a board to the end of that spacer to make lining up even simpler **(I)**.

End Rabbet with a Router and Rabbeting Bit

Special bearing-mounted rabbeting bits cut end rabbets very efficiently. These bits now come with changeable bearing sets to change the width of the cut. Choose the bearing for the size rabbet you wish to cut **(A)**.

Set the full depth of the rabbet **(B)**. Move the bit into the work until the bearing contacts the edge of the board. Feed the board at a moderate pace and work from left to right along an edge (into the rotation of the bit) **(C)**. Make the cut almost all the way across the board, but stop just short of the end to avoid tearout. Feed back into the board for that short distance to clean up the rabbet. For deep rabbets, take several progressive cuts until the bearing contacts the edge of the board.

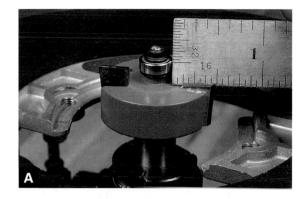

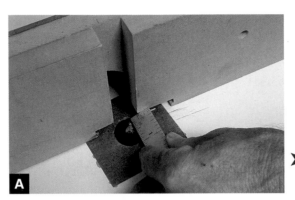

End Rabbet on the Router Table

Cutting an end rabbet on the router table is similar to cutting it with an edge guide, but there are some important differences.

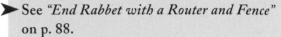
➤ See *"End Rabbet with a Router and Fence"* on p. 88.

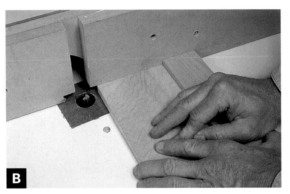

The router is under the table, so the feed direction is opposite: from right to left, into the rotation of the bit. The angle of the fence isn't critical, since the edge of the board will ride against the fence, ensuring a square cut.

[TIP] **Use a fence with a dust-collection system so the chips won't blow back and clog the cut.**

Set the fence for the width of the rabbet you wish to cut **(A)**. Holding the work firmly against the fence, feed the work from right to left. Use a board to back up the cut and prevent tearout **(B)**.

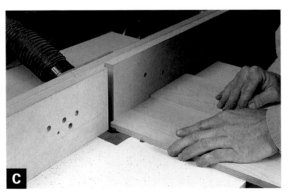

You can also package narrow boards together followed up by a backer to make a cut across the bit **(C)**.

Edge Rabbet on the Table Saw

Use the table saw to make through edge rabbet cuts with ease and accuracy. An effective, if slow, method is to hold the workpiece flat to the table and make a series of passes with the single blade. Another technique uses just two through cuts. Place the board flat to the table to make the first cut. Always know where the exit point of the blade is so you can keep your hands well clear **(A)**.

Use an auxiliary fence attached to the saw fence to help support the board.

Then make a second pass holding the work vertically **(B)**.

> ⚠️ **WARNING** Don't trap the offcut piece between the blade and the fence or you'll get kickback.

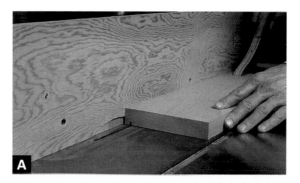

Edge Rabbet with a Dado Blade

Dado blades make easy work of through rabbets and can cut in one pass. Assemble the dado head to the size of the rabbet to be cut **(A)**. An auxiliary fence can capture the dado blade edge within it so the cut can be made right up to the edge of the board **(B)**. Set the fence so the cut is made on the edge nearer the fence **(C)**. This helps prevent kickback, particularly if the work rides up on the dado blade. Keep the feed rate slow and use a push stick.

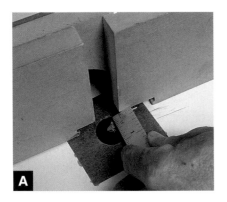

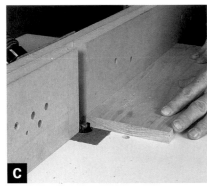

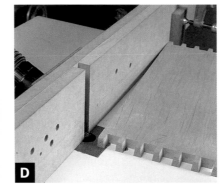

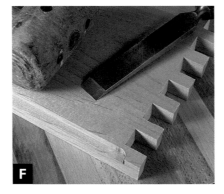

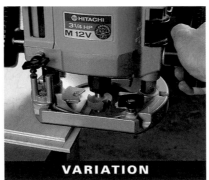

VARIATION

Edge Rabbet on the Router Table

Use a straight bit in the router table to make edge rabbets. Straight bits work well because their small diameter leave very little wood to clean up. Place the router table fence just at the proper distance from the cutting edge of the bit to the fence **(A)**. Rotate the bit so one cutting edge is farthest from the fence. The fence itself does not have to be parallel to any edge of the table for your cut to be parallel to the edge of the board. Photo **B** shows how a bit that's larger than the required rabbet is captured in the fence. Holding the edge of the stock firmly against the fence, feed the work from right to left **(C)**.

To make a stopped rabbet, clamp a stop onto the fence or router table to stop the cut **(D)**. Move into the stop slowly at the end of the cut to avoid jarring the weak short grain of the board.

Routing a rabbet in solid wood can often cause tearout at the edges of the cut. This is especially true when the cut goes against the grain of the wood. Slow down your feed rate, take small depths of cut, and consider a climb cut to pre-score the grain **(E)**.

Stopped rabbets on a cabinet back will leave you with some cleanup work, but this is preferable and far safer than making a table saw stopped cut **(F)**.

[VARIATION] Make your rabbeting cuts topside with the proper size rabbeting bit. Move left to right along the edge.

Through Groove on the Table Saw

The table saw is well suited for making through groove cuts. Make certain the workpiece edge is flat and that there is no debris along the saw fence. Use a push stick on small boards. A combination or rip blade makes groove cuts easily in solid-wood or sheet-good stock **(A)**. A wider groove can be made with a single blade by making a series of cuts. Just move the fence over after each pass to establish the extra width **(B)**.

[**TIP**] **If the groove cut is centered in the workpiece you can make a cut, flip the board edge for edge, and make a second cut with the same fence setting.**

Remove the remainder of the waste material with a chisel or router plane, or just move the fence over in very small amounts each time to remove every bit of waste.

[**VARIATION**] **Dado blades were designed for jobs like cutting through grooves. They remove large amounts of wood in a hurry, but take care to feed the work through at a moderate rate. Also use a push stick or hold-down device to keep the workpiece flat to the table. Make a deep groove in a series of passes rather than in one large deep cut.**

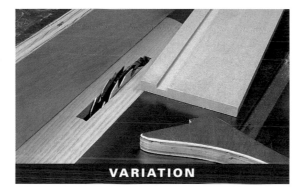

VARIATION

Groove on the Router Table

The router table is the best tool for making stopped groove cuts. You can use stops clamped onto the fence or table, and there is less cleanup and little or no danger of kickback.

Always match the bit width to the stock that goes in the groove **(A)**. Most sheet-good material these days is undersize rather than oversize, so check the thickness of the stock carefully before routing a groove. Take a practice pass in scrap wood, and remember that it's always better to cut a little less than the thickness of the stock. Adjust the bit cutting height to ⅛ in. for most materials. Set the fence distance to the bit with the bit rotated so one cutting edge is closest to the fence **(B)**. Holding the work firmly against the fence, feed from right to left across the bit **(C)**.

When making a stopped groove, carefully mark the fence to show you where to begin and end the cut. Hold a piece of scrap up to the bit. Then rotate the bit until it pushes the scrap away from it. Where the scrap stops moving is the position of the outer edge of the bit. Mark this on the fence and square this line up so you can easily see it. Do the same on the other side of the bit, and you'll have two lines on the fence that indicate the width of the bit **(D)**.

Mark the stopped cuts on the workpiece. Line the first stopped cut line with the left edge of the bit as marked on the fence. Then clamp stops on the fence or table at the rear end of the board **(E)**. Move the board along to line up the second cut against the right edge of the bit and clamp another stop for it.

[TIP] **Chips are likely to bunch up against the far stop on the outfeed side of the router table fence as you make a cut. Put a fat shim, such as a piece of ¼-in. plywood, underneath the stop before clamping. Then remove the shim so the debris can be blown away as you cut.**

With the workpiece above the bit, carefully lower the right end against the stop block to the right. Now lower the left end into the bit. To prevent burning as the bit cuts to depth, slide the workpiece back and forth for just a short distance as you drop down onto the bit until you reach full depth **(F)**. When you're at depth, move all the way back to the first stop to make sure it's cleaned and then proceed with the cut. Lift the board off the bit at the far end of the cut by pushing into the fence firmly but gently **(G)**. This keeps the board in line with the cut. You can also push into the end stop to help lift the wood off the bit.

After cutting the stopped groove, clean the round corners with a chisel. Line up a wide chisel flat against the side walls of the groove and walk it over to the stop mark to establish your lines **(H)**. Then chop down to depth.

Step 1

Set the workpiece down onto the bit; then move it back and forth until the cut is at full depth. This will prevent burning.

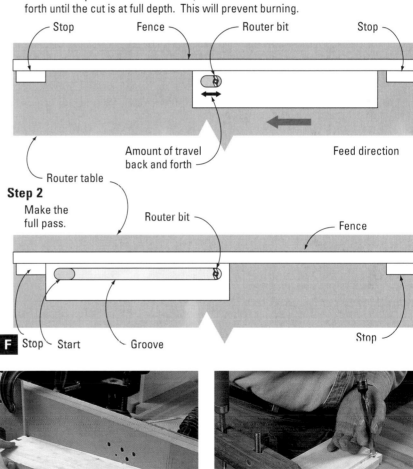

Stop — Fence — — Router bit — Stop

Amount of travel back and forth

Feed direction

Router table

Step 2

Make the full pass.

Router bit — — Fence

F Stop — Start — Groove — Stop

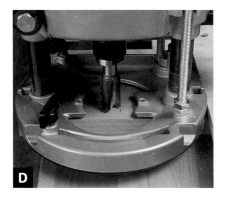

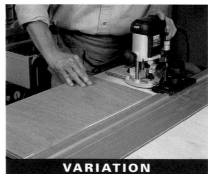

VARIATION

Through Dado with a Router

A topside dado pass with the router on a wide panel needs careful alignment. A right-angle jig guides the cut for a through dado. Select a bit for cutting the dado. When making a housed dado, don't assume that the bit will perfectly match your material. Leave the dado slightly undersize and trim the part that slides into it until it fits (**A**). Measure the distance from the edge of the router baseplate to the edge of the bit (**B**). Place the jig on the work, making sure it is square (**C, D**). Run the base tight to the jig or put in a template guide and run it tight to the edge of the jig (**E**).

[**VARIATION**] **Commercial clamps or fence systems can be used to guide the work, especially for sheet-good material. The fence system shown here (by Festool®) uses a straightedge fence that is placed in position onto the plywood; the router rides along the guide rail. Use a spacer board to set the fence in exactly the correct position. It lines up flush with the edge of the panel. Make the cut and then use the spacer to line up the matching cut on the opposite panel.**

Through Dado on the Router Table

Set the fence for the distance from the edge of the board to the dado **(A)**. Cut the dado on the router table using a straight bit.

To make a dado that's wider than your widest bit, use a spacer block during the first pass. Put the spacer in place between the workpiece and fence. This pushes the work just a bit farther away from the fence. Then remove the spacer to make the second pass. This ensures that you will always be cutting into the rotation of the bit when moving from right to left on the router table **(B)**. Use a backer board to support the pass and to protect the exit hole from tearout. As you make the pass, be sure all the boards are lined up tight to the fence and don't let them angle or shift **(C)**.

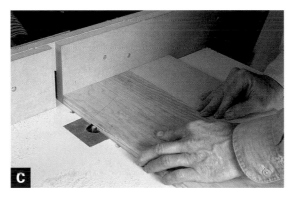

VARIATION

Through Dado on the Table Saw

To cut a through dado on the table saw, use a crosscut jig to make a series of passes. Set up stops for each side of the dado cut. If all your work is cut perfectly to length, then all the dadoes will be the same size **(A)**. Be sure no debris gets between the end of the board and the stops, as this will cause an inaccurate cut. Make a pass and then move over just a little for each subsequent pass.

On a narrow board, it's simple to make the two end cuts, cut away all the remaining wood in the middle, and then clean the dado with the saw-blade **(B)**. After making all the rough cuts, move the jig so the board is sitting right over the top of the blade. Then move the board back and forth over the blade between the stops to clean up the cut. Do this in a series of passes.

[VARIATION] A familiar method for cutting through dadoes on the table saw is to use a dado set. Match your dado package to the stock thickness. If you don't have a designated crosscut jig for dadoing, use a miter gauge to move the work past the dado blade.

Stopped Dado with a Router

Stopped dadoes do not show through at the end of the board. They are best made with the router, and you can do this topside with an auxiliary fence attached to the router fence. Begin by marking out the joint clearly **(A)**; then trust your eye and steady hand with the router to stop the dado pass in the right spot **(B)**. If you can't see through the router base to the joint mark on the workpiece, mark the position of the router base instead. Place the router just over the end of the joint with the bit properly rotated. Use a pencil to mark the position of the base and bring the router to that point with each pass **(C)**. You could also use a right-angle fence to guide the router **(D)**.

➤ See *"Through Dado with a Router"* on p. 96.

Drawer Lock Joint

On the router table, make the horizontal cut for a drawer lock joint in a piece of scrap plywood (**A**). Next, make the vertical cut with the bit just emerging from the fence.

[**TIP**] **Use a zero-clearance fence with dust collection and run your router at its lowest speed.**

Play around with the bit height to get that perfect fit and check the setup in some scrap (**B**). Adjust the bit lower if the joint is too tight, because the dado cut in the joint is always the same width. The tongue gets smaller with less bit showing at a lower height. I find that just about ¹⁵⁄₃₂ in. is optimal for a good fit, but remember that you can also adjust the fit by the placement of the fence. Set the fence too far from the bit, and the joint may fit but the corner won't be flush. Set it too close, and the joint won't fit properly. Keep moving the fence while adjusting the bit height until you get the joint to fit.

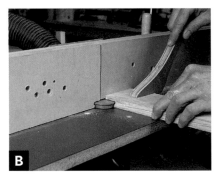

Rabbeted Drawer Lock Joint

It is possible to make a rabbeted version of the drawer lock joint by exposing more of the bit. Waste some of the wood first on the table saw set up with a dado blade (**A**). Then place the fence at the proper distance and feed the board slowly past the bit (**B**). The rabbeted drawer face will allow you to use a full or partial overlay drawer (**C**).

Tongue-and-Groove Joint on the Router Table

Place a bearing-mounted slotting cutter in the router table for cutting the groove. Make sure that the depth of cut—the distance from the bit edge to the bearing—is right for your job. You can change out bearings to adjust the depth of cut as required **(A)**. Or you can hide the cutter inside an adjustable fence so only as much bit as needed pokes out **(B, C)**. Slotting cutters will also cut the tongue. Adjust the bit height so you're cutting a rabbet first on one face and then the other **(D)**.

The stock has to be flat with parallel faces for this method to work. Make sure you press the work down flat to the table as you pass it by the bit.

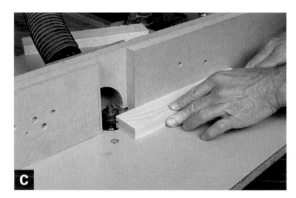

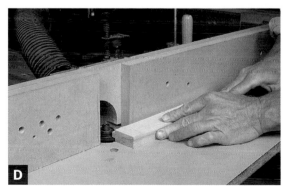

Hand-Cut Tongue-and-Groove Joint

Combination planes work well for plowing a through groove cut. The no. 45 plane shown here, like all combination planes, needs careful alignment so the iron is well supported during the cut **(A)**. Don't let too much blade be exposed or you'll experience chatter.

Tongue cuts can be made with a rabbeting plane **(B)**. Keep the plane square to the edge of the board so the shoulder remains square to the tongue. Set the plane fence so the tongue is almost as deep as the groove.

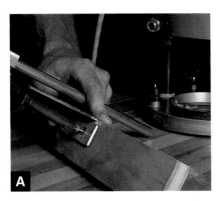

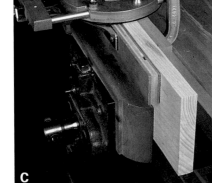

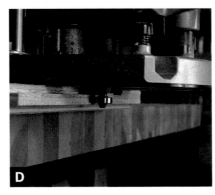

Tongue-and-Groove Joint with a Router

The groove is cut using a straight bit chucked in a plunge router. Using a plunge router allows you to easily control the depth of cut. The cut is guided by the router's edge guide fitted with an auxiliary fence **(A)**. Since edge cuts like this are precarious, mount another board next to the workpiece to support the cut **(B)**.

You could also use a slotting cutter in a router table to make the groove cut. Or you could clamp on a second fence to the router base and trap the workpiece between the fences **(C)**.

Use a rabbeting bit topside to cut a tongue on a plywood panel **(D)**. Make sure that the cut is deep enough to hold but not so deep that it weakens the tongue.

Making a Loose Tongue

Another method of tongue and grooving is to use a loose tongue that fits into grooved boards **(A)**. A loose tongue is simply a spline glued in between two groove cuts. Make it fit snugly, with just a little room for glue. The tongue shouldn't fall out of the joint when testing its fit; nor should you have to hammer it in place, except when you apply the glue. When using any sheet-good material, you can use a plywood tongue, as there is no concern with shrinkage. Solid-wood tongues can be used for joining solid-wood sides. Run the spline with short cross-grain for the greatest strength.

Make through groove cuts on the table saw or with a straight bit and plunge router.

► See *"Through Groove on the Table Saw"* on p. 93.

Or make stopped groove cuts on the router table with a straight bit **(B)**. Clamp stops onto the fence and drop down onto the bit. Have the bit set at full height and use ⅛-in. to ¼-in. table inserts to raise the board up. After each pass, pull out an insert. Or reset the bit height after each pass. Be sure to index off the face side of each board for the groove cuts.

Fit splines that are too thick by scraping or planing them. Not only will sanding round their edges but also it is too difficult to control with any hand-held sander **(C)**. Check the fit of the tongue along the entire length of the grooves.

(Continued on p. 104.)

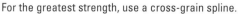
For the greatest strength, use a cross-grain spline.

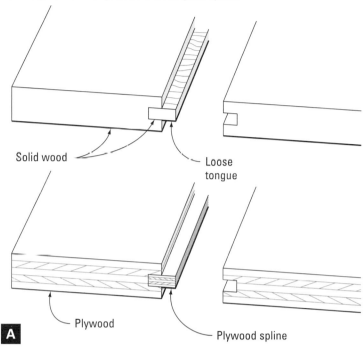

Solid wood · Loose tongue · Plywood · Plywood spline

A

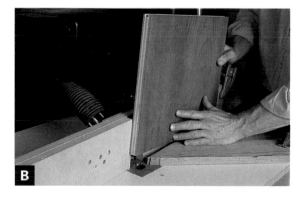

B

C

A solid corner joint can also use loose tongues, but this is only possible with plywood or sheet-good case sides. The shrinkage of solid sides to a solid corner running cross-grain would cause the joint to fail or the case to rack horribly out of square.

Use a slotting cutter on the router table, but match its groove cut to the thickness of the spline, if you can (**D**). Grind a cutter down to match undersize plywood if you need to make a number of these joints for a project. Remember to make the corner stock a bit larger than the plywood stock as well, to give strength to the corner after grooving. You don't want those groove cuts meeting up inside your corner block.

Through groove cuts can be dressed up with a false tongue fitted at the outside of the joint. Make a false tongue out of a nice contrasting material, such as mahogany (shown here) or walnut (**E**).

Tongue-and-Groove Joint on the Table Saw

The table saw makes through groove cuts like any other rip cut. Keep the workpiece held flat to the table and fence and use a moderate feed rate. If necessary, support the workpiece with an auxiliary fence (A). A single pass over the blade will cut a ⅛-in.-wide groove. A dado set will, of course, make a large groove much more quickly. Flip the board face for face to center a larger groove cut.

A single blade will cut the tongue. Make the first two cuts horizontally to establish the shoulders of the tongue (B). These cuts are made like two rabbet cuts with their shoulders lining up. Make the second pass holding the workpiece vertically to cut the sides of the tongue (C), but keep the waste piece away from the fence so it's not trapped by the blade, causing kickback. Set the blade height for just under the shoulder cut. Clean up any leftover waste with a chisel. Use an auxiliary fence for better support of the workpiece. Check the fit of the tongue before committing all your cuts.

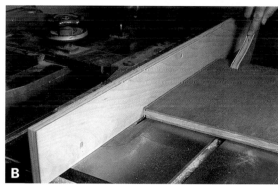

You can also use a dado blade with an auxiliary fence to cut the tongue. The auxiliary fence allows you to zero the dado blade right next to the fence (D). By doing this, you minimize the danger of kickback, but remember to use a push stick. Make sure the workpiece edge is square so the tongue shoulders are square and in line with one another. Do this cut in scrap, checking the fits of the shoulder and the tongue separately. Adjust the fence setting and blade height accordingly.

A

B

Biscuit-Reinforced Miter

For biscuit-reinforced miters, first make the miter cuts using your preferred cutting method.

Biscuits placed across a miter joint do a good job of adding strength and are not visible **(A)**. Check your cut first on a piece of scrap stock to make sure the biscuit joiner is set for the right depth of cut. You don't want the biscuit slot to go through the board. Clamp the workpiece securely before making the biscuit cut.

Next, size the miter joint with a light application of glue. Then put glue in the slots and across the faces of the joint and finally bring the boards together **(B)**.

Splined Miter

The first step to making a splined miter is to cut the miters on the table saw **(A)**. The blade angle for cutting the spline is already set after making the miter cuts. Place a fence close to the blade and, using the miter gauge, run the workpiece past the blade. Double-check the blade height and fence settings in scrap material **(B)**. For saws that tilt toward the fence, place the fence on the opposite side of the blade.

Splined compound angle miters require that the cut be made vertically past the blade with the blade set at its determined cutting angle **(C)**.

[**VARIATION**] **Make up an angle jig to support a mitered board as it moves across the router table. The one shown here is made of medium-density fiberboard (MDF) and has enough room so the workpiece can be securely clamped to it. Place a straight bit in the router table and pass the jig past the bit. For deeper splines, make several passes to get to a full depth of cut. Pass the jig from right to left into the rotation of the bit, which will push the jig in tight to the fence.**

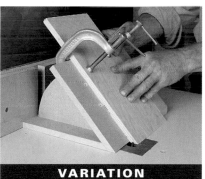

VARIATION

Plywood Splines

Use plywood splines for miters cut in sheet-good materials, such as plywood and medium-density fiberboard (MDF). It's much better if the plywood is already pretty close to the proper thickness. Then all that's required is to scrape it to fit the spline cut **(A)**. Dress up a plywood spline miter joint by placing a bit of hardwood just at the end of a cut **(B)**. Run the grain direction of the wood spline the short way across the joint.

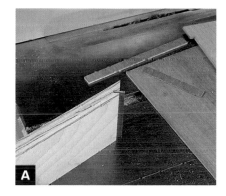

Solid-Wood Splines

Use solid-wood splines in boxes or cases made of solid wood. Mill them out of a straight-grained piece of stock. The grain direction must run the same way as the sides of the box so their shrinkage directions are the same. This means you'll be working with wide short-grain pieces that are hard to mill with a jointer or planer and that tend to break along their width. However, in their length where they need to be strong to hold the joint together, they are impossible to break.

First mill up a board as wide as your box or even a bit wider. Then crosscut a section to length on the table saw. Take this wide piece to the bandsaw and trim it close to the required thickness of the spline, using a fence to run against (**A**). Use a pencil as a push stick. A practice cut will show you if you're close enough in thickness.

Set the spline onto a bench hook and use a block plane to finish off the fitting (**B**). Be careful not to break the short grain; but if you do break a spline, the pieces will still work in the joint. The break won't be seen and the joint itself won't be compromised.

Double-check the length of the spline and trim it if needed in place on the joint (**C**). If the spline is close in length, a few passes with a block plane should be all that's necessary to clean it up. Leave the splines a bit wide and, after gluing, you can clean the ends off with a file, chisel, or plane. Spline miters make gluing a miter joint a bit easier, because the joint can't slip around during assembly (**D**).

Keyed Miter on the Router Table

You can make key cuts on the router table using a straight bit and a key miter jig. The jig supports the box during the cut. It's made of one flat board with a fence mounted to it at a 45-degree angle.

[TIP] Keep any fasteners you use to mount the fence higher than the highest possible height of the router bit.

Mark out the locations of the keys on the box. Then set the fence in position next to the jig, and measure from the jig (A). If the cuts are placed symmetrically, you can make one pass, flip the box around edge for edge, and make a second pass. You will have to support the box in tight to the jig as you pass it over the bit.

[VARIATION] For better support, make a miter jig with a 90-degree cradle in it to hold your box or case. Hold this in tight to the fence and pass the whole jig by the bit. You'll have to measure off the fence with the jig in place.

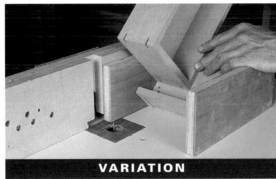

VARIATION

Keyed Miter on the Table Saw

To cut keyed miters in large cases on the table saw, make a larger cradle to hold the carcase. Clamp the key miter jig right to the crosscut jig. The support pieces that hold the jig arms to-gether also act as stops for locating the case in the jig **(A)**. A backer board prevents tearout on the face side of the carcase. Use double-sided tape to hold the backer board in place and clamp the workpiece securely to the jig **(B)**.

[**VARIATION**] Use the small key miter jig against the table saw fence to make key cuts in small boxes.

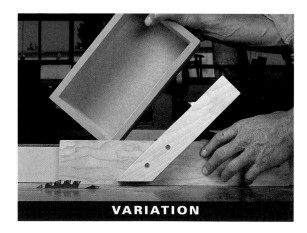

VARIATION

Hand-Cut Halved Joint

To begin a hand-cut halved joint, use a marking gauge to lay out all the shoulder cuts. These will run along the cross-grain of the boards. Mark both faces of each board and don't forget to mark across the edge that connects these faces. The cheek cut, which runs with the grain, can be just penciled onto the face. Do this for just half of each joint **(A)**. Place the board in the vise vertically and low enough so there's no movement or vibration as you saw. Saw to the waste side of the line straight down to the gauge line **(B)**.

After sawing, chop on the gauge marks with a chisel. Drag the chisel along until you feel it just drop into the gauge line. Make a light chopping cut; then turn the chisel over and clean up the cut. Make several more light passes and then move to the other face. Keep the cuts perfectly vertical. Then put the board in the vise and chop on the gauge line that's on the edge of the board. This will connect all three chopping lines together and form the plane that you want the shoulder to lie in **(C)**.

Then use the saw again to saw close to the marks to remove the waste. Now use a wide chisel to clean the shoulder cut down to the gauge lines. You can undercut the shoulder a little, but do so away from any edge or face **(D)**. Check the fit of the shoulder and cheek to see that they're square and flat **(E)**. Then you can mark to the other mating piece with a marking knife. Push one board into a bench dog or stop, and butt the other piece right up to it, lining up its shoulder cut on the inside face of the other board. Be sure to indicate which corners go together so you can find this easily during assembly **(F)**

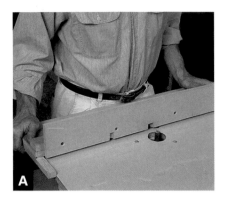

Finger Joint on the Router Table

To make larger or variably spaced finger joints or when working with wide boards, make the joints on the router table. Use a sliding table that fits around the edge of the router table or use a miter gauge, if you have a slot for one in your table **(A)**. Mark out the finger joints on one board **(B)**, and trim away most of the waste in the finger sockets on the bandsaw **(C)**. Mount a wide straight bit in the router and set it for the full depth of cut.

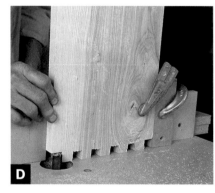

Position the stock in the jig so it sets the first finger cut in exactly the right spot and clamp a stop block onto the jig. Then take a pass for the first finger. For symmetrical fingers, flip the board edge for edge to make the second cut **(D)**. A spacer block will move the stock away from the stop for the second cut. Use a series of spacer blocks as wide as the finger cuts to move the board over for successive cuts **(E)**. Use a spacer block exactly as wide as your router bit to index the matching cuts off the existing stop. Use paper shims between the stop and spacer to adjust the fit of the fingers **(F)**.

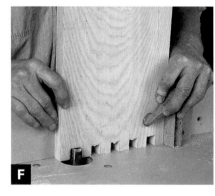

Finger Joint on the Bandsaw

Don't rule out the bandsaw for making finger joints. It can do surprisingly good work if the blade is sharp and you have a good adjustable fence on it.

Lay out the finger spacing and mark out the joints. Also lay in a gauge line (**A**). You must be able to accurately and easily adjust the fence on your bandsaw to make these finger joint cuts. Clamp a stop on the fence to limit the depth of cut (**B**). Make the first finger cut. Flip the board and make the matching cut on the other side of the board. Now do all the cuts on the two sides or end pieces (**C**).

For the matching board, use a spacer between the fence and the board that's as wide as the bandsaw blade (**D**). Then make the matching board cuts. For more fingers re-adjust the fence and cut the rest of the fingers along with their matching cuts until all the cuts have been made.

Next, rough out the waste on the bandsaw. Use a narrow blade to make the tight curve cuts (**E**). Trim as close to the gauge line as you can freehand. Then set the fence to cut right to the line. It will be easier to do this on the board with a finger socket at its edges (**F**). Don't cut into the fingers. For sockets between fingers, put the blade as close as you can to the gauge line and let the blade start to cut. With a slow feed rate, it will eventually move over to the line (**G**).

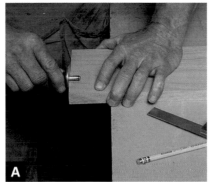

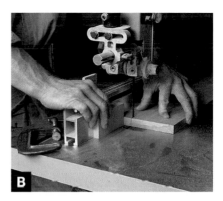

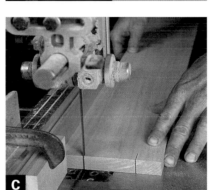

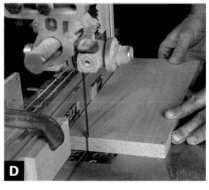

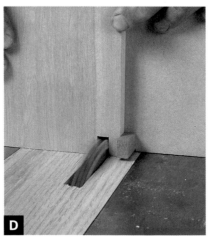

Finger Joint on the Table Saw

Set up a dado blade as wide as the fingers you want. Be sure to make the carcase or box as wide as some multiple of the finger cut so you end up with full fingers at both edges of the piece. Use a miter gauge with miter gauge blocks fit to it to take up any slack (such as a Tru-Fit system), or put an auxiliary fence between two miter gauges. Then take a single pass through the fence with the dado blade **(A)**.

Next, mill a piece of scrap that is exactly as wide as your dado package. This will be your indexing pin. Make it out of a hardwood, like maple, and long enough that you can cut it in two. Put one indexing pin in the slot cut into the fence by the dado blade **(B)**.

Move the auxiliary fence over to the left of the blade by the thickness of one finger cut. Use the second indexing pin as a spacer between the blade and first pin to measure that distance precisely **(C)**. Be careful here, because if you move the pin too far from the blade your fingers will be too tight. Have the second spacer pin pressed in right between the blade and indexing pin. Clamp or screw the auxiliary fence right in place here.

[TIP] **You can also take one or two passes with a handplane on the spacer to shrink the fingers slightly, making them a bit looser.**

Put the first board snug up against the indexing pin and take a pass **(D)**. Then set the finger slot you just cut over the indexing pin and make the second pass **(E)**. Continue with this process until all the finger cuts are made. Always keep the boards vertical and square to the saw table **(F)**.

To make the matching cuts on the second piece use the spacer pin again. Set it between the indexing pin and the blade. Then place the board up next to it. This will set the board the proper distance away from the pin for its first pass **(G)**. After making the first pass, just butt the finger slot right up to the indexing pin for the second cut. Continue as before, lifting the board up and onto the indexing pin after each pass has been made. The fit should be snug enough to hold together on its own, but not so snug you have to hammer it together **(H)**.

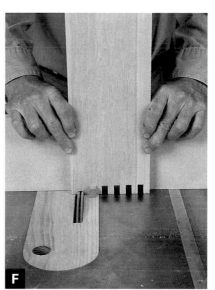

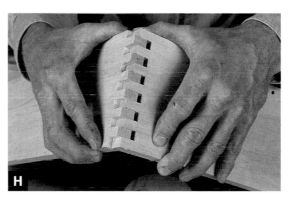

A

B

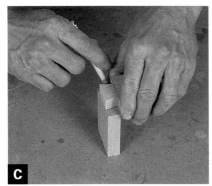

C

D

E

The 5-Minute Dovetail

Use this exercise to warm up before cutting your actual workpieces. You will need a dovetail saw, a pencil, a chisel, and mallet.

First, mill two small pieces of stock: $\frac{5}{8}$ in. by 2 in. by 3 in. Use a soft hardwood, such as soft maple or alder. Mark out the thickness of each piece on the other with a pencil **(A)**. Then place one piece vertically in a vise.

Begin by sawing the tail. Saw down to the pencil line but at a slight angle. Remember: straight across and at an angle down to the pencil line. Cut first one side and then the other. Don't worry about how the tail angles turn out. You will mark out whatever their shape is onto the pin piece. Then turn the piece in the vise and make the straight shoulder cuts **(B)**.

Mark out the tail board onto the pin piece **(C)**. Put a pencil mark on what wood needs to come out. Also mark the face of each piece for ease of reassembly. Remember that you're making a right-angle corner here. Then place the pin board in the vise vertically.

Saw to the waste side of the lines down to the pencil line. You'll saw at an angle but straight down. When you've made the cuts for the tail socket, notice that you've also created two half pins **(D)**.

With a chisel, chop out on the pencil mark to remove the waste. Chisel from both faces in toward the middle and use a cleaning pass every once in a while to remove the waste **(E)**. Fit the tails and pins together.

Hand-Cut Through Dovetail

To begin hand-cut through dovetails, set the marking gauge for slightly less than the thickness of the stock. Put lines around the four sides of the tail boards but only on the faces of the pin boards. The half pins don't require any gauge lines at the outside edges **(A)**.

Set up a sliding bevel for the tail and pin angle. For best results, keep the angle ratio somewhere between 1:5 and 1:8. Lay these angles out on a square-edged board. Measure up 5 in. and over 1 in. to get a 1:5 slope **(B)**. Lay out the tails on the gauge line. Mark out all the tails on the face sides of the boards. Then square the lines across the end grain as well. Mark these angles down the far side of the board with the sliding bevel as a double-check for your sawing.

[TIP] When cutting thin boards, stack the two together in the vise with their edges and ends lined up.

Cut the tails with a small-kerf dovetail saw. Keep the board straight in the vise and learn to angle the saw for the tail cut. Start the cut on the far edge, cutting in the reverse direction of the saw-teeth to establish the cut. Then gradually lay the saw down across the end of the board, making sure it's square across the board. Next, tilt the saw to cut the tail angle and saw just down to the gauge line **(C)**.

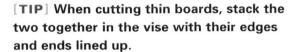

Remove the waste by holding the chisel right on the gauge lines. Sight to the side of the chisel when chopping. This way you can see that you're holding the tool truly perpendicular for the start of the cut. Make sure the corners of the tails are

(Continued on p. 118.)

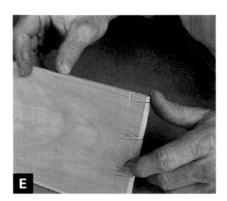

clean and the shoulders are flat or even a bit undercut. After completing a few chopping passes, angle the chisel just a little to undercut the shoulders **(D)**.

Chop the half pin sockets from both faces and the edge to establish three flats all in one plane. Then saw off the waste close to these cuts down to the tail. Finish up by paring the end grain down to those lines. You can undercut the shoulder just past the first chopping marks as well **(E)**. Get all the tails right and ready before moving to the pins.

Mark the tails out onto the pin board. Mount the pin board high enough in the vise so you can easily line up its edges with the tail board and another flat board. I put a handplane on its edge and rest the tail board on it. Use a sharp marking knife to transfer the tail shape onto the end grain of the pin board **(F)**. Draw square lines from those marks to the gauge lines.

Cut the pins at an angle to the face but straight down the board to the gauge line **(G)**. Remember to stay on the waste side of the line with your saw.

Chop away the waste on the pin board with a chisel. Make the first chopping passes very light; flip the chisel bevel side down and clean up the waste. Make sure the board is securely fastened to the benchtop with a clamp or pushed up against a bench dog or stop **(H)**.

A well-cut dovetail joint should go together with hand pressure and have just enough room for the glue, which swells the wood a bit. After checking the fit, use a scrap block and hammer or use a dead-blow hammer to carefully take the joint apart **(I)**.

Through Dovetail with Mitered Shoulder

The advantage of a through dovetail with a mitered shoulder is a more refined look than the standard through dovetail. Although the end grain still shows on both sides, the front edge meets in a clean miter rather than a butt joint **(A)**.

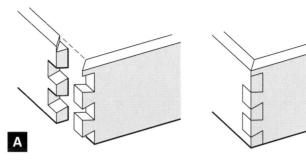

A

Lay out the dovetail joint to allow for the miter at one edge. Place gauge lines on both faces and only one edge of the tail board. Lay out the miter cut at the other edge of the board with a pencil and the miter square on a combination square. Then cut the through tails, but don't angle the last cut near the miter. It's a straight-sided cut **(B)**. Next, cut the miter with a dovetail saw. Make the pin cuts after marking them out from the tails **(C)**.

B

C

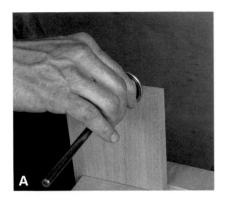

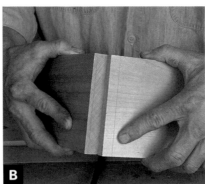

Hand-Cut Half-Blind Dovetail

Half-blind dovetails are commonly used for building drawers. The joint shows from only the drawer side, where it is lapped into the drawer face.

The joint requires two different gauge lines on the drawer face because it doesn't come through. One line marks out the thickness of the tail stock as usual. Gauge a line on the inside of the drawer face at just less than the thickness of the drawer side. The other gauge line marks out the depth of the lap. Put it in on the drawer face end at about three-quarters of its full thickness **(A)**. Use this last gauge setting to mark out the tail boards across their faces and edges **(B)**.

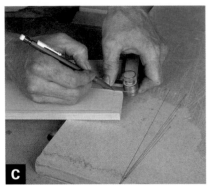

Lay out and mark the tails onto the drawer sides. Set a sliding bevel for the angle, between 1:5 and 1:8 is common. The size of the tails is generally two to three times the size of the pins, but above all be sure to make the pin size convenient for chopping out **(C)**.

Cut the tails with the board held perfectly vertical in the vise. Angle the saw to make the tail cuts straight across the board. Practice will improve your ability to make these cuts accurately **(D)**.

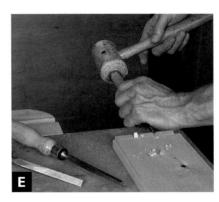

Use a chisel to chop out on the gauge lines. Make the first passes fairly light, because the chisel acts as a wedge and can move off the line if you're too heavy with the hammer blow. Clean up the waste with some cuts made straight into the board **(E)**. Make sure the corners of the tails are clean and that the area across the pin sockets are all flat. You can undercut this area a little to help with the fitting.

Clamp the drawer face in the vise. Set the tail board or drawer side onto it and use a handplane on edge to support the other end of the tail board. By raising both boards up, you can more easily line up their edges with a flat piece of scrap. Line up the end of the drawer side with the gauge line on the end of the drawer face. Use a knife to mark out the tails on the end of the pin board while holding the tail board down tightly (F). No matter how the tails came out, their shape is now transferred to the matching board.

Reverse the pin board in the vise. Cut the pins holding the saw at an angle. Cut down to both of the gauge lines and no farther (G).

Then clean up the cuts with a chisel. Make the first chopping cut very light; then clean up the waste by holding the chisel bevel side down (H). Continue removing the waste from both directions until you're down to the gauge lines. Make these surfaces slightly undercut to create a goodlooking joint (I).

Fit the joint one tail at a time and don't force the work. Always look for the shiny spots that indicate where a joint is rubbing. Pare these spots first. Work from one end of a board to the other when adjusting the fit (J).

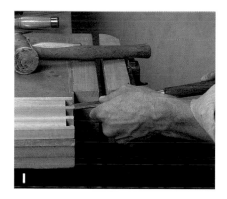

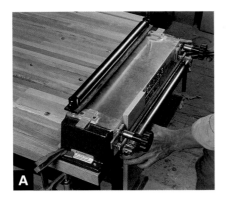

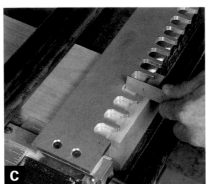

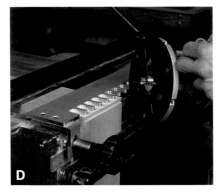

Half-Blind Dovetail with a Router and Omnijig

The Omnijig® cuts half-blind dovetails in both boards at once using a finger template, ½-in. dovetail bit, and ⅝-in. template guide. Mount the template guide first; then insert the dovetail bit into the router. Set the bit depth for approximately $^{19}/_{32}$ in. Loosen all the sliding stop bars and move them out of the way. Check the manual for final side stop adjustment. Adjust the clamp bars for the thickness of the stock.

For this example, I'm cutting half-blind dovetails for a drawer. Place the drawer side vertically in the jig with its inside facing out. Raise it higher than the surface of the jig and butt it up against the side stop **(A)**. Place the drawer face flat in the jig with its inside facing up and its end butted up to the face of the drawer side. Then reset the vertical piece so its end lines up flush with the top of the horizontal piece **(B)**.

Set the bracket spacers so the bottom of one of the template finger slots sits approximately $^{19}/_{32}$ in. from the end of the drawer face. Check this depth and check the side stop placement so the two boards are offset by $^{7}/_{16}$ in. **(C)**. Make a climb cut first across the outer face of the vertical board, moving from right to left to prevent tearout **(D)**. Then rout between each of the fingers carefully, from left to right. Make sure to go fully into each of the fingers **(E)**.

Half-Blind Dovetail with a Generic Jig

Generic jigs cut both boards at once. You will need a dovetail bit and the proper template guide to ride in the finger assembly. Always make practice cuts in scrap wood before cutting your good stock. The depth of cut is crucial here for a good fit.

Place the tail piece, or drawer side, vertically in the jig with its inside facing out. Set it in high and butt the pin board, or drawer face, right up to it with its inside facing up. Make sure both boards register against their side stops **(A)**. Reset the vertical board's end to line up flush with the face of the horizontal board and clamp it firmly in place **(B)**.

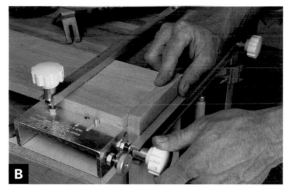

Place the bit in the router and set its height. This is the critical part for the fit of the joint; so when you find the right height setting, make up a height block to index the bit each time. Or dedicate a router and bit to that jig and never change the bit **(C)**.

Turn the router on, set the edge of the base down on the edge of the finger template, and move into the work. Don't come straight down onto the finger assembly and do not tip or lift the router while making the cut **(D)**. Make a first pass across the face of the vertical board, moving from right to left. This climb cut will help prevent tearout. Then move into each of the fingers, carefully moving from left to right. The final step is to come back and retrace the cut, making sure you've entered into each of the fingers as deeply as you can go.

Through Sliding Dovetail

Before starting to cut sliding dovetails, make sure the stock is flat and remove all the milling marks. If you handplane, sand, or scrape your work after you cut the joint, you will affect its fit **(A)**.

Make the dovetail slot first. For a ½-in. dovetail, use a ¼-in. straight bit on the router table to rough out the slot. Leave this cut just short of full depth. Run the end of the board against a fence set so that the straight bit is centered in the final dovetail slot position **(B)**.

Mount the dovetail bit and set it to full depth. You get only one try with this cut at full depth. Make a pass, keeping pressure down on the board to keep the cut consistent in depth. Run the pass twice if you have any doubts about it. Use a backer board to prevent tearout or cut the stock ⅛ in. oversize in width so there will be enough wood to cut away the inevitable tearout. Use a table insert in the router table to cover up as much of the bit as possible **(C)**.

Cut the tail section on the router table, holding your workpiece vertically. Don't reset the bit height. It will perfectly match the first cut. Set the fence over the bit so only a portion of it is showing. Cut one face side of all the joints and then cut the other faces. Fine-tune and adjust the fence by cutting into a piece of scrap that's the same thickness. If you need to cut more off the tail, use a pencil to mark the fence position on the table, loosen the fence clamps, and then tap it a little away from the pencil mark to expose more bit. Each movement of the fence will give you two possible cuts, one on each face **(D)**.

If you think you're very close with the fit but don't want to risk it, hedge your bet by placing a paper shim between the fence and the workpiece. This will kick the work out a few thousandths of an inch from the fence. A dollar bill gives you a 0.003-in. shim **(E)**. If the joint is still too tight, remove the shim and take another pass. On narrower boards, a handplane pass off the board's face will put you that much closer to the bit for a slightly narrower tail cut.

Before starting to fit the joint, take a single handplane pass off the end grain of the tail **(F)**. This gives you just a little sliding room and some room for glue. Alternatively, you could set the bit depth for the male cut just a hair lower than the height of the female cut. If the tail still binds up in the slot, double-check the depth of the cut with a depth gauge. Or use a combination square as a gauge. Make sure the depth is consistent **(G)**.

> ⚠ **WARNING** Always be aware of the exit point of the bit on the router table. Place your hands in a safe spot—away from this hole.

Frame Joinery

Butt Joints

➤ Butt Joint Reinforced with Screws (p. 128)

➤ Butt Joint with Pocket-Hole Screws (p. 129)

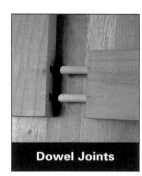

Dowel Joints

➤ Butt Joint with Blind Dowels (p. 130)

Biscuit Joints

➤ Frame Joint with Biscuits (p. 132)

➤ Frame Joint with Multiple Biscuits (p. 133)

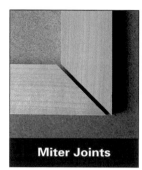

Miter Joints

➤ Miter Joint (p. 134)

➤ Miter Joint Reinforced with Nails (p. 135)

➤ Biscuited Miter Joint (p. 136)

➤ Splined Miter Joint on the Router Table (p. 137)

➤ Splined Miter Joint on the Table Saw (p. 138)

➤ Mitered Slip Joint (p. 139)

➤ Keyed Miter Joint (p. 140)

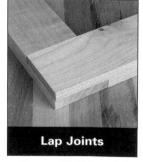

Lap Joints

➤ Corner Half-Lap Joint on the Table Saw (p. 142)

➤ Corner Half-Lap Joint on the Router Table (p. 143)

➤ T or Cross Half-Lap Joint on the Table Saw (p. 144)

➤ Dovetail Lap Joint (p. 145)

➤ Mitered Half-Lap Joint with a Router (p. 146)

➤ Mitered Half-Lap Joint on the Table Saw (p. 147)

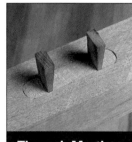

Through Mortises

➤ Through Mortise on the Drill Press (p. 173)

➤ Through Mortise with a Plunge Router and Fence (p. 174)

➤ Through Mortise with a Plunge Router and Template (p. 175)

➤ Wedged Through Tenon (p. 176)

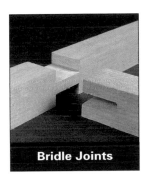

Bridle Joints

Scarf Joints

Splice Joints

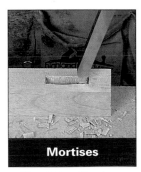

Mortises

Tenons

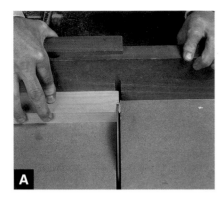

Butt Joint Reinforced with Screws

Butt joints have the simplest requirements, which are, nevertheless, quite important for good results. Make sure the stock is flat, not twisted or in-winding, and keep all the crosscuts square across the width and face of the boards. Also make sure the edge of the stock is milled square, especially where it will butt into the end of another board **(A)**.

Drill through the frame stile with a wide enough diameter bit so the screw head will easily enter the hole. Measure the screw head first to avoid marring the hole. Keep the depth of the holes consistent and deep enough so the screws will have some grab **(B)**.

Drill pilot holes for frames when working with thin stock or when using very hard wood. Some screws with an auger-type tip will enter without splitting the wood, but try one out first on a piece of scrap to see how it performs. Be sure to make the pilot hole just smaller than the root of the screw. The root is the part of the screw that is not threaded **(C)**.

Put glue on the end grain of the rail for just a little extra holding power. Then drive the screws with the frame flat on the workbench. Push the frame against the bench dogs or a clamped board to prevent it from moving. Lubricate the screws with a bit of wax for easier entry **(D)**. Or glue and clamp the frame, let it set up, and then drive the screws **(E)**. Fill the countersunk holes with plugs if the frame edges will be visible.

Butt Joint with Pocket-Hole Screws

Pocket holes eliminate any concerns that the screw's countersunk hole will show, because they're applied from the inside face of the frame. They're very quick to apply since the screws are self-tapping. You use only one bit to cut the countersink and the short pilot hole. Pocket screws also eliminate the need for clamping the frame.

Mount the wood into the pocket-hole jig and drill the pocket hole with the supplied bit **(A)**. Set the depth-stop collar on the bit before drilling the first hole. Put a shim on the jig and run the bit's tip into it. Then lock down the depth stop. This will prevent you from accidentally drilling into the jig or dulling the bit **(B)**.

Drill down to depth and then clear the waste out of the bit and hole **(C)**. The drill bit has enough of a pilot bit leading the cut that a small pilot hole will be created for the screw. Set the pocket screw in that hole and drive it home. Remember to glue the end grain of the rail **(D)**.

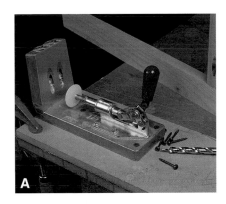

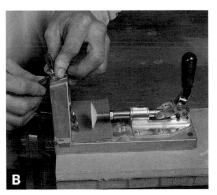

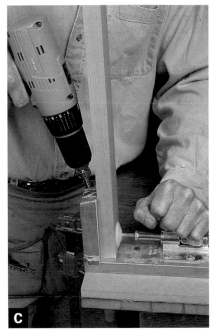

A

B

C

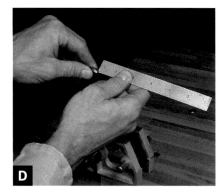

D

E

Butt Joint with Blind Dowels

Dowel a frame together using a doweling jig to help locate the dowel holes. Be sure to double-check the settings and drill as straight into the wood as you can. Dowels that go in on an angle cause twisted frames. Mark the dowel positions when the face frame is on the bench **(A)**.

Place the rail securely in the vise and then set the doweling jig on the end of the rail **(B)**.

Align the marks on the jig for the proper-size dowel to the pencil marks on the frame **(C)**. Here, I'm using a ¼-in. dowel for a ¾-in.-thick frame. Use a brad-point bit with a centering point to drill the dowel holes. Be sure to take the point into account when setting the bit depth. On larger-diameter bits this amount of protrusion can be significant. No frame will clamp home if the dowels are too long for the dowel holes **(D)**. Mark the bit depth with a piece of masking tape **(E)**.

Drill each of the rail holes to depth, making sure to line up the pencil mark accurately to the jig mark each time **(F)**. Then drill the stiles with the stile mounted in the vise. Use the same depth setting **(G)**.

Check the dowel size to the drill bit. If the dowels have shrunk oval, as they're apt to, they may not fit the hole. A quick fix is to cook them a little in a shop oven. They'll shrink enough to make insertion easier. When the glue hits them, the dowels will expand back and lock themselves into place **(H)**.

Use dowels with spiral- or straight-cut glue slots. These allow the glue to escape as the dowels are inserted. Put glue at the mouth of a dowel hole. As you put in the dowel, it will push the glue down into the rest of the hole **(I)**. Have clamps ready when gluing up a doweled frame. You will have to apply some pressure to get the frames to butt together completely **(J)**.

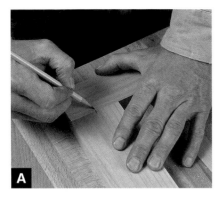

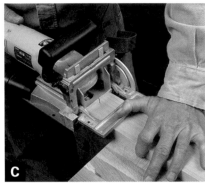

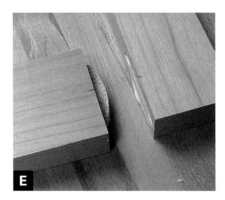

Frame Joint with Biscuits

Use biscuits for a strong and invisible frame joint. Keep the biscuit cut centered in the thickness of the frame. Also index off the face sides of all the frame pieces to ensure a flat frame. Be sure to use a small enough biscuit that the cut doesn't show through at the ends of the board, or offset the cut to one edge if that edge won't be visible. Make a practice cut first to see what diameter cut will be made.

Mark the location of the biscuits onto the frame **(A)**. Push the boards into a clamped backer board or bench dogs so they're well supported. Cut the biscuit slots on the stile edge **(B)**. Then make the biscuit slots on the rail end. Always keep the biscuit joiner flat on each piece so the slot goes in straight **(C)**.

Put glue in the slots using a brush so enough glue gets in **(D)**. Have clamps ready to pull the frame together, because the biscuits start to swell as soon as the glue comes into contact with them **(E)**.

Frame Joint with Multiple Biscuits

For thicker frames, use multiple biscuits. The biscuit slots are close to the two faces of the boards. Mark the biscuit location across the frame members **(A)**. Then mark the depth of the biscuit cuts on the side of the board **(B)**.

Set up the biscuit joiner for the first cut and cut all the boards **(C)**. Then re-adjust the fence for the second cut **(D)**. Make the second set of cuts on all the boards **(E)**. Instead of changing the fence adjustment, you can use a flat shim under the fence to raise the biscuit joiner after making the lower cut. The shim has to be flat and of the proper thickness so the upper cut is in the correct position.

[TIP] If you mill the stock accurately, you can make the first biscuit cut and just flip the board to make the second cut. You'll need two sets of pencil marks, one on each face.

Before gluing the biscuits into the frame members, have clamps ready to pull everything together **(F)**.

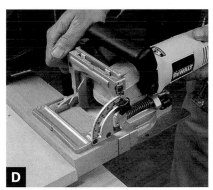

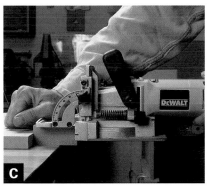

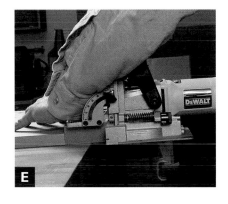

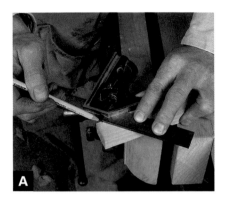

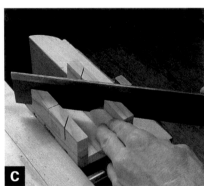

Miter Joint

Lay out the 45-degree miter line with a combination square. Hold the square tight to the edge of the board. You can square the miter line down the sides of the board, if you want, for another aid when cutting **(A)**.

Cut the miter with a handsaw, but remember that you're always cutting in two directions: across at the angle and straight down the board. Here, practice definitely makes for perfect **(B)**. Miter boxes are old stand-bys for roughing out miter cuts. Finish carpenters use them for doing trim work in a house. Line up the saw tight against the 45-degree slot while making the cut **(C)**.

Trim the miter by taking very light passes with a block plane. If you're careful and the plane is tuned and sharp, this cleanup pass will improve the miter in a matter of seconds. Be sure to hold the plane square to the face of the board **(D)**.

Miter Joint Reinforced with Nails

Simple frames can be strengthened using nails or brads across the joint. Cut the miters using a handsaw or compound miter saw **(A)**. Glue up the frame and use a band clamp or miter clamps. After the glue has set overnight you can nail the joints.

Very hard woods should be predrilled to avoid splitting. Keep the frame well supported on the bench over a bench leg so the vibration of the hammering gets taken up by the leg **(B)**. Brad nailers also work well for pinning miters. Shoot multiple brads in from the same side so they won't run into each other. Also make very sure to aim truly so the brad stays centered in the frame. Avoid knots and keep your fingers well away from the joint when using a brad nailer **(C)**.

Finally, set the nails or brads with a nail set and put putty in the holes before finishing **(D)**.

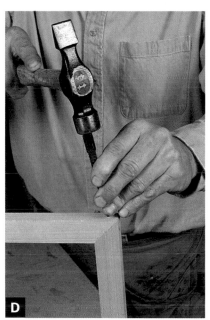

Biscuited Miter Joint

Use a biscuit across a miter joint to improve its strength. To keep it hidden, the biscuit should be shorter than the length of the miter. The biscuit slot is cut into long grain, so the biscuit will make a good glue joint.

Mark the biscuit location on the face side of the miter joint **(A)**. Cut the biscuit slot into each mitered frame member, centering the biscuit slot in the thickness of the frame. If you don't hit dead-on center, remember that as long as you reference off matching faces the slots will line up. Hold the biscuit joiner steady and flat on the face of the frame when cutting **(B)**.

Put enough glue in the biscuit slot to allow the biscuit to swell and lock the joint in place. Remember to size the end of the miter joint with glue before gluing in the biscuits **(C)**. Have clamps ready to pull the miter together **(D)**.

Splined Miter Joint on the Router Table

Make spline cuts along the length of the miters for a loose spline. Match the grain direction of the spline to that of the frame, so they'll shrink in the same direction. The spline can be made of a contrasting wood or the same wood; but remember it will always show, because the exposed grain is part end grain.

You can use the router table for spline cuts that aren't too deep. Mount a straight bit for the size spline required **(A)**. Measure for the spline location on a frame member and center this as best you can. Double splines can be used in thicker frames and should be measured for them accordingly **(B)**.

You'll cut the spline slot using a spline miter jig **(C)**. Set the fence distance off the pencil-marked frame member with the jig in place. Clamp the router table fence down securely **(D)**. For deeper slots, don't take one full pass to make the cut. Make several passes to get down to depth. You can clamp the frame member onto the miter jig or hold it securely onto the jig and pass it over the bit for a series of cuts **(E)**. Make the second pass using a second fence on the miter jig. Use this fence for boards that have to index off the same face side. This way, even if the slot isn't centered in the frame member, the cuts will match **(F)**.

[**VARIATION**] Use a slotting cutter in the router table to cut the spline slot. Capture the cutter in a zero-clearance fence, exposing only as much bit as is required. Stack several frame members together for the cut and use a backer for even better support. Remember to index off matching faces.

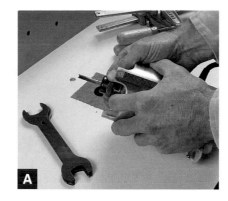

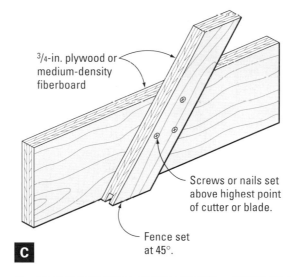

3/4-in. plywood or medium-density fiberboard

Screws or nails set above highest point of cutter or blade.

Fence set at 45°.

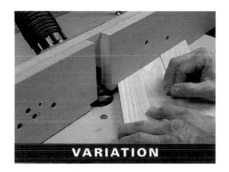

VARIATION

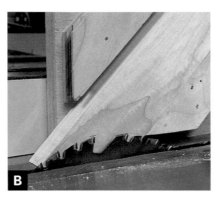

Splined Miter Joint on the Table Saw

Loose spline miter cuts on the table saw are all made with the blade at full height. Set the fence distance with the board marked out for the cut. Hold the miter jig in place when setting the fence. The cut shown here will yield a simple ⅛-in.-wide slot with a regular sawblade. A thin-kerf blade will cut an even smaller slot **(A)**.

Set the blade height for the full height of the slot **(B)**. Make the first spline cut by passing the board at a moderate speed over the blade. Too slow a speed and you might end up burning the wood **(C)**. Make the matching cut using the miter jig with a second fence on it. Clamp the frame member to the jig or hold it firmly in place as you pass it by the blade **(D)**.

[VARIATION] Use a dado blade for wider spline cuts. Clamp the frame member to the jig. If you're getting tearout with this cut, use a backer board or put in a gauge line on the back edge of the frame member.

Pinning the splines with dowel pins gives the joint even more visual interest and strength. After gluing the miter, drill through the spline on the drill press using a brad-point bit. Glue and hammer in the dowels; then clean them flush with a chisel **(E)**.

VARIATION

Mitered Slip Joint

The mitered slip joint is more like a slot mortise-and-tenon joint than a miter joint. But the result shows a mitered joint to the world. Each matching board for the joint is cut differently. Miter cut one board's end and crosscut the other board square. The penciled-out areas on the boards shown in photo **A** indicate what wood has to come out. You'll cut a mortise slot square across the mitered board and make two mitered shoulder cuts on the squared board to establish the tenon.

Use a dado blade and the tenoning jig to make the slot cut straight across the mitered board. Clamp each mitered board vertically in the tenoning jig. Set the blade height so the bottom of the slot is in line with the end of the miter cut. Make all the slot cuts **(B)**.

Use the miter jig to cut the mitered shoulder tenon. Set the blade height to start cutting just at the corner of the frame board **(C)**. Make the first cheek cut with the miter jig. Make the same cut on all the square-end boards **(D)**.

Make the second cut after resetting the saw fence. Since this cut comes all the way out to the face of the board, use a spacer to push each board out just a bit from the jig. Then the blade will make the cut without marring the jig **(E)**.

[**VARIATION**] **Instead of cutting the tenon in the miter jig, use the miter gauge and a dado blade to cut the tenon boards, holding them flat on the saw table. Make a series of passes to cut each tenon cheek.**

Fit the slip joint carefully so it slides together with just hand pressure. You can clamp across the faces once it's together **(F)**.

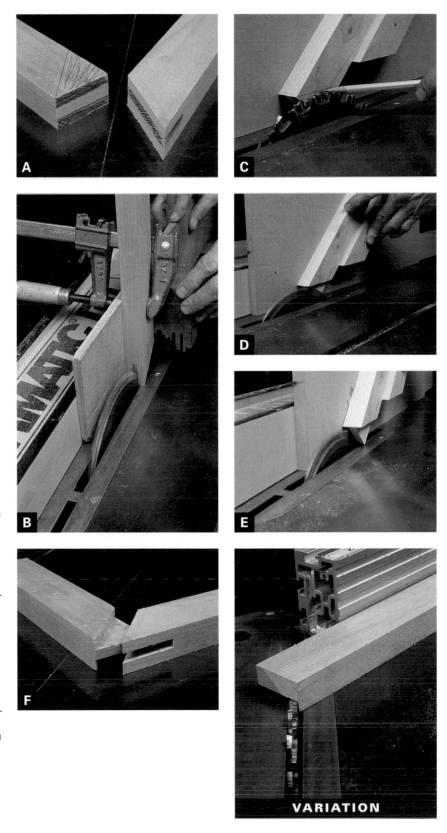

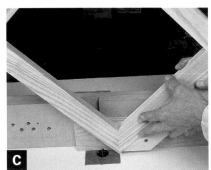

Keyed Miter Joint

When constructing a keyed miter joint, make the key cuts after the frame has been glued together **(A)**. Measure for the key position after cleaning the faces of the frame with a handplane, scraper, or sander. Place the board in a vise to hold it while marking **(B)**.

Make the key cut using a straight bit in a table-mounted router. This will create a nice flat-bottomed cut. Use the miter jig to support the frame as you pass it by the bit. Set the bit for the full depth of cut, but don't try to cut at that full depth in one pass. Instead, make a series of passes. Either clamp the frame in the jig or hold it up high in the jig for the first pass and then gradually lower it after each pass for a deeper cut. After each key slot is cut, rotate the frame in the jig to cut the next corner **(C)**.

[VARIATION] To make a deeper key cut on wider frames, use the table saw and hold the miter jig up against the fence. It's up to you to hold it tightly to the saw fence.

Mill the key stock on the bandsaw. Rough out the thickness and width on a long stick of wood. Use a contrasting wood to make a nice design element in the frame **(D)**.

Cut the key stock to thickness on the table saw. Use a push stick to move the stock past the blade **(E)**. You should leave the width oversize and cut the keys oversize in length as well. There's no need fussing with the dimensions, because you'll cut the keys off flush after they are glued in place.

Plane the keys to fit on a bench hook using a block plane to trim them to size. The block plane will be small enough to work easily on the key stock. Put one key behind another to support the sole of the plane **(F)**. When the key fits hand snug in the slot, you can glue it in place. Make sure it fits all the way down into the bottom of the slot, and don't trust a blob of glue as evidence that it's seated. Check to see that the key is flush across the slot **(G)**. After the glue has set, trim the overhanging keys on the bandsaw. Then handplane or sand the keys flush to the frame edges **(H)**.

[**TIP**] **Cut down away from the corner in each direction for handplane cleaning. Otherwise you'll be cutting uphill on the key, causing tearout at the corner.**

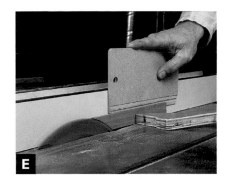

Corner Half-Lap Joint on the Table Saw

To make a corner half-lap joint on the table saw, mark out the shoulder location and depth of cut on the board. These should be set for just under the full width and half the thickness of the stock, which will make clamping and cleanup easier. Set the blade height and clamp a stop on the crosscut jig for the shoulder cuts **(A)**.

Make a series of passes to cut the cheek and finally the shoulder **(B)**. Most saws with an alternate-top bevel grind leave behind small grooves. Clean those up by moving the board just over top dead center on the blade and moving it back and forth over the blade. Push it forward to cut the next sideways pass and so on until you've trimmed the entire cheek **(C)**.

[VARIATION] Use the miter gauge with a dado blade to cut lap joints quickly. Move the workpiece past the saw and set the fence up as stop to index the shoulder cut. Keep the feed rate moderate.

VARIATION

Corner Half-Lap Joint on the Router Table

With a wide bit mounted in the router table, you can cut a half-lap joint fairly quickly. Set the bit height to cut just under half the thickness of the stock. First, rough out the joint on the bandsaw so you can set the bit height to its final depth (**A**). Set the fence to make the shoulder cut by using one of the boards as a guide. Clamp the fence in place just under the width of the stock. Have the bit rotated so one of its cutting edges is at a point farthest away from the fence and line up the board just outside that cutting edge (**B**).

Use two or more boards packaged together to make the cuts. You can also use a backer board to help prevent tearout at the rear of the cut. Start at the end of the boards and make full passes across them. Depending on the bit diameter, you may need to make several passes (**C**). Finish up the lap joint cut with the boards running right against the fence (**D**).

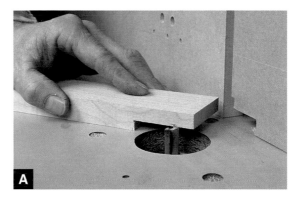

A

B

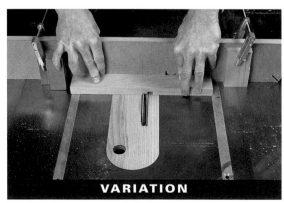

C

VARIATION

T or Cross Half-Lap Joint on the Table Saw

Use this method of cutting a T or cross half-lap joint when joining boards of the same width. Mark out one board for the cross half-lap joint just under the full width of the stock. Also mark out the depth of cut for just under half the thickness of the stock. Set up two stops on the crosscut jig for each shoulder of the joint **(A)**.

Make a series of passes to cut the joint and then move the workpiece right over the blade. Move it back and forth between the stops at top dead center to clean up the entire face of the joint **(B)**.

➤ See *"Corner Half-Lap Joint on the Table Saw"* on p. 142.

[VARIATION] You can also set up a dado blade to make lap cuts. Use a moderate feed rate to move the boards over the blade.

Fit the cross half-lap joint to width by taking hand-plane passes along the edges of the board. Check the fit by turning the board over and placing it in the joint **(C)**.

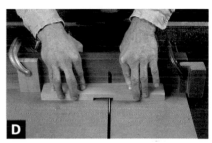

Dovetail Lap Joint

The first step for making a dovetail lap joint is to cut the lap shoulder on the table saw almost to full depth. Then cut the cheek using the bandsaw with a fence **(A)**.

[VARIATION 1] Cut the cheek on the router table. Always rough out the cut first on the bandsaw. This way you can set the bit depth to its full height.

Mark out and cut the tail on the bandsaw. Rough cut the shoulder up to the dovetail line and then cut just up to that line. Clean the shoulder cut with a chisel **(B)**.

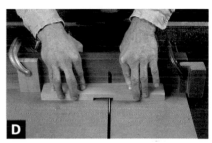

[VARIATION 2] Cut the dovetail cheek and shoulder by hand with a dovetail saw.

Mark out the mating piece by setting the dovetailed board in place on it. Place its shoulder tight up against the edge. Support the back end of the board with a block to level out the dovetailed board **(C)**. Rough out the interior of the joint with cuts on the table saw **(D)**. Then saw out the shoulders by hand. This will ensure that you'll follow whatever angle you've cut into the tail **(E)**. Clean out the remaining wood with a chisel down to depth **(F)**.

[VARIATION 3] You can also use a straight bit in the router to cut the lap joint down to depth. Make the cut freehand, being sure to stay away from the shoulders of the joint. If the joint is deep enough, use a top-mounted flush-trimming bit and run the bearing against the shoulders to make the cut.

VARIATION 1

VARIATION 3

VARIATION 2

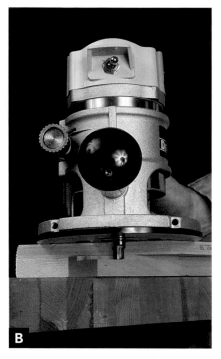

Mitered Half-Lap Joint with a Router

To cut half-lap joints with a router, first crosscut one of the boards with a miter cut and the mating board with a square cut. Rout the joint on the square-end board using a miter jig and flush-trimming bit. Clamp the jig in place on the board and set the bit depth for the first pass **(A)**. Make sure the top-mounted bearing runs into the fence of the jig **(B)**. Drop the bit height to make the second pass. The bearing will run against the first cut you made. Cut to just under half the thickness of the joint **(C)**. Cut the mating part of the joint with a right-angle jig clamped onto the piece with the mitered end.

Use the same bit and get down to full depth in a series of passes, as before **(D)**.

With this joint, not only do you get the benefit of the lap joint and its gluing surface but you can also carry a molded edge detail right through the face edge of the joint **(E)**.

Mitered Half-Lap Joint on the Table Saw

Mitered half lap joints on the table saw are cut in pairs. One side of the joint has a square end with a mitered shoulder on the lap cut. The other side has a mitered end with a square shoulder. Make the miter cuts on the ends of two opposite parts of the frame.

Cut the mating boards square and to length **(A)**. Make the square shoulder cuts using the miter gauge on the table saw. Set the blade for just under half the thickness of the stock and set the shoulder stop for just under the full width of the stock **(B)**. Make the mitered shoulder cut on the square-end board. You won't have to change the blade height. Set a stop so the cut starts just at the tip of the board **(C)**.

Make the cheek cuts next. Cut the cheek on the square-end board using a tenoning jig with a 45-degree fence on it **(D)**. Cut the cheek on the mitered-end board with a regular tenoning jig; hold the piece vertical.

A

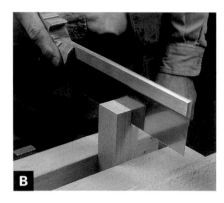

B

C

D

E

F

G

Hand-Cut Corner Bridle Joint

Bridle joints, or slot mortise and tenons, can be laid out with the slot one-third the full thickness of the stock. I prefer to size the tenon a bit smaller, closer to one-quarter of the thickness. But make the slot close in size to one of your chisels for ease in chopping out the waste.

Mark out the depth of the slot on both faces of the boards with a marking gauge. Pencil in the cheek lines across the end of the piece and square those lines down to the gauge line (A).

Saw to depth using a backsaw. Keep the sawcut on the waste side of the line (B). Chop out the bottom of the slot while holding the chisel vertical. Sight it from the side of the board to make it easier to see how you're holding the chisel. Make your first passes very light and, after each chopping cut, remove the waste. Chop from both faces in toward the middle. You can slightly undercut the slot once you get the cut started (C).

Set a combination square off the mating piece for the matching shoulder cut. Lock the square down just under the full width of the stock (D). Then use the square to set the fence for the shoulder cuts on the tenoned piece. Make sure the fence is square across the board (E).

Cut the first cheek of the tenoned board with a ripsaw down to the shoulder lines (F). For a bridle joint with flush faces on the mating boards, check the fit off the first cheek cut. Reverse the cut, placing it against the outside face of the mortised board. If the slot lines up with the outer face of the tenoned piece, the cut is in the proper spot. If it's not deep enough, use a handplane to bring it down to size (G).

T Bridle Joint

Cut the slot mortise while holding the work vertically in a tenoning jig.

▶ See *"Corner Bridle Joint on the Table Saw"* on p. 151.

Mark a gauge line on the board to prevent tearout **(A)**. Next, cut the bridle joint to fit that slot.

▶ See *"T or Cross Half-Lap Joint on the Table Saw"* on p. 144.

Set up a stop on the crosscut jig to locate one shoulder cut and raise the blade height close to the marked height. Make a series of passes **(B)**. Put a spacer between the end of the rail and the stop to cut the second shoulder. Finish up the cut on the first face **(C)**.

Flip the board over and make the passes on the second face. Use the spacer again for the second shoulder cut. Check the fit of the tenon to the slot before continuing **(D)**. Raise the blade height, if necessary.

[VARIATION] Clean the waste out exactly to depth with a topside router cut. Clamp another board of the same height close by to support the router base. Use a straight bit and cut freehand or use a top-mounted flush-trimming bit to make the cut if it's deep enough. Clean up any parts you miss with a wide chisel.

Fit each part of the joint separately. Flip the board and check the width of the slot to the board. Use a handplane to trim the board to fit **(E)**.

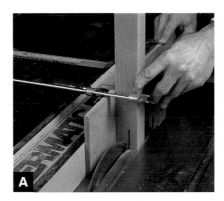

A

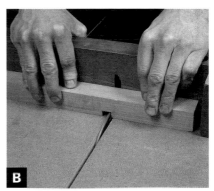

B

C

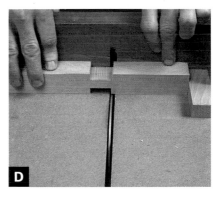

D

VARIATION

E

VARIATION

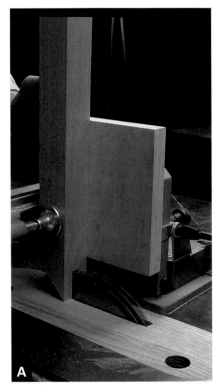

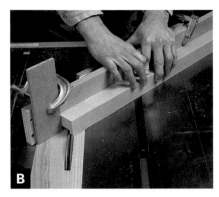

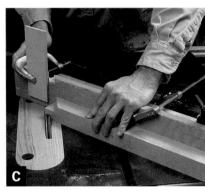

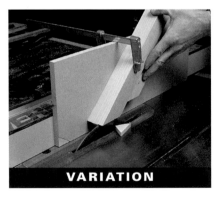

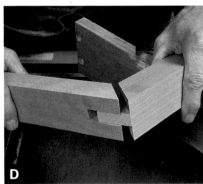

VARIATION

Mitered Corner Bridle Joint

One board in the mitered corner bridle joint will have a mitered-end cut. The other will be cross-cut square at its end. Cut the slot into the mitered-end piece with the dado blade. Clamp the board vertically into the tenoning jig (**A**). The tenoned board will have mitered shoulders. Use the dado blade to cut the cheek and mitered shoulder, holding the workpiece against the miter gauge angled at 45 degrees (**B**).

After the first cheek is cut, flip the miter gauge to the opposite 45-degree setting and make the second cheek cut. Use stops to index the cut for other boards (**C**). The joint should slide together with light pressure (**D**).

[**VARIATION**] If you don't have a good dado blade, cut the slot with a regular sawblade and chop out the bottom of the slot with a chisel. Cut the mitered shoulders for the mating piece using the miter gauge. Then cut the cheeks using the angled tenoning jig. Rough out the inside cheek cut on the bandsaw to avoid a flying offcut. The outside cheek will simply fall off when you make the cheek pass.

Corner Bridle Joint on the Table Saw

Lay out the bridle joint so the mortise slot is slightly less than one-third the thickness of the stock. Mark out the depth of cut with a marking gauge to help prevent tearout. Use a tenoning jig to support the board, cutting almost to full depth **(A)**.

[**TIP**] **An alternate-top bevel blade won't leave a smooth enough surface at the bottom of the cut. Use a flat-grind blade instead.**

Make a series of passes until the slot is cut. For the best-looking joint, clean up the bottom of the slot with a chisel **(B)**.

[**VARIATION 1**] **Use a dado blade to cut the slot in one or two passes. Move the stock past the blade at a moderate feed rate and support the piece well. Put a gauge line on the board or use a backer board to prevent tearout.**

Cut the shoulders for the tenon first. Clamp a stop to the crosscut jig fence and set the blade height to cut just under the required height **(C)**.

[**VARIATION 2**] **Rough out the cheeks on the bandsaw so you don't have offcuts flying around on the table saw. Use the offcuts for clamping blocks or to glue back onto a tenon that you cut too small. The grain and color will match perfectly.**

Trim the cheeks using the tenoning jig **(D)**. Check the fit of the first cheek pass by reversing the tenoned board on the slotted piece. If the slot lines up with the face of the board, the cut is in the right spot **(E)**.

A

B

C

D

VARIATION 1

E

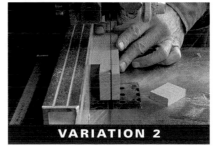
VARIATION 2

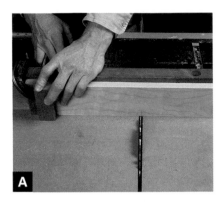

A

B

C

D

E

Halved Joint on the Table Saw

The first step to making a halved joint on the table saw is to mark it out for a little less than the width of the stock and a little less than the height of the stock. You will fit this joint by planing the long grain of the boards left proud by these setups.

Put a stop on the crosscut jig off the marked-out joint (**A**). Make a series of passes and check the fit against the mating board; it should be just short of fitting (**B**). Set up a second stop for the other side of the halving cut and locate it precisely; then make the cut (**C**).

Next, make the mating cut on the other board. If you're not sure that the stop is in the proper spot, put a shim at the end of the board. This will push the board away from the stop a few thousandths of an inch. If the cut is still too small, remove the shim for another pass (**D**).

Fit the joint using a handplane to trim wood off the faces of the boards. This will not only remove the milling marks but will more precisely fit the halved joint. Fit each board separately so you'll know where the joint is tight; then put the two together correctly (**E**).

Hand-Cut Scarf Joint

To begin a hand-cut scarf joint, set the sliding bevel to an angle between 1:8 and 1:10, and mark out the boards **(A, B)**.

Clamp the boards securely when making the sawcuts **(C)**. If you stack the boards together when sawing, they will line up almost automatically **(D)**.

To finish, clean up the cuts with a handplane **(E)**.

[VARIATION] You can use a chopsaw to make the scarf cuts.

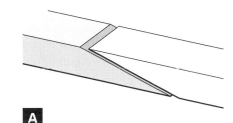

A

B

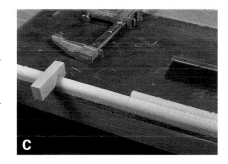

C

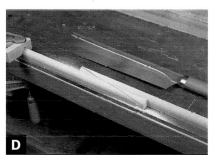

D

E

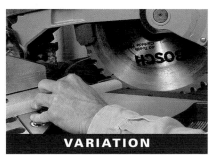

VARIATION

Scarf Joint with a Router

Scarf joints can be cut with a handheld router. Clamp the board to be scarfed in the scarf jig **(A)**. The jig's sides are angled at the proper degree for scarf joints. A plunge router rides in a carriage that rests on top of the angled sides.

Rout the scarf, taking several passes to get down to depth. Start up at the beginning of the scarf joint and gradually move down the jig **(B)**. With a good, wide straight bit, you should have very little cleanup work to do on the joint **(C)**.

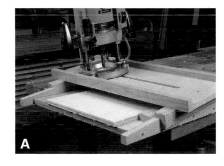

A

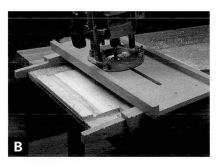

B

C

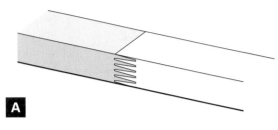

A

Tapered Finger Splice Joint

Tapered finger joints are showing up in lots of lumberyards these days as we stretch our resources to continue to provide building material **(A)**. These joints offer plenty of gluing surface and some mechanical resistance as well.

Set up the finger-joint bit in the speed-controlled table-mounted router. Run the speed down to around 10,000 rpm. Align the cutters to the stock thickness. Both cuts made on the matching boards will be done with one setup **(B)**.

Make the pass on the first board with its face side up **(C)**. Make the pass on the second board with its face side down. Adjust the bit height and depth of cut until the boards perfectly line up on their faces and the joint closes all the way up **(D)**.

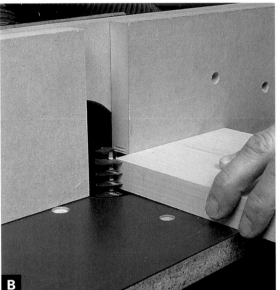

B

C

D

Lapped Dovetail Splice Joint

Lapped splice joints can be cut using a dovetail **(A)**. Mark out the dovetail using a sliding bevel. Don't make the angle too severe, as this will leave weakened short grain out at the end of the tail. Keep the angle between 1:5 and 1:8 **(B)**. Mark the shoulder's lines with a marking gauge.

Clamp the piece in the vise and make the shoulder cuts down to the tail lines **(C)**. Cut the sides of the dovetail with the piece held vertically in the vise. Clean up the cuts with a chisel **(D)**.

You can also use the table saw to create the dovetail. Tilt the blade to the proper angle and use the tenoning jig to hold the workpiece in place. You'll make two passes to create the tail sides **(E)**.

Mark out the tail piece for the lap cut and then make the shoulder cut with a crosscut saw. Cut the lap cheek down to the shoulder line **(F)**. Clean up the lap cuts with a wide chisel. Make sure the cuts are straight and square to each other **(G)**.

Mark out the tail onto the pin piece. Put a scrap block under the end of the tail board to support it during marking out **(H)**. Cut the matching shoulder and cheek for the lap part of the joint. Clean up those cuts **(I)**.

Saw out the pin at an angle. Saw as deeply as you can go without cutting past the lines. You can chop out a stop at the end of the tail socket and run the saw gently into that **(J)**. Finally, chop out the tail socket and fit the joint **(K)**.

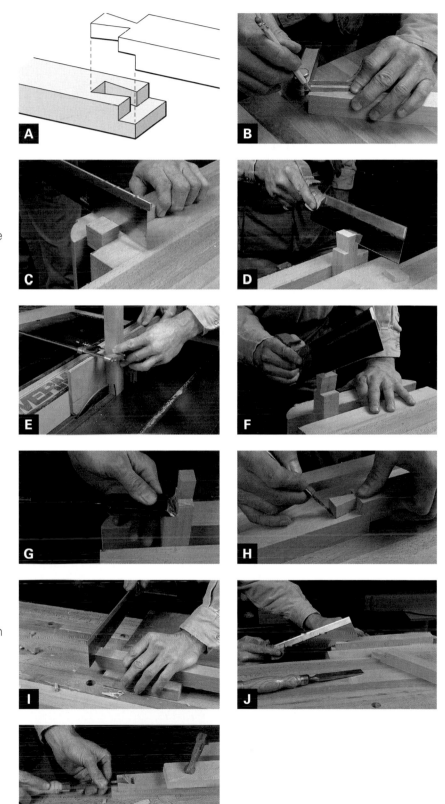

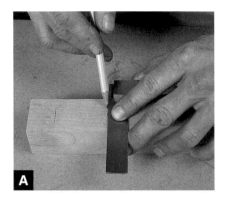

A

B

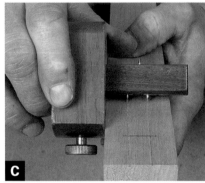

C

D

E

F

Hand-Cut Mortise with a Mortising Chisel

To make a hand-cut mortise, first mark out its position on the board by measuring with a ruler or tape measure from the board's end. Square lines across the board to indicate the ends of the mortise **(A)**.

Next, set up a mortising gauge or marking gauge to mark out the width of the mortise. Use your mortising chisel as a guide for this. Place the chisel just between the two points on the gauge **(B)**. Then set the head of the gauge to place the mortise where you want it in the thickness of the board. Mark out the mortise, holding the gauge tight to the edge of the board throughout. Don't mark past the pencil lines at the bottom of the mortise **(C)**.

Make your first chopping cut in the center of the mortise with the chisel set just between the mortise lines. Rely on the width of the chisel to establish the side walls but remember to chop down square to the face of the board **(D)**. Continue chopping with cuts at an angle in toward the center of the mortise until you get to the full depth of the mortise. Chop and lever out the waste until you get close to the ends of the mortise. At the ends, chop straight down on the lines. You can undercut the ends of the mortise a bit to help the tenon enter the joint **(E)**.

When the mortise is cut, clean the side walls and check all along the width of the mortise, using what I call a drift. This is just a thin piece of wood that you push into the widest part of the mortise **(F)**. Where it won't go in is where you need to remove more wood. As you pare, remember to keep the side walls flat and parallel to each other.

Mortise on the Drill Press

An accurate method of removing the waste in a mortise is to drill it out on the drill press with a fence. Mark the ends and center of the mortise on the board. Set up and clamp the drill press fence using the marked board as a guide. Line up the center of the bit to the center of the mortise **(A)**. Set the bit depth by zeroing the bit on the workpiece. The tip of the brad-point bit, which extends beyond its cutting edges, needs to be figured into this measurement **(B)**.

First, drill the two outer holes all the way to depth **(C)**. Then finish up the middle of the mortise with more boring. Always make sure there's wood for the center of the bit to bite into or the bit will drift off line. If you're careful and slow, you can drill out the very small remaining portion of wood with a good brad-point bit **(D)**.

Finish mortising by coming back with the bit and removing all the small arcs left by the first cuts. Make sure the workpiece is held securely when you drill. Clean up the mortise with a sharp, wide chisel.

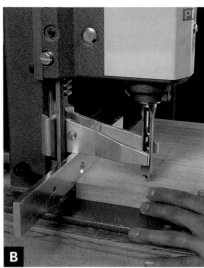

Mortise with a Hollow-Chisel Mortiser

A hollow-chisel mortising machine is designed for one job only: mortising. It uses superior leverage in its control arm to allow you to push through the wood with the chisel while you drill out most of the waste with a drill bit. This bit and chisel arrangement, however, does require perfectly sharpened and tuned bits and chisels for results. After honing the bit and chisel, set the bit through the chisel with a bare $\frac{1}{32}$ in. or so between the bottom of the cutting edge of the bit and the chisel points. Otherwise, you will end up burning the steel or not getting through the wood. Also make sure the hollow chisel is properly aligned, parallel to the fence **(A)**.

Mark out the mortise on the board and set the fence to place the hollow chisel in the right position over it **(B)**. Set the depth of the mortise cut and then clamp the board down in place using spacer blocks if needed under the clamp. First, make the two outer cuts in each mortise and then finish up the middle of the mortise. Be sure to have some wood for the bit and chisel to center on or else the bit will drift off line as you plunge down **(C)**. Remember to keep the hollow chisel exit hole pointed to the side to keep the hot chips off your hand or set up a dust collector right near the exit hole **(D)**.

[VARIATION] You can place a hollow-chisel mortising attachment on the drill press. You will have to remove the chuck to attach the chisel holder and then reattach it.

VARIATION

Mortise with a Plunge Router and Fence

When mortising narrow stock with a plunge router, clamp several boards together on the bench to provide good support for the router.

First, mark out the mortise **(A)**. Use an auxiliary fence mounted to the router fence to give you better support and greater accuracy when cutting **(B)**. Zero the bit onto the workpiece **(C)**. Then measure up on the depth scale to the depth of the mortise to be cut **(D)**. Set and lock down the fence so the mortise is accurately placed in the thickness of the board. Plunge down about ⅛ in. or so with each pass.

To be able to stop the router pass accurately at the ends of the mortise use a simple pencil mark on the wood. Line up the bit at the end of the mortise and then mark the position of the router base on the stock. Come up to this mark each time when you're mortising **(E)**.

A more guaranteed method is to clamp a stop to the board that the router base will run into **(F)**. Rout between the pencil marks or stops until you're all the way down to full depth **(G)**.

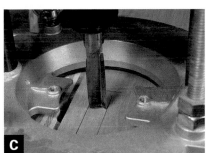

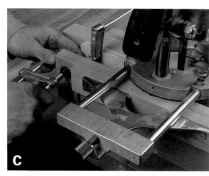

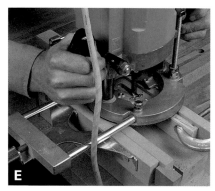

Mortise with a Plunge Router and Universal Jig

Use a universal mortising jig to register the plunge router and fence to make mortising cuts. With a good-size jig, you can cut mortises in material of almost any size or shape. The router fence rides against the outside of the jig while the bit cuts the board, which is clamped to the inside of the jig. Use support blocks under the workpiece, if necessary, to raise it high enough to rout (**A**).

Mount the bit and fence for the plunge router. Set the bit in line with the end of the marked-out mortise. Because my jig has one end stop permanently mounted, I run my fence into this stop and then locate and clamp the mortise under the bit (**B**). The router fence always runs into this stop to establish one end of the mortise.

Next, move the bit to the other end of the mortise and clamp on a stop to the jig to limit the travel of the router. This stop sets the length of the mortise cut (**C**). Zero the bit onto the board; then measure up on the depth scale of the router to set the depth of cut (**D**).

Rout to depth between the stops, being especially careful to keep the router fence tight to the jig (**E**). To index subsequent cuts, clamp on a stop at the end of the board.

Mortise on the Router Table

Use the router table for shallow mortising. Locate the mortise by measuring the distance from the edge of the bit to the router table fence. Rotate the bit's cutting edge so it's at a point closest to the fence **(A)**. Set the bit height for a first pass at ⅛ in. **(B)**. This shallow cut lightens the load on the router. Clamp on stops to the fence to limit the travel of the workpiece **(C)**. This will set the length of the mortise.

Rout by setting one end of the board against the far stop and slowly dropping down onto the bit. Hold the workpiece tight to the fence as you move down into the bit. As you drop down, move the board back and forth a little until you are finally down to depth. This will minimize any burning caused by a router bit without a center cutting edge **(D)**. After the first pass, reset the bit for another ⅛-in.-deep cut **(E)**.

[**VARIATION**] **For most fixed-base table-mounted routers, the depth of cut cannot be adjusted consistently. So you'll often see steps in the cuts, because the bit doesn't stay centered in the base. To increase your accuracy and to speed up the mortising, set the bit at its full depth of cut and use table shims to create each new depth setting. Pull one shim out after each pass. These shims can be made of any flat sheet-good material with a bit slot cut into it.**

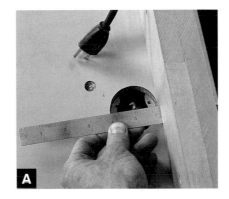

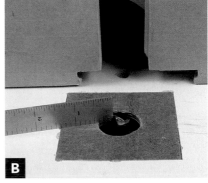

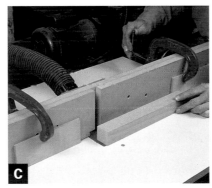

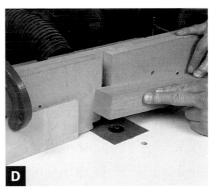

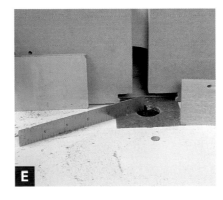

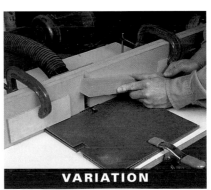

Hand-Cut Tenon

A

Hand-cut tenons demand careful marking out, sharp tools, and patience in the fitting. Always cut tenons after making the mortises. It's much easier to trim a tenon to fit an existing mortise than vice versa.

Mark the length of the tenon or shoulder position with a marking gauge. A wheel-type cutter works best for marking out cross-grain **(A)**. Mark out both faces of the board. Lay out the thickness of the tenon or the cheek cuts with a pencil and rule or use the marking gauge again **(B)**. Mark both edges as well as the end of the board.

B

Cut the shoulders first, holding the workpiece tight to a bench hook or with the board clamped to the bench **(C)**.

[VARIATION 1] Run the saw against a fence clamped onto the board. If you're careful aligning the fence on both faces and hold the saw tight to the fence, you'll get nice consistent shoulder cuts. Use a combination square as a depth gauge to set the fence.

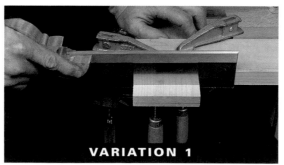

C

VARIATION 1

After making the shoulder cuts, saw the tenon cheeks with a tenon saw or backsaw. On wider boards, cut the cheeks in a series of cuts so you're not faced with one wide cut that might go awry. Start the cheek cut with the board angled in the vise so you can see the lines on both the end and the near edge of the board **(D)**. Saw down close to the shoulder cut. Flip the board around in the vise and make a second cheek cut down to the shoulder cut **(E)**. Then finish the sawing by placing the board upright in the vise and cutting straight down to the shoulder **(F)**.

[VARIATION 2] For narrower boards, saw straight across to make the cheek cuts.

After making the first cheek cut, I find it better to clean it up with a shoulder or bullnose plane before moving on to the next cut. If you've taken off too much wood, you can then adjust the second cut.

After both cheek cuts are made, check the fit of the tenon. Try to leave the tenon a bit fat so you can clean the cheeks with a handplane or chisels for a final, perfect fit **(G)**.

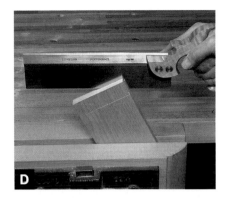

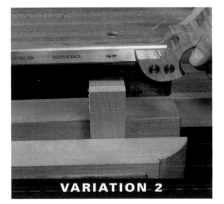

VARIATION 2

Tenon with a Router and Right-Angle Jig

Cut tenons topside with a router running against a clamped-on fence or right-angle jig. First measure the distance from the cutting edge of the bit to the edge of the router base. This is the crucial distance for setting the fence (**A**). Clamp the workpiece down to the bench. Place another board close by it to support the router base and right-angle jig. Use a square as a depth guide to place the jig; clamp it in place (**B**). Set the router bit to cut the tenon in a series of passes, or set it for full depth if you need just a shallow cut.

Start routing first at the end of the board moving left to right across it, gradually working in toward the shoulder. If you cut too slowly, the end grain will burn; so keep the feed rate moderately fast.

For the shoulder cut, hold the router base with one consistent spot on it riding against the jig. Move almost all the way through the shoulder cut. Stop just short of the end; then pull the router away from the jig and off the board. Next, rout back into the shoulder cut for the last 2 in. to prevent tearout at the edge of the board (**C**).

Vertical Tenon on the Router Table

Cut tenons vertically on the router table if the stock is wide enough to move smoothly across the router table and table insert. Narrow boards have a tendency to dip into the bit. Use a push block to help move the workpiece smoothly. Feed the work from right to left across the bit, moving into its rotation.

First, trim the outer face of the board to prevent tearout (**A**). Next, reset the fence to cut a centered tenon and make the full tenon cuts (**B**).

> ⚠ **WARNING** Keep the bit captured in the fence to avoid trapping the workpiece between the bit and fence. Otherwise, when making a trim cut like this, and feeding the piece right to left, the workpiece can be jerked through the cut or pulled from your hands.

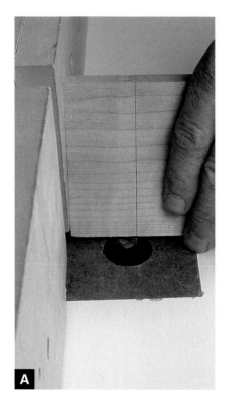

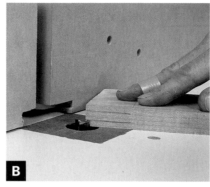

Horizontal Tenon on the Router Table

The first step to cutting a horizontal tenon on the router table is to mount a wide bit in the router. Rotate the bit so the cutting edge is at a point farthest from the fence. Measure this distance or set the marked-out tenon up to the bit to locate it and clamp down the fence **(A)**. Set the bit height to the full depth of cut, using the marked-out tenon as a guide **(B)**.

First, trim the tenons on the bandsaw to eliminate wear and tear on the router bit **(C)**. Save the offcuts, just in case you cut a tenon too small. Simply glue the offcut back onto the tenon and recut it.

Use a backer board to support the workpiece when cutting on the router table. Otherwise, this narrow board will rock against the fence. Start cutting at the end of the tenon, moving from right to left across the bit. Gradually work your way in toward the shoulder **(D)**. Make the final pass to establish the shoulder by running the board and backer right up against the fence **(E)**.

Tenon Crosscut on the Table Saw

Cut tenons flat on the table saw using a crosscut jig. Set the blade height off a marked-out tenon **(A)**. Next, clamp a stop onto the jig fence to index the shoulder cuts. I always mark the tenon length on the edge of the board closest to the sawblade so I can line this up easier **(B)**.

Make a series of passes with the sawblade until you've cut the entire cheek. Flip the board to cut the remaining cheek **(C)**.

These cheek cuts usually end up with numerous ridges, owing to the alternate-top bevel grind of combination sawblades. To clean up these ridges, first wet your fingertips so you can grip the board well. Then move the board right over top dead center on the blade and slide it back and forth over the blade. You will move the board right into the stop, so there's no fear of moving past the shoulder. After one pass, move the jig just a bit farther over the blade and take another pass. Take your time with this, and you'll eventually clean up the entire tenon **(D)**.

[**VARIATION**] **The dado blade, of course, can quickly remove a great deal of wood. Make sure the dado is cutting a nice flat-bottomed cut. Use the miter gauge. And for this type of cut, you can use the saw fence as a stop for the shoulder cut.**

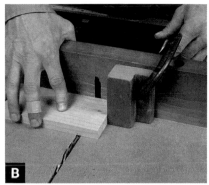

A

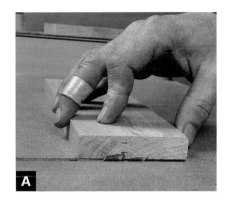

B

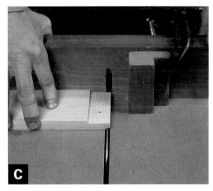

C

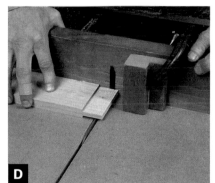

D

VARIATION

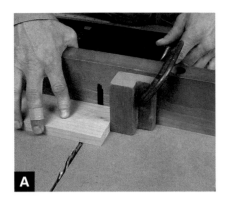

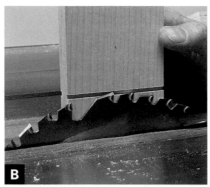

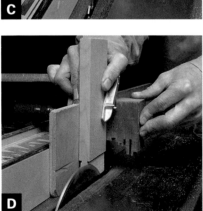

Tenon on the Table Saw with a Shopmade Jig

Before using a shopmade tenoning jig on the table saw, crosscut the tenon shoulders using the crosscut jig with a stop mounted on it. Keep the cut just under the full depth of the cheeks (**A**).

[**TIP**] **Remove most of the cheek waste on the bandsaw. This will prevent any off-cuts from flying around the table saw and will make the tenon cut easier and more accurate.**

Set the blade height for just under the full depth of the shoulders (**B**). You'll use a shopmade tenoning jig to support the tenon board. Place the board and jig next to the blade to set the fence distance (**C**). Clamp the tenon board to the jig and get a firm grip on the jig. Keep it close to the saw fence and perfectly upright when making a pass.

If the tenon is centered, flip the board around to cut the other cheek; then check the fit (**D**). If the tenon is just a hair too large and you don't want to change the fence setting, use a shim for a trimming pass. Place a paper shim between the board and the jig to kick it out toward the blade just a bit (**E**).

Tenon on the Bandsaw

Before cutting the tenon on the bandsaw, mark it out on the board. Set the bandsaw fence to cut the tenon shoulders first. Be sure to line up the pencil-marked shoulder with a sawtooth that's pointing away from the fence **(A)**.

Saw the shoulders up to the cheek marks, using a backer board for support against the fence **(B)**. Narrow boards like the one shown here have a tendency to rock their ends against a fence unless they have support. Or you can feed the work with a miter gauge, if you have one for the saw.

Next, saw the tenon cheeks, slowing the feed rate down as you come up to the shoulder cut. It is common to pop through this last bit of wood and into the shoulder if you're not prepared for it. You could, of course, clamp on a stop to the fence to prevent this. If the tenon is centered, make one cheek cut and flip the board for the second cut. Save the offcuts for your friends who cut their tenons too small: The offcuts can be glued back on and the tenons recut **(C)**.

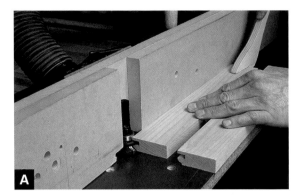

Mortise and Tenon with Cope and Stick Bits

Cope and stick bits come in a wide variety of patterns and a few configurations. These matched bit sets all cut a stub mortise-and-tenon joint that's in line with a panel groove and a molded edge for frame-and-panel doors. Because of the small amount of gluing surface in these joints, do not expect great strength from them unless you also dowel or screw across the joint.

Cut the stile groove and its molding or sticking with the grooving bit on a speed-controlled table-mounted router. Run the motor speed down around 10,000 rpm. Cut some practice boards to get the bit height just right and remember to use a push stick **(A)**.

[**TIP**] **For safety, use a fence lined up with the bearing.**

Cut the tongued profile or coped piece on the rail with the tongue bit across the end grain of the rail piece. Use a backer board to prevent tearout and to give you better bearing surface across the fence **(B)**.

[**VARIATION**] **Use a reversible bit set to cut both sides of the joint. These bits are less expensive but take some time to reverse the cutter positions.**

Drawbore Tenon

Drawboring is more suited to timberframe construction than to fine furniture making, but the joint can be used for furniture if done carefully. The hole drilled into the tenon is offset a bare $\frac{1}{32}$ in. toward the shoulder from the hole drilled into the mortise **(A)**. When you put in the dowel pin, the tenon shoulder is drawn in tighter to the mortise. For a bridle joint or slot mortise, the tenon hole is closer to the shoulder and higher on the tenon, which pulls the tenon in and down to the mortise. If the offset is too great, the pin won't make it through the holes or will end up stretching out the tenon hole instead of pulling the joint tight.

Cut the mortise and fit the tenon to it.

> See pp. 156-169 for cutting methods.

Take the joint apart and drill through the mortise with a brad-point bit on the drill press. To prevent tearout inside the joint, drill slowly or place a piece of scrap inside the joint **(B)**.

Put the joint back together and mark the hole center on the tenon with the same brad-point bit **(C)**. Remove the tenon and remark the hole center just a bit closer to the shoulder **(D)**. Drill through the tenon using a piece of scrap under it to prevent tearout and to support the cut **(E)**.

Put a heavy chamfer on a dowel pin, which is cut extra long. After you glue in the tenon, bang the dowel through the joint so the chamfer comes all the way through. A chamfered bolt driven through from the other side will help pull things together **(F)**.

Drawbored Tenon

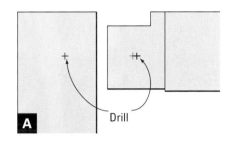

Drill

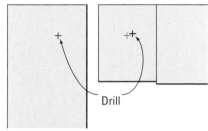

Drawbored Slot Mortise

Drill

B

C

D

E

F

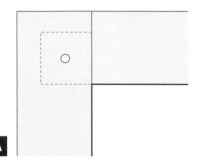

A

C

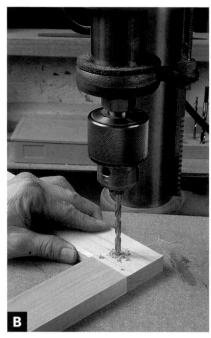

B

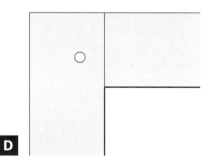

D

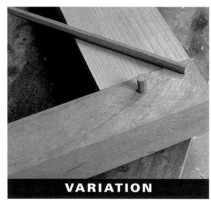

VARIATION

Pinned Tenon

To ensure a tenon will hold over time, run a pin through it **(A)**. Even if the glue fails, a pinned tenon will remain together.

After gluing up, drill the joint with a brad-point bit. If you want the pin to show through on both sides, use a piece of scrap under the frame to prevent tearout when you drill through. If not, carefully set the depth of cut so the centering point doesn't come through the back **(B)**.

Chamfer the end of a dowel pin and add just a bit of glue to the hole before pounding the dowel home **(C)**. A more rustic approach is to use octagonal pins in round holes **(D)**.

[VARIATION] The pins shown here lock themselves into place because their corners cut into the surrounding wood. Shape the pin stock with a block plane and chamfer the end before inserting it into its hole; avoid making the stock too large.

Through Mortise on the Drill Press

The drill press accurately cuts through mortises with the aid of a fence.

➤ See *"Mortise on the Drill Press"* on p. 157.

Drill from one side all the way through the board. Put an auxiliary table on the drill press table and a piece of scrap on top of that so you can drill into it. Clamp these both in place so they don't move around on you as you drill **(A)**. Set the bit depth of cut so it drills all the way through the board and a little way into the scrap **(B)**.

Drill the two outside holes first; then drill the remaining wood in the center of the mortise **(C)**. Always have some wood for the centering point of the bit to grab into so the bit doesn't wander. Leave the mortise ends round and round the tenon or chop the mortise ends square with a chisel.

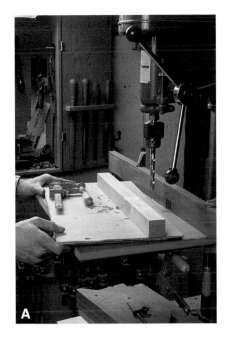

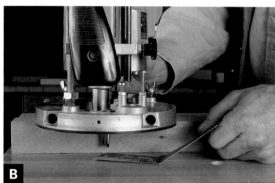

Through Mortise with a Plunge Router and Fence

Use a plunge router to cut through mortises with round ends.

➤ See *"Mortise with a Plunge Router and Fence"* on p. 159.

You'll have to round the tenon to fit the mortise. Use a bit that's long enough to cut through the wood without marring the topside of the mortise with the shank of the bit or the collet nut. You can rout through into a piece of scrap or stop the cut just short. I prefer the latter method, as it prevents errant cuts into the benchtop. Support the plunge router with boards the same height, putting one at the side and another at the end of the cut.

Mark out the mortise on one face. Set the router fence off these marks **(A)**. Using a cardboard shim on the bench as a guide, set the bit depth to come almost through the board. Push the plunge router down to the shim and lock the depth stop rod **(B)**. Rout through the mortise. The little bit of wood that's remaining is easily pushed through with a pencil **(C)**.

Clean up the remaining bit of wood with a chisel and round file.

Through Mortise with a Plunge Router and Template

Through mortises can be cut with a handheld router and a template.

You'll have to round the tenon to fit the round end of the mortise. Make sure the bit is long enough to cut through the board and that the collet nut doesn't run into the template guide. Use a piece of scrap under the workpiece to prevent tearout when routing through or stop the mortise just short of coming through. Set the template in place, and put the plunge router on top of it to set the bit depth. Place a piece of cardboard or paper on the benchtop, push the bit down until it hits the cardboard or paper, and lock down the depth stop rod **(A)**.

Rout to depth just short of the other face, remove the template, and punch through the remaining wood **(B)**. Clean up the exit side of the through mortise with a chisel and round file.

A

Wedged Through Tenon

A tenon wedge should be aligned so it applies pressure against the end grain of its mortise rather than the long grain. This will avoid any tendency for the long grain to split out. First, cut the mortise and fit the tenon cheeks.

> **See pp. 156-169 for cutting methods.**

Next, cut the tenon to height so it just fits inside the length of the mortise. Use the bandsaw to trim it down to size. Check the fit from end to end of the mortise (**A**). Then round the tenon ends if the mortise has round ends.

Because of the pressure that a wedge exerts on a tenon, especially in dry wood, don't widen the mortise. This increases the risk of splitting out the tenon when you apply the wedge. Keep the mortise at one length throughout and concentrate on a smaller wedge doing its job of creating pressure.

To avoid the risk of splitting out the bottom of the tenon with the wedging pressure, drill a ³⁄₁₆-in. relief hole about two-thirds of the way back from the end of the tenon on the drill press (**B**). This hole will spread out the wedging pressure around a circumference instead of concentrating the pressure at the bottom of the wedge slot, where cracks will occur. Cut the wedge slot down to this hole on the bandsaw, using a fence to guide the cut (**C**). Make the kerf about ³⁄₃₂ in. wide.

B

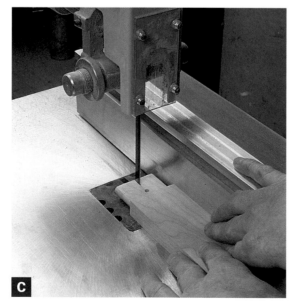

C

[VARIATION] For a design detail, use diagonal or double wedges in the through tenon. Cut a diagonal kerf in the tenon with a handsaw.

Make the wedge from a harder wood than your tenon. Cut the wedge to about twice the thickness of its slot and make some extra wedges that are a bit thicker. If you find that your wedges are going in too easily, use the thicker wedges for the remaining tenons. Cut the wedges to length at about three-quarters of the full length of the wedge slot. You'll find that the wedging force will tend to fill up most gaps that show at the edge of a through joint.

Put glue in the wedge slot and use a hammer to drive the wedge. When the sound changes from a thud to a ping you've gone as far as you can with the wedge (**D**).

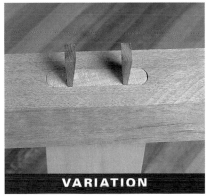

VARIATION

Shaping Wood

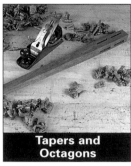

Tapers and Octagons

Arc, Circles, and Ellipses

Curves

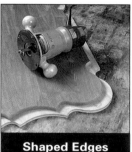

Shaped Edges

Coves

Turning Shapes

Bending

Two-Sided Taper Freehand on the Bandsaw

Begin by laying out the taper on the stock **(A)**. To simplify construction, tapers usually don't extend into the area of joinery **(B)**. It's best to lay out and cut the leg mortise while the stock is still square **(C)**.

Next, mount a wide blade, such as ³/₄ in., on the bandsaw. Using a wide blade greatly reduces the tendency for the blade to wander in the cut **(D)**. Start at the foot and closely follow the layout line **(E)**. Turn the leg 90 degrees and make the second cut **(F)**. After all the cuts are made, remove the saw marks with a sharp bench plane **(G)**.

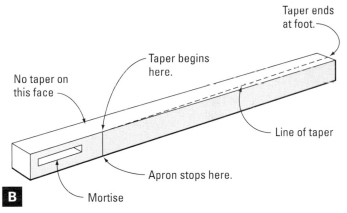

Taper ends at foot.

Taper begins here.

No taper on this face

Line of taper

Apron stops here.

Mortise

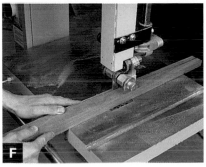

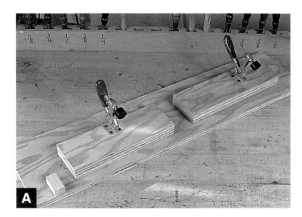

A

B

Taper on the Bandsaw with a Jig

If you've got a lot of stock to taper it makes sense to construct a jig to speed the process along. Although the table saw is a good choice for tapering, I prefer the bandsaw for tapering thick stock such as bedposts. This technique uses a template that follows a guide adjacent to the bandsaw blade. Best of all, you can create one-, two-, or even four-sided tapers with this technique.

First, make the jig to the desired degree of taper **(A)**. The guide is simply a stick with a notch for the blade **(B)**. Make certain that the guide is clamped firmly in position before you begin **(C)**.

To use the jig, keep the base in contact with the guide throughout the cut **(D)**. You'll need the off-cuts for support during the second cut. Afterward, rotate the stock to make the second taper **(E)**.

You can use a guide and templates to rapidly bandsaw any number of identical parts.

Guide

This curve should match the tightest curve in the pattern.

C

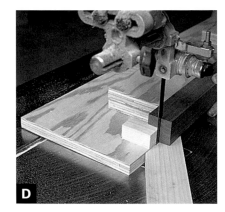

D

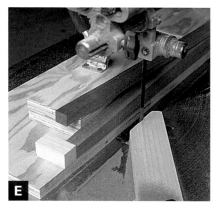

E

Two-Sided Taper on the Table Saw

Once you've made the jig and milled the stock, set the blade height so that the teeth are just above the workpiece **(A)**. Next, set the fence at a distance from the blade that corresponds to the width of the jig **(B)**. Position the stock for the first cut. As you feed the jig and workpiece into the blade, it's crucial to maintain contact with the fence **(C)**. A splitter will dramatically increase safety during any ripping procedure such as this **(D)**. Finally, rotate the leg and cut the second taper **(E)**.

➤ See *"Taper on the Bandsaw with a Jig"* on p. 180.

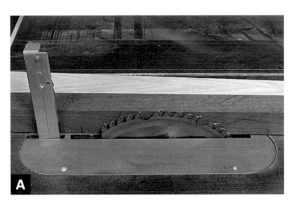

A

B

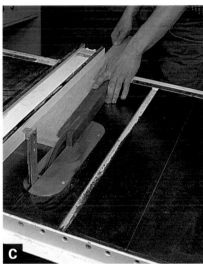

C

D

E

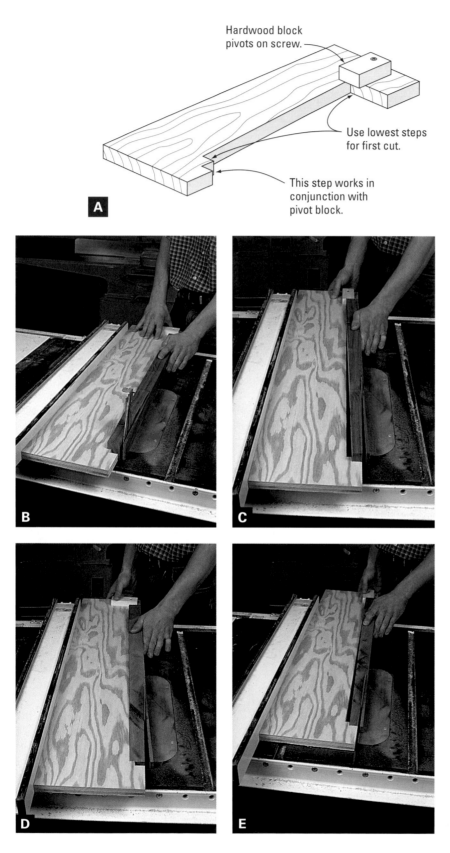

Hardwood block
pivots on screw.

Use lowest steps
for first cut.

This step works in
conjunction with
pivot block.

A

B

C

D

E

Four-Sided Taper on the Table Saw

The process for cutting a four-sided taper is much like the procedure for cutting a two-sided taper. The difference is the jig. There are two steps on the jig: one for the first two cuts and another for the final two cuts **(A)**.

To use the jig, first pivot the stop block out of the way and cut two adjacent tapers **(B, C)**. Then pivot the stop into position and use the second step of the jig for the last two tapers **(D, E)**. Remember to use a splitter on your saw and keep the jig in contact with the fence.

Eight-Sided Taper on the Router Table or Shaper

Before shaping a tapered octagon, always begin by drawing two full-size octagons. The first represents the start of the taper; the second drawing represents the end.

Next, lay out a four-sided taper on the stock **(A)** and cut the four tapers using your favorite method **(B)**. Now you're ready to chamfer the corners to create the eight-sided taper. But first smooth away the saw marks with a handplane or jointer **(C)**.

To chamfer the corners, first build a jig to support the stock during the cut. Next, mount a chamfer cutterhead or bit on your shaper or router table **(D)**. Adjust the bit height for the full depth of cut according to the drawing you made earlier **(E)**. The jig will raise and support the small end of the stock to create the necessary amount of chamfer at each end **(F)**.

Position the work in the jig with the trailing end of the stock resting firmly against the stop. Now feed the workpiece and jig past the cutterhead to cut the tapered chamfer **(G)**. When you reach the end of the taper, stop and make a mark on the table or fence **(H)**. This gives you a reference point when cutting the three remaining chamfers.

A

B

C

D

E

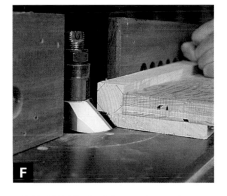
F

G

H

Arcs, Circles, and Ellipses Freehand on the Bandsaw

Unless I've got a large number of pieces to cut, I prefer to do the cutting freehand on the bandsaw. Cutting freehand is surprisingly fast and, with a little practice, accurate. The key is to use the widest possible blade and follow the line closely **(A)**. If your saw's table is small, space your hands farther apart to support the stock **(B)**. After sawing, smooth the edges with a spokeshave **(C)**. If you're careful to watch the grain direction, you'll avoid tearout.

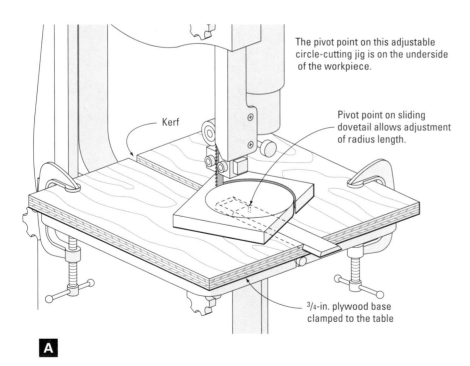

The pivot point on this adjustable circle-cutting jig is on the underside of the workpiece.

Kerf

Pivot point on sliding dovetail allows adjustment of radius length.

3/4-in. plywood base clamped to the table

Circles on the Bandsaw with a Jig

When cutting a number of true circles, you'll find it helpful to use a jig that allows you to rotate the stock. Build the jig shown here **(A)**. The pin's location is adjustable by sliding the board that holds the pin to the desired distance from the blade. The pin-to-blade distance represents the radius of the circle. Make a small hole in the stock at the center of the circle you wish to cut. This will ride on the pin as you pivot the stock through the blade of the bandsaw **(B)**.

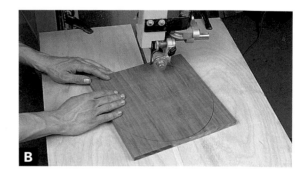

Bandsawing Tight Curves

Bandsawing should always begin with a pattern. This allows you to work out proportions and create smooth, flowing curves.

Begin by carefully tracing the pattern onto the stock **(A)**. If there are slight imperfections in the wood, you can often orient the pattern to locate them in areas of offcuts.

The example for this technique is two bracket feet joined by molding. Shape the molding before bandsawing, while the straight reference edges are still intact **(B)**. The long, straight section that spans the feet is difficult to cut with a bandsaw. Instead, make a stop cut on the table saw. The stop block prevents kickback **(C)**, and a second cut from the opposite face will reach into the corners **(D)**.

[**VARIATION**] **You can get a straighter line between the bracket feet if you use the table saw instead of the bandsaw. It's called a stop cut, and the way to do it safely is with a stop block clamped to the fence or table.**

(Continued on p. 186.)

A

B

C

D

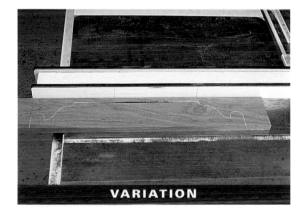

VARIATION

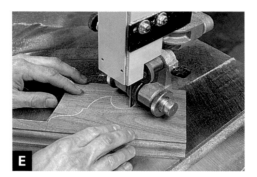

Before bandsawing, mount a blade that will turn the tightest contour without binding. Then plan the cutting sequence to avoid trapping the blade **(E)**. Backing out of the turn is a sure way to pull the blade off the wheels **(F)**.

You can avoid tedious cleanup of the surface by carefully sawing to the layout line **(G)**. When the bandsawing is complete, smooth the curves with a spindle sander **(H)** and clean up the intersections with a chisel for a crisp, defined look **(I)**.

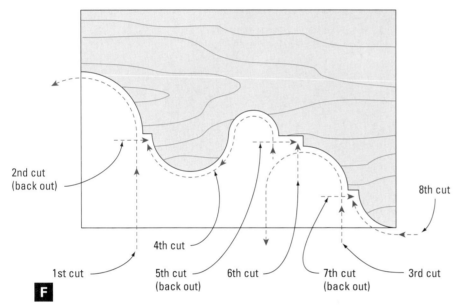

2nd cut
(back out)

8th cut

4th cut

1st cut

5th cut
(back out)

6th cut

7th cut
(back out)

3rd cut

F

Sawing Curves with a Coping Saw

A coping saw has a frame to tension a narrow blade for sawing tight contours. If you need to saw scrollwork only occasionally, a coping saw is an inexpensive way to go.

The key when using a coping saw is to provide support for the stock. Make a simple device called a *bird's mouth* **(A)**. It is a board with a deep V cut into one end. To use it, clamp it to the benchtop with the V overhanging the edge. Position the workpiece over the V and begin sawing **(B)**. As you follow the outline, reposition the work as necessary to provide support close to the cut.

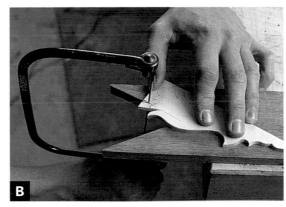

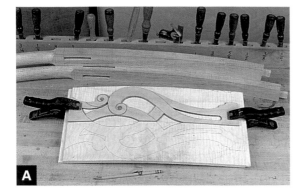

Interior Cuts with a Scrollsaw

The scrollsaw is the tool of choice for interior cuts. (A jigsaw can also be used, but it won't be as accurate and will require more cleanup with a file and sandpaper.) The blade of a scrollsaw can be unclamped at one end and threaded through a hole in the workpiece. Because the blade is clamped securely at each end, the cut is precise with minimal flex.

As an example of this process, I'm using a curved chair back. When tracing the pattern, it's necessary to flex it so it conforms to the curve of the work. You can hold it in position with clamps while tracing the outline (A).

Next, drill a small hole at each interior cutout for threading the blade (B). When sawing, take your time and follow the layout lines closely; this greatly reduces the amount of tedious cleanup later (C).

To create the illusion of thinness and delicacy, scrollwork is sometimes beveled on the edges. It's time-consuming work, but the refined appearance is worth the effort.

[**VARIATION**] **You can also use a coping saw or fretsaw to cut interior curves by loosening the blade and freeing it so that you can enter the work through the drill hole.**

Chamfer with a Block Plane

Hand tools are a pleasure to use and are surprisingly efficient, especially when only a few pieces need to be shaped.

First, lay out the chamfer with a pencil to use as a guide while cutting **(A)**. A combination square will guide the pencil and keep the layout consistent **(B)**.

Next, begin chamfering the stock on the end of the board **(C)**. Hold the plane at an angle that corresponds to the desired angle of the chamfer. As you approach the layout lines, you can adjust the angle if needed. Finish the surface with one continuous light pass. Any tearout that occurs will disappear when you chamfer the edges **(D)**.

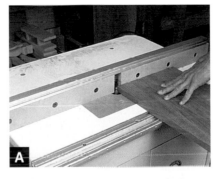

A "Worn" Table Edge

A worn, rounded surface is friendly to the touch and has a familiar look. Any surface can be worked to create an appearance of age; but the square, utilitarian edges of a tabletop work well for this technique.

First, use a ¼-in. roundover bit to remove the excess stock on the top and bottom of the edge **(A)**. Next, use a coarse file to gently round and soften the corners **(B)**. Be careful not to overdo it, or it can look artificial. A light pass with a scraper completes the job **(C)**.

Shaped Edge with a Handheld Router

One of the advantages of a router over a shaper is that it is lightweight and portable. Profiling the edge of large, awkward stock such as a tabletop can be difficult without a helper—but with the router it's a snap. The chamfer shown here is just an example of the many edge treatments you can cut with a router.

First mill the stock to size and clamp it to your workbench. If you're creating a large chamfer, you may want to shape it in two passes. Otherwise, set the bit for the required cutting depth and guide it around the perimeter of the top in a counterclockwise direction. To avoid unsightly tearout on the edges, shape an end first **(A)** and slow the feed rate as you approach the corner. As you finish with the sides **(B)**, any slight tearout will be shaped away.

Shaped Edge on the Router Table

The router table has replaced the shaper for most small tasks. Shaping a chamfer with the router table is a prime example.

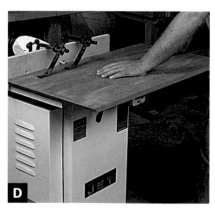

Begin by adjusting the bit height **(A)** and set the fence tangent to the guide bearing on the bit **(B)**. Then, starting with an end, feed the stock from right to left **(C)**. When shaping the ends, slow down the feed as you approach the corner to avoid excessive tearout. When you shape the edges, any minor tearout will be shaped away **(D)**.

Entire Edge of a Curved Shape on the Router

Anytime you shape a curved surface with a router, the rub bearing on the bit must follow a curve to guide the bit and limit the cutting depth. When only part of the edge is shaped, the portion that remains can serve to guide the bearing. However, when the entire edge is shaped, a template is needed to guide the cut **(A)**.

After making the template, trace it onto the workpiece. Now saw the outline slightly proud of the line, which will provide extra stock to be removed by the router bit. If the top is large and your bandsaw is limited in size, you may opt to use a portable jigsaw **(B)**. If so, clamp the work to the bench to keep it stationary while sawing.

Next, attach the template to the underside of the top with screws **(C)**. The screw holes will later be hidden, but make certain that the screw doesn't penetrate the full thickness of the top.

Before shaping, set the bit height with an offcut from the top **(D)**. Now you're ready to make the cut. To have complete control of routers and shapers, it's important always to feed in the opposite direction of the cutter rotation **(E)**. When hand feeding a router, move it counterclockwise around the top's perimeter.

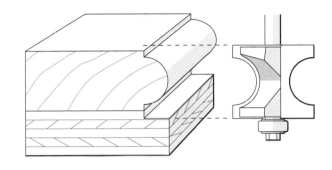

A Because the entire edge is removed, a template is needed when shaping this profile on a curved surface.

B

C

D

E

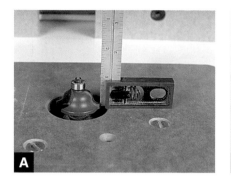

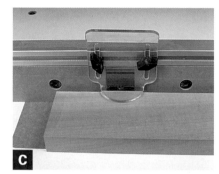

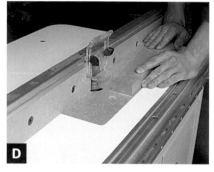

Molding on the Router Table

Anytime you're shaping strip molding on the router table you'll want to select wide stock to distance your hands safely from the spinning bit. After securing the bit in the collet, set the height to create the cutting depth you desire. A small, graduated square works well for gauging the bit height **(A)**.

Next, set the fence in position by aligning it tangent with the bearing on the bit **(B)**. Now set the stock in place and lock the guard in position **(C)**.

When you've finished these steps, make the cut by feeding the stock from right to left **(D)**. Listen to the router for an indication of the proper feed rate and rotations per minute (rpms). After shaping, rip the molding free on the table saw **(E)**. The finished molding is now ready to apply **(F)**.

Cove Cut on the Table Saw

The first woodworker to use this technique has been long forgotten. In fact, I suspect that cove cutting on the table saw is as old as the saw itself. It's a great technique that has a multitude of uses.

Begin by milling the stock and drawing the cove on each end. Next, adjust the blade height on the table saw to equal the depth of the cove **(A)**. Now you're ready to set the fence angle.

Position the fence so that the blade enters the stock on one edge of the cove **(B)** and exits on the opposite edge **(C)**. Then clamp the fence securely to the table saw. Now check the fence once more. If necessary, make minor adjustments to the angle. Then lower the blade to ⅟₁₆ in., and you're ready to make the cut.

Use push blocks to safely distance your hands **(D)**. As you push the stock over the top of the blade, maintain contact with the fence **(E)**. Before each successive pass, raise the blade approximately ⅟₁₆ in. **(F)**. For the final pass, take a very light cut and feed the workpiece slowly to achieve the smoothest surface possible **(G)**.

Afterward, remove the saw marks with a curved scraper and sand the cove smooth **(H)**. By tilting the blade, you can create asymmetrical coves **(I)**.

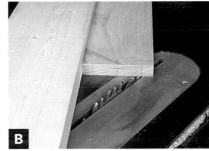

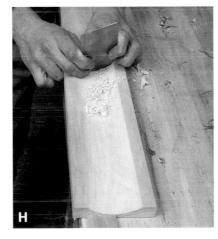

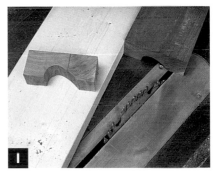

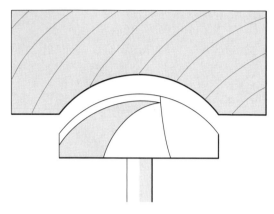

Even a large router bit can't shape a very large cove.

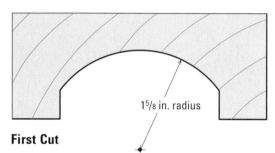

First Cut

1⅝ in. radius

Instead use two large router bits with different radii to create a large elliptical cove.

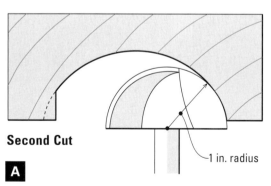

Second Cut

1 in. radius

A

B

C

D

Cove Cut on the Router Table

Even the largest router bits will not cut a very deep cove. But there's a practical way to increase the size of the cove. Use two bits of different radii and create an elliptical cove **(A)**. This will greatly increase the depth and width of the cove and enable you to create a large molding profile. As an added benefit, an elliptical cove is more appealing than one with a constant radius.

Begin by making multiple light passes with the first bit **(B)**. It's important to keep each cut light; heavy cuts are prone to kickback and tend to cause overheating of the router. Use featherboards to keep the workpiece in position.

After making the first portion of the cove, switch bits and complete the cut **(C)**. Adjust the fence position and the bit height to blend the curves from each of the two router bits. The final cove should be a smooth, continuous curve **(D)**.

Turning a Cylinder

Turning a cylinder involves removing the four corners of the stock to produce a smooth, uniform surface. It's typically the first step in producing a spindle turning, such as a leg or post. Because the stock contacts the tool only four times per revolution, the initial stage of this process is naturally rough. The best tool for the job is a massive, square-end gouge aptly called a roughing gouge.

Begin by securely mounting the work in the lathe. To begin the cut, start with the gouge handle low and gradually lift the handle until the cutting begins **(A)**. Once the chips begin to fly, slide the gouge along the tool rest to shape the entire length of the stock **(B)**. To keep the stock uniform in diameter, limit the cutting depth by bracing your fist against the tool rest.

[TIP] **When rounding square stock to form a cylinder, you can quickly and easily check for roundness by holding the middle of the gouge on the spinning stock. If it bounces lightly there's still a flat spot remaining.**

To shape the stock next to a pommel, rotate the gouge **(C)** and cut with the corner **(D)**. As you approach a true cylinder, you can check the stock for roundness by placing the middle portion of the tool on top of the spinning work **(E)**. This speeds the process by avoiding switching the lathe off and on again. The finished cylinder should be uniform and smooth, and its diameter should match the major diameter of the object you plan to turn.

A

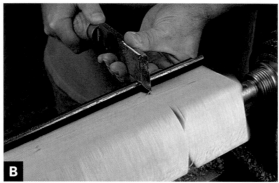

B

C

Turning a Pommel

A pommel is the square corner on a post or leg where a turned section intersects a square section. It's created by shearing a V into the square stock with a skew.

Begin by squaring the stock and milling it to size. Next, locate the center at each end of the stock by drawing diagonal lines. Mark the center with an awl to ensure accuracy. Then mount the work securely in the lathe.

Before turning, mark a layout line to indicate the location of the pommel. With the stock spinning relatively fast, nick the corners of the stock with the point of a skew. Next, make the cut deeper and wider by working the skew from the left and from the right **(A)**. Each time you make a cut, lever the edge of the skew into the work **(B)**. Use only the point of the skew to avoid catching the work and spoiling it. The pommel is complete when the cuts at each corner meet to surround the circumference of the work **(C)**.

Bead Turned with a Spindle Gouge

A bead is a convex curve made up of one-quarter or one-half of a circle or ellipse.

Begin by establishing the size of the bead. First cut the fillets that flank the bead **(A)**. Then cut the bead to the required diameter.

The next step is to shape the bead. Always work from the center toward the edges, or downhill. First, position the gouge so that the bevel rubs the spinning stock and then lift the handle until cutting begins. Now, roll the gouge to form one-half of the bead **(B)**. As you roll the gouge, lift the handle and pivot the handle in the direction you are cutting **(C)**. The three movements—roll, lift, and pivot—must be done simultaneously. It takes a bit of practice, but you'll soon begin to develop a feel for it. As you roll the bead, watch the top of the work so that you can view the bead as it is shaped.

After you've shaped half of the bead, start at the center once again and shape the second half **(D)**.

If the gouge catches during the process, you've most likely pivoted the handle too far, lifting the bevel from the work. The result is that the unsupported edge digs in, an occurrence referred to as a *catch* by woodturners. If the cutting action stops before you've shaped the bead entirely, it's because you didn't pivot the handle far enough and consequently the edge is not making contact with the stock.

A

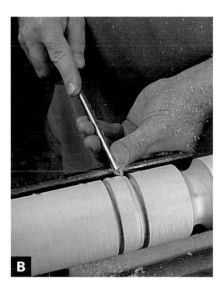

B

D

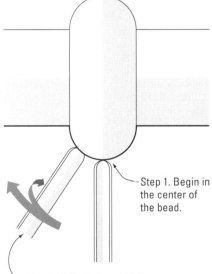

Step 1. Begin in the center of the bead.

Step 2. Roll, pivot, and lift the handle simultaneously.

Step 3. Repeat the process on the opposite side.

C

A

B

C

D

E

F

Bead Turned with a Skew

As you've probably heard, the skew is a difficult tool to master. It can catch easily and often. So why not shape a bead with a spindle gouge? Sometimes a bead is positioned adjacent to an ogee, pommel, or another bead. A gouge won't work in these tight situations; but the sharp, narrow point of a skew will.

[TIP] Keep a block of paraffin at hand and periodically rub a coat on the tool rest. You will get more control, because the tools will slide much easier across the rest.

There are some remedies for reducing the risk of a catch. First, keep the skew sharp. Sharp tools will always give you better control. Second, as you grind the skew, use a grinding method that keeps the bevel flat or hollow ground. A faceted, convex bevel will leave the edge unsupported, which will likely result in a catch.

To begin shaping a bead with a skew, first incise the width of the bead with the point **(A)**. Next, cut V's at the incisions to remove the excess stock **(B)**. Now, you're ready to shape the bead.

Using the heel of the skew, start off-center of the bead to take a light cut **(C)**. Let the bevel rub, and lift the handle until the cutting begins. Then roll the skew, lift the handle, and pivot it. After the first light cut, start at the apex of the bead and repeat the process **(D)**. The motions are very similar to those used with the spindle gouge **(E)**. After shaping the first half, begin at the apex of the bead and shape the second half. The finished shape should be full and round **(F)**.

Turning a Cove

The cove is a concave or hollow profile. The process of turning a cove is similar to turning a bead with a spindle gouge. The difference is that the profile and movements are reversed **(A)**.

Begin by making two slight incisions with the point of a skew **(B)**. These light cuts define the width of the cove and provide a notch to rest the gouge when starting the cut.

Next, remove some of the excess wood from the center of the cove with the spindle gouge. Let the bevel of the gouge rub **(C)** and lift the handle until the cutting begins; then cut a small hollow area **(D)**.

Now you're ready to shape the cove. Position the gouge horizontally on the rest, with the gouge rolled to the side. Point the tip of the gouge toward the center of the work. Now, enter the stock **(E)**. As you make the cut, simultaneously roll the gouge, pivot the handle, and lower the handle **(F)**. To avoid a catch don't attempt to cut uphill; instead, end the cut at the bottom of the cove. Now repeat the process for the second side. As you shape the cove, view the top of the turning to watch the shape as you create it.

To enlarge the cove, repeat the process until the final width and depth are reached **(G)**. Check the diameter at the bottom of the cove with a spring caliper.

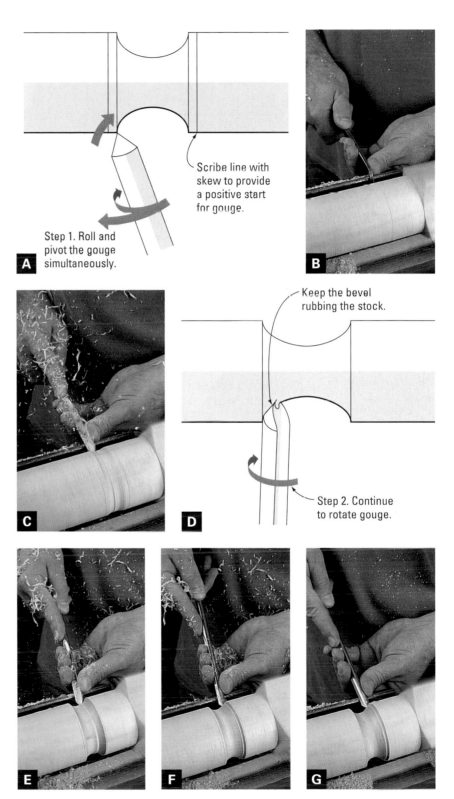

Scribe line with skew to provide a positive start for gouge.

Step 1. Roll and pivot the gouge simultaneously.

A

B

Keep the bevel rubbing the stock.

Step 2. Continue to rotate gouge.

C

D

E

F

G

Steam Bending

To find the examples given in this section on steam bending, I visited Brian Boggs at his shop in Berea, Kentucky. A long-time chairmaker, Brian has taken steam bending to a science. He uses a pressure cooker to supply the steam, and his steam box is stainless steel. The steel steam box is fitted within a well-insulated wooden box. His forms are sophisticated, too. Built up of layers of plywood, the forms have stainless-steel straps that fit over the outer portion of the bend to prevent failure from the extreme stresses that occur when bending.

Begin by selecting the stock and working it to rough size. It's important that the grain is straight and runs in the same direction as the stock. The stock can be rived (split) or sawn, as long as the grain direction is parallel with the edge and face **(A)**. After rough sizing, mill the stock to final size.

The next step is to steam the parts. A rule of thumb is to steam the parts 1 hour for each inch of thickness. Make certain that the steam box is hot before loading the parts **(B)**.

Take advantage of the time while the parts are steaming to make preparations for bending. Make certain your form is in place and that you have the necessary clamps at hand. Once the parts are sufficiently pliable to bend around the form, remove them from the steam box.

> ⚠️ **WARNING Wooden parts coming out of a steam box are very hot! Protect your hands with a pair of leather work gloves.**

Bent Lamination with a Two-Part Form

Begin by resawing stock for the laminae (A). Experiment to find a thickness that easily conforms to the curve of the plywood form. After sawing, scrape or sand the surfaces to smooth away the saw marks. If you choose to sand, it's a good idea to remove the fine dust from the pores of the wood with compressed air.

The next step is to prepare for glue-up. If you use plastic resin glue, you'll need measuring cups and a stirring stick. A small foam paint roller works well for glue application. I like to have the clamps I'll be using ready and waiting (B). These simple steps make the gluing process proceed smoothly and without fuss.

After spreading the glue, stack the layers and position them within the form. Then apply clamp pressure from the center and work toward each end (C).

> **⚠ WARNING** Plastic resin and other two-part adhesives cure by chemical reaction as the two parts are mixed. During this process, toxic chemical fumes are often released. Protect yourself by having good cross-ventilation.

A

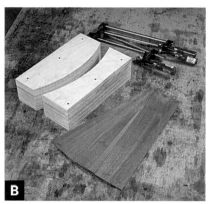

B

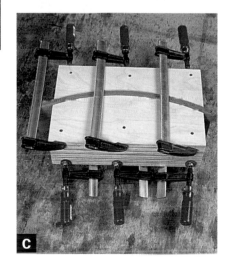

C

Construction

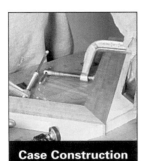

Case Construction

Shelves

Drawers

Doors

Locks and Catches

Bases

Backs

Tops

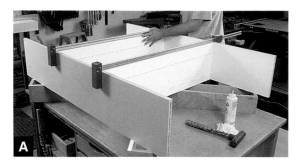

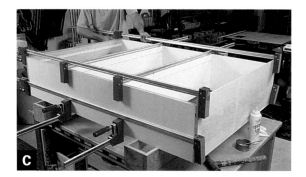

Assembling a Case

For most cabinets, there's a basic assembly sequence that will guarantee success—or at least a more comfortable heart rate. The trick is always to begin assembly from the insides out. In most instances, this means assembling any interior dividers or partitions to the top and bottom of the case. If the case is wide, clamp one side of the work while it sits face down on the bench **(A)**. Then flip the assembly over and clamp the opposite side **(B)**.

Tackle the outside of the case, often the sides or ends of a cabinet, after you've clamped all the interior assemblies. Depending on the type of clamps you use and the design of the cabinet, you might have to wait for the glue to dry on the interior parts before clamping the outside of the case. When possible, use long-reach clamps, because they can reach over existing clamps and let you clamp the entire case in one assembly session **(C)**.

Clamping Corners

Corner joints constitute most of the casework in furniture—including small boxes and drawers—and it's necessary to find an effective way to clamp across what is typically a wide surface. Like edge work, the answer is to use cauls to help distribute clamping pressure.

When joints protrude at the corners, such as in through dovetails or box joints, use notched cauls to bring the corner together **(A)**. Make the notch cuts on the bandsaw or table saw. The blocks gain purchase and don't interfere with closing the joint, and they center over the joint to avoid bowing the sides.

Miter joints have a way of not closing at the most inappropriate times. To get good purchase on what is often a very slippery joint, there are several clamping strategies. The tried-and-true method is to clamp all four corners of a mitered frame at once with bar clamps. The deep throats of Bessey® K-body clamps make it easy to get over and under the joint **(B)**. Tighten each clamp a little at a time, like tightening the lug nuts on a car wheel. Make sure to check the frame for square before letting the glue dry.

The block-and-rod frame system shown here (from Lee Valley Tools) gives you very precise control when closing four miters at a time, and it doesn't require lots of clamping force **(C)**. Like the bar clamp approach, tighten each corner a little at a time to align the miters.

One of the simplest ways to close the joint is to clamp shopmade blocks to the frame before assembly. Cut out the blocks on the bandsaw so that the clamping surfaces are parallel to each other when the frame is assembled **(D)**.

A picture framer's vise is handy for closing one miter at a time **(E)**. This is useful when you're nailing or screwing the joint, since you can assemble the frame one piece at a time.

Web clamps allow you to glue up all four corners at once, and they work well on both flat frames and boxes **(F)**. You can use heavy-duty web clamps for large cases, but plan on having several on hand to close the joints.

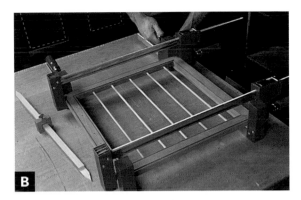

B

C

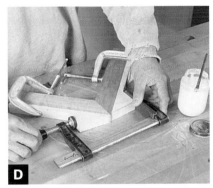

D

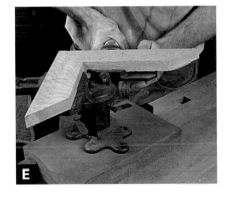

E

F

Building Face Frames

One of the easiest ways for constructing a frame is to mill square stock; then join it using biscuits. This technique works well when the case won't be seen at the top and the bottom, such as a base cabinet that will be covered with a counter-top or a wall cabinet hung at eye level. Cut all the stiles and rails to length; then dry-fit the parts and use a biscuit to lay out the joints. If you draw a centerline on the biscuit, you can mark the stiles and rails by eye if you position the biscuit so it won't protrude inside the frame (**A**).

Cut half slots for the biscuits with a plate joiner. On such narrow pieces, use a shopmade fixture to secure the stock so your hands are out of the way (**B**). Slot all the stiles and rails using the fixture, aligning the center mark on the joiner with the marks you made on the stock (**C**).

Spread glue in the half slots, insert the biscuits, and clamp the frame together (**D**). Then saw the protruding biscuits flush with a backsaw (**E**).

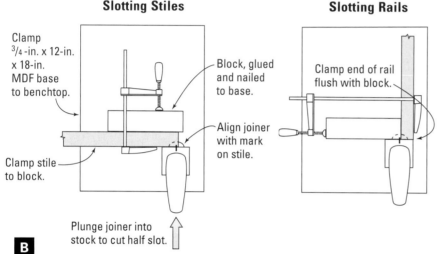

Slotting Stiles

Clamp ³/₄-in. x 12-in. x 18-in. MDF base to benchtop.

Block, glued and nailed to base.

Align joiner with mark on stile.

Clamp stile to block.

Plunge joiner into stock to cut half slot.

Slotting Rails

Clamp end of rail flush with block.

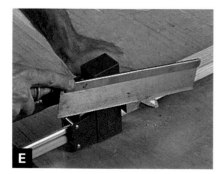

Attaching Face Frames

Although you can certainly nail a face frame to the front of a case, gluing the frame with clamps is a cleaner alternative. Because of the frame's relatively thin and narrow members, it can be difficult to apply sufficient clamping pressure over the frame for tight joints. The trick is to use some scrap cauls, about 2 in. wide, between the clamps and the frame to distribute the pressure. Spread glue on the edges of the case and carefully align the frame to the case. There should be about 1/16 in. of overhang on either side. Now position the cauls and apply clamps every 6 in. or so (**A**). If you see any gaps at the joint line, add more clamps.

Once the glue has dried, clamp the case on its side and use a bench plane to trim the small overhang (**B**). By keeping the body of the plane on the work and skewing the plane so the cutter is over the frame only, you avoid planing into the side of the case. Smooth any difficult spots and remove plane tracks with a hand scraper (**C**).

Finish by sanding the edge with 180-grit sandpaper wrapped around a felt block. If you're careful with your grain selection when picking the stiles of the frame, you can make the joint almost disappear (**D**).

This dovetail dado-routing jig serves double-duty to rout $^{11}/_{16}$-in. dovetail sockets and $^3/_4$-in. dadoes in case sides. Using a $^1/_2$-in. dovetail bit in the first router, add shims on either side of the guide rails that provide $^3/_{16}$ in. of side-to-side play between the router and the rails. Rout the dovetails by moving the router from left to right as you push it away from you. To rout dadoes, remove the shims and install a $^3/_4$-in. plunge-cutting straight bit in a second router with a larger baseplate.

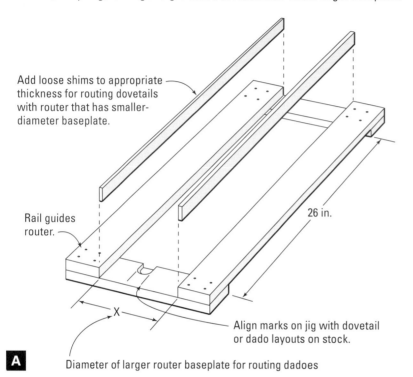

Add loose shims to appropriate thickness for routing dovetails with router that has smaller-diameter baseplate.

Rail guides router.

26 in.

X

Align marks on jig with dovetail or dado layouts on stock.

A

Diameter of larger router baseplate for routing dadoes

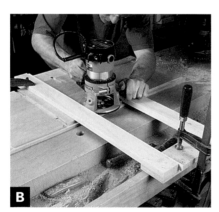

B

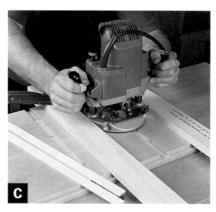

C

Web Frames

A web frame stiffens a case and creates a strong platform for housing drawers—all without adding excess weight to a cabinet—and its design allows for the movement of cases with solid-wood sides.

Start by sizing and cutting the frame parts to fit the interior dimensions of the cabinet. Prepare for the case joinery by first cutting mortise-and-tenon joints in the frame parts. Then cut the dovetail sockets and dadoes into the case sides. For accuracy, use one jig to cut both joints at the same time—but with two routers with different diameter baseplates **(A)**. Shims placed on either side of the smaller router accommodate the difference in base diameter. Size the shims to suit your particular router. You can use this jig to cut both joints using only one router, but you'll have to either change bits (and bit depth) between cuts or reposition the jig for each cut.

Rout an $^{11}/_{16}$-in.-wide by $^5/_{16}$-in.-deep dovetail socket for the horizontal drawer divider using a $^1/_2$-in. bit. Using a bit that's smaller than the desired slot width puts a lot less strain on the bit and makes a cleaner cut in the wood. Place the shims on either side of the router and move the router in a clockwise direction, making contact with the shim on the left side and then with the shim on the right. Pencil lines mark the length of the socket, so it's a simple matter of stopping the cut when the bit reaches the mark **(B)**.

Next, rout the dadoes for the drawer runners. Remove the shims and use the same jig and the second router, which has a larger baseplate. Use a $^3/_4$-in. plunge-cutting straight bit to cut a shallow $^1/_8$-in. dado between the dovetail slots **(C)**.

Working from the front of the cabinet, install the front dividers by gluing the dovetails into the sockets and clamping across the joints **(D)**.

Next, turn the case over and install the drawer runner from the back by gluing it into the mortise in the front divider. Don't glue the runner into the dado. Instead, drive a screw through an oversize hole in the center of the runner and into the case side **(E)**. On wider cases, use two or three screws through the runner. Adding screws may sound unconventional, but the technique stiffens the overall frame and—more important—helps keep the case sides flat over time.

Glue the back divider into the dovetail sockets at the back, but don't glue the rear tenons on the runners. Make sure to size the runners so you leave an ⅛-in. gap between the shoulder of the runner and the back divider **(F)**. This arrangement allows for movement of the case sides. Waxing the rear tenons is also a good idea to promote easy movement of the runner. On the case shown here, where pairs of drawers run side by side, vertical dividers were dovetailed at the front of the case. Add wide runners behind the dividers using the same dry-tenon technique. Later, glue narrow guide strips onto the runner to guide the sides of the drawers.

➤ See *"Drawer Runners"* on p. 210.

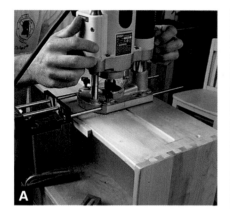

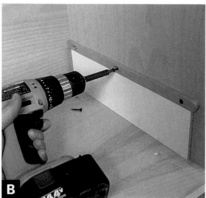

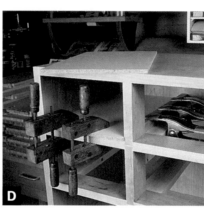

Drawer Runners

If the cabinet contains drawers, some guide system is necessary. For the simplest cabinet, the side itself can guide the drawer. But guides are required, for example, when a face frame extends beyond the side of a cabinet or when a vertical divider divides two or more drawers side by side.

When your case doesn't involve horizontal front dividers and you want to maximize usable space, you can hang drawers directly above and below each other by attaching solid-wood strips to the sides of the case and then routing matching grooves in the drawer sides.

Rout a ¼-in.-deep stopped groove in the drawer side (**A**). Attach the strip to the case with screws. A piece of plywood registered against the case bottom keeps the strip parallel and helps align pairs of strips (**B**). Slide the drawer onto the strips and all you see is the grooves in the drawer sides (**C**). In the case of an extended face frame, just pack out the space with a plywood strip to accommodate the frame overhang; then screw the hardwood guide strip to the side of the case.

[**TIP**] **When a drawer has free space above the sides, install a kicker above the sides to prevent tipping. A couple screws or some spots of glue attach the kicker to the case.**

For divided drawers, rip and plane a strip equal to the thickness of the divider and mortise it into the front and back of the cabinet, or glue it directly to the web frame. To help align the guide strip square to the opening, use a pair of scrap boards cut to the exact width of the drawer openings. Clamp the boards in position with the guide strip between them. Then remove one board and glue and clamp the strip to the frame (**D**).

Dust Panels

There are two primary reasons for adding dust panels inside your cabinets: In bureaus, a panel helps prevent clothes from getting tangled in drawers above. It also helps seal the cabinet from airborne dust.

Before assembling the frame, groove the web members for the panel. It's quick to rout the slots with a slotting cutter on the router table **(A)**.

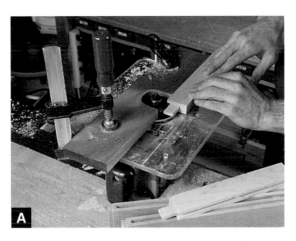

After installing the front divider and the runners, slide the panel into the grooves from the back. For extra rigidity, you can glue the panel into the front and side grooves, as long as you make it from plywood **(B)**.

Add the rear divider by gluing only its dovetails into the sockets. Be careful not to glue the divider to the panel or the tenons on the runners to allow for movement of the case sides **(C)**.

This tapered-dovetail socket jig is sized to rout a $5/16$-in.-deep by $5/8$-in.-wide dovetail in a case side up to 14 in. wide, using a $1/2$-in. dovetail bit. The dovetail tapers $1/16$ in. over its length. For wider cases, use the same amount of taper and make the guide boards wider.

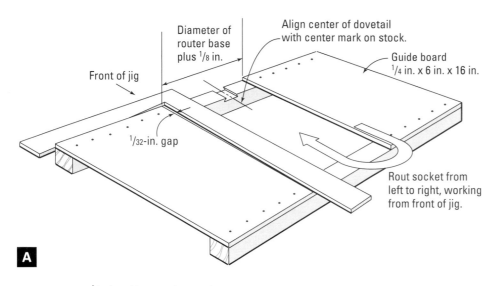

Diameter of router base plus $1/8$ in.

Front of jig

Align center of dovetail with center mark on stock.

Guide board $1/4$ in. x 6 in. x 16 in.

$1/32$-in. gap

Rout socket from left to right, working from front of jig.

A

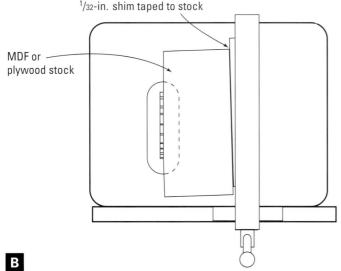

$1/32$-in. shim taped to stock

MDF or plywood stock

B

Tapered Sliding Dovetail

The strongest connection is to dovetail the shelf to the case sides, tapering the joint along its length.

Cut the tapered dovetail sockets in the case first. Use a shopmade jig (**A, B**) to guide the router and a $1/2$-in. dovetail bit. To reduce tearout, rout a notch into the back edge first, before routing the full width of the panel (**C**).

Next, tape $1/32$-in.-thick shims to both sides of the shelf stock (**D**).

Using the same bit you used to cut the socket, rout the pin by making one pass on the router table on each side of the stock. Be sure to rout in scrap first to fine-tune the fit, moving the fence in or out from the bit, or adjusting the shim thickness, until the widest part of the tail almost—but not quite—fits into the wider end of the socket. Beams clamped to the stock remove any possible warp (**E**).

The dovetail pin should tighten as the joint is brought home. Having to tap the last $1/2$ in. into the socket means a tight-fitting joint. Glue is optional, although with solid wood it's a good idea to glue about 2 in. at the front of the joint to keep the shelf flush with the case despite any wood movement (**F**).

C

D

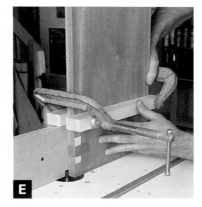

E

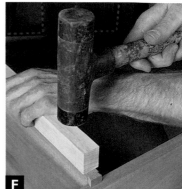

F

Through-Dado Shelf

A strong shelf connection is to attach the shelf permanently to the case sides. This approach strengthens the case itself and helps stiffen the shelf and prevent it from sagging under a load.

The simplest method for making a fixed shelf is to cut through dadoes in the case sides to receive the shelf. Rout the dadoes with a straight bit guided by a straightedge. For a clean cut, plunge rout the dado in successively deeper passes to reduce tearout **(A)**. Make your dadoes shallow—about ¼ in. deep in a ¾-in. panel—to keep the case sides strong and to leave enough material for nailing or screwing through the joint.

A tight-fitting joint is important for strength and good looks. Most plywood comes about ¹⁄₆₄ in. under nominal thickness, so you'll need to cut dadoes slightly undersize for a tight fit. The dado shown on the right in photo **B** was routed with a conventional straight bit, which resulted in a loose joint with a small gap. The bit on the left of the photo is specially sized for an exact fit with standard ¼-in. hardwood plywood, so the joint is strong and tight.

For a finished appearance, simply glue and clamp the joint **(C)**. For case sides that won't be seen, add screws or nails through the side to ease assembly and to strengthen the joint.

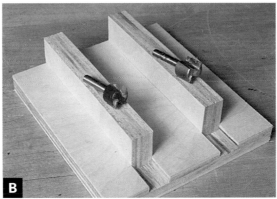

Wood Brackets for Open Shelves

Attached to the wall or placed in an open cabinet, wooden brackets can support a lot of weight and add a custom look.

If you're making one or two brackets, you can draw the desired shape on the stock and saw it out on the bandsaw. For multiple brackets, use a plywood template to trace the shape onto the stock **(A)**.

Saw out the shape by cutting to the line on the bandsaw **(B)**. Clean up the saw marks on the drum sander, sanding "downhill" to the grain for the smoothest surface **(C)**. Pare the shoulders and flats with a sharp chisel.

When possible, screw through the back of the case or the backboard and into the brackets to conceal the connection **(D)**. If necessary, you can also screw through the brackets themselves and into the backboard; then plug the screw holes for a finished appearance.

You can simply let the finished shelf sit on the brackets or secure it from behind the backboard and below the brackets with screws or finish nails **(E)**.

Ledges for Open Shelves

Display shelves often call for a ledge in the middle of a board, which can be screwed in place from behind.

To elevate your ledge from rectilinear boredom, first scroll the ends of the stock on the bandsaw **(A)** and then clean up the sawn surfaces with a drum sander or by hand.

For a more delicate feel, chamfer the underside of the stock on the router table. Use a piloted chamfer bit and begin the cut safely by rotating the stock against a starting pin. Don't rout the full chamfer in one pass; make successively deeper cuts by raising the cutter after each pass **(B)**.

For a low-profile look, counterbore the stock with a ¼-in. Forstner bit and use trim-head screws to attach the shelf to the backboard **(C)**. Once the shelves are secured, spread glue on a ¼-in. wooden plug and tap it into the counterbored hole. A mark on the plug indicates grain direction **(D)**.

Once the glue has dried, pare and sand the plug flush with the edge of the shelf **(E)**. Because the plug's grain runs parallel to the shelf's grain, the plug blends in seamlessly.

Custom-fitted ledges can make a distinguished statement. As shown here, I store my larger handplanes on shelves scrolled to the outline of each plane **(F)**.

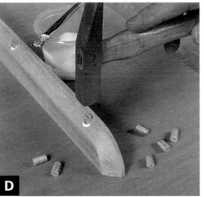

Use this template-rounding jig on a router table to cut half-circles on the ends of wooden supports or anywhere you need a specific radius on the ends of stock. Rip the stock to finished width and about ⅛ in. over length; then bandsaw a curve on the ends slightly bigger than the desired radius. Using a top-bearing template or pattern bit, rout each support in four consecutive passes, each pass cutting one corner of the support.

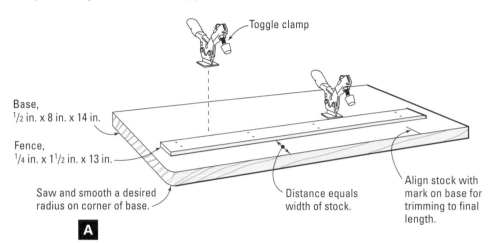

Toggle clamp

Base,
½ in. x 8 in. x 14 in.

Fence,
¼ in. x 1½ in. x 13 in.

Saw and smooth a desired radius on corner of base.

Distance equals width of stock.

Align stock with mark on base for trimming to final length.

A

Wood Support and Edge Strip

An elegant solution to adjustable shelving is to support each shelf on support cleats that nestle into half-holes drilled into wooden strips. The system is simpler to make than it looks, and a template-rounding jig helps you accurately make the round-ended supports **(A)**.

Starting with a pair of 2-in.-wide boards, drill a series of 1-in.-diameter holes along the center of each board using a Forstner bit on the drill press **(B)**.

Rip each board in half on the table saw to create two strips **(C)** and nail the strips into the corners of the case. A pneumatic brad gun makes for fast work **(D)**.

After sizing the cleats to about ⅛ in. longer than the finished size, use a template-rounding jig and a pattern bit to reach the finished length, rounding the ends at the same time **(E)**.

Install the supports between the edge strips at the desired height. The finished shelf sits on top of the supports **(F)**. You'll have to notch the shelf to fit it around the edge strips.

> ⚠️ **WARNING** Always remove rings and other jewelry when operating a drill press. Rings caught by a spinning drill chuck or bit can rip the flesh right off your finger.

B

C

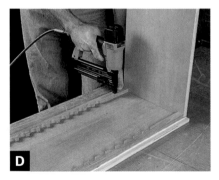

D

E

F

Adjustable Shelves

For maximum versatility in a cabinet or book-case, a shelf that simply rests on supports is the way to go. With this approach, you can easily reconfigure shelves on the fly. The type of support you choose is mostly an aesthetic decision, from simple pins that fit into holes drilled into the case, to more elaborate wooden hangers that add flair to your furniture.

Wood cleats used to support shelves are simple and effective. To improve their looks, keep the cleats as thin as possible (⅜ in. thick is about minimum) and install them with finish nails or small screws.

After ripping and crosscutting the stock to width and length, round over the front and bottom edge on the router table. Use a starting pin to begin the cut safely **(A)**.

It's easier if you secure the cleats before fully assembling the case. Use a square to ensure each cleat runs dead square across the case **(B)**.

The finished shelf rests on top of the cleats **(C)**. To adjust the shelf, simply place it over another set of cleats.

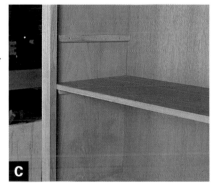

This simple hole-layout jig allows for accurate layout of shelf-pin holes. To use it, align the bottom edge with the bottom of the case side or with the case's joinery, such as a dado or biscuits. Use an awl or a center punch to mark the hole locations by pushing the punch through the jig and into the workpiece.

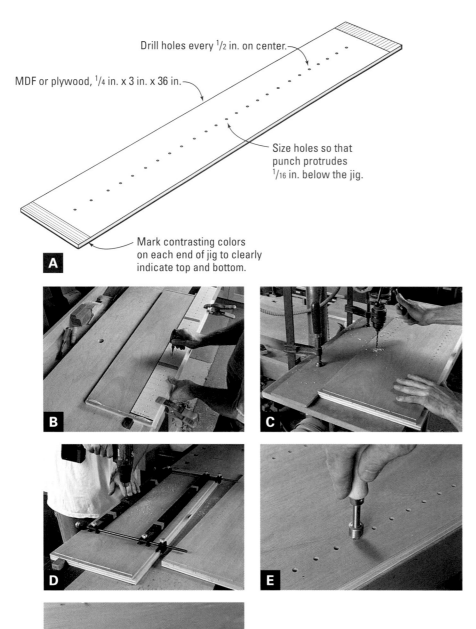

Drill holes every 1/2 in. on center.

MDF or plywood, 1/4 in. x 3 in. x 36 in.

Size holes so that punch protrudes 1/16 in. below the jig.

Mark contrasting colors on each end of jig to clearly indicate top and bottom.

A

B

C

D

E

F

Pins and Holes

Drilling a series of holes in the case and using pins to support the shelves is another simple yet good-looking solution to adjustable shelving. But make a mistake in the hole layout and you'll end up with wobbly shelves. The key is to use a simple jig that lets you lay out dead-accurate holes in the case sides **(A)**.

Clamp the jig to the case side with its edge flush with the edge of the panel. For this example, I used the biscuit joinery in the panel to help align the end of the jig. Use a center punch or an awl to mark the stock through the jig. Masking tape applied to the jig defines the row of holes you want to drill **(B)**.

Drill the holes on the drill press using a fence clamped to the table and a brad-point bit. The fence is rabbeted so wayward chips don't interfere with alignment **(C)**.

[**TIP**] **Shavings from a drill press (or a router table) have a nasty habit of lodging between the workpiece and the fence, most likely spoiling the work. A rabbet cut into the bottom of the fence provides a channel for the shavings and allows the workpiece to contact the fence.**

If you don't own a drill press, a good drilling option is to use a commercial drilling rig like the Veritas® jig shown here. There's no marking out; just secure the jig to the stock and drill into the work through hardened steel bushings **(D)**. Masking tape wrapped around the bit guides it to the correct depth.

A nice touch is to lightly chamfer the drilled holes with a handheld countersinking bit. Be sure to use the same number of rotations per hole for a consistent look **(E)**. Brass pins provide a clean look **(F)**.

Pilasters and Clips

Pilasters offer an easy way to incorporate adjustable shelves into cabinets, and they usually allow for incremental height changes of ½ in. or less—a real benefit for configuring shelves exactly where you want them. Some pilasters can be surface mounted, but recessed pilasters have a cleaner look.

Plow grooves in the stock for the pilaster using a dado blade or router, making sure to test the fit first in scrap (A).

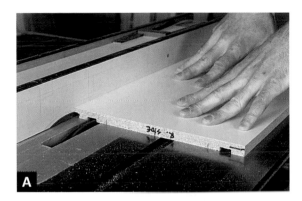

Crosscut the pilaster strip to length using a crosscut-style carbide-tipped blade for aluminum, brass, or plastic (B). For steel, you'll need to use a hacksaw. It's important when using any style of pilaster that the slots or holes for the clips are equidistant from the ends of each pilaster, so measure carefully when cutting to length.

Tap the pilaster strip into the groove, using the assembled top and bottom of the cabinet to help register the strip (C).

With the cabinet fully assembled, you can hang the shelves. The plastic clips twist securely into this style of pilaster (D).

This wire support drilling jig lets you drill a pair of accurately spaced holes for a wire support. To use the jig, hold the fence firmly against the front edge of the stock and drill through the correct holes in the acrylic.

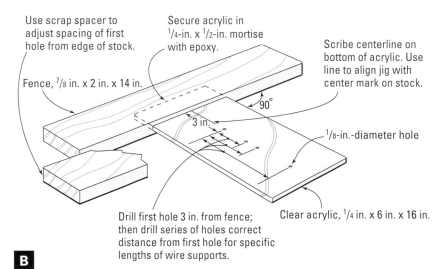

Use scrap spacer to adjust spacing of first hole from edge of stock.

Secure acrylic in $^1/_4$-in. x $^1/_2$-in. mortise with epoxy.

Scribe centerline on bottom of acrylic. Use line to align jig with center mark on stock.

Fence, $^7/_8$ in. x 2 in. x 14 in.

90°

3 in.

$^1/_8$-in.-diameter hole

Drill first hole 3 in. from fence; then drill series of holes correct distance from first hole for specific lengths of wire supports.

Clear acrylic, $^1/_4$ in. x 6 in. x 16 in.

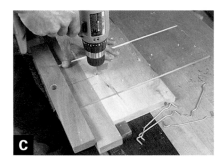

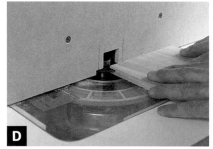

Wire Supports

These imaginative little strips of wire—sometimes called invisible or "magic" wires—work great when you need to make removable dividers or partitions.

A pair of small bent wires engage slots cut into the ends of the shelf and small holes drilled into the case. To position the shelf, you simply slide it over the wires from the front of the case. There are two benefits to using wire supports: First, the holes you drill in the case are small ($^1/_8$ in. diameter), so they don't intrude glaringly into your design. Second, once the shelf is hung, you won't see any visible means of support.

Wire supports are available in roughly 6-in. and 9-in. lengths. If you need longer wires, for wider shelves, you can double up the wires to gain the necessary support. For narrow shelves, use shorter wires that you make yourself. Clamp a piece of stiff $^1/_8$-in.-diameter wire—or an existing longer wire support—into a bending jig in a metal-working vise to form the bends (**A**).

Use a drilling jig to drill the $^1/_8$-in. holes accurately in the case side for the wires (**B**). Tape placed on the drill bit lets you know when you've reached the correct depth (**C**).

Cut a groove in the ends of each shelf, stopping it about $^1/_2$ in. from the front edge so you don't see the groove when the shelf is installed. Use an $^1/_8$-in. slotting cutter on the router table and adjust the fence for the correct depth of cut. Pencil marks on the fence indicate where to start and stop the cut (**D**). The finished shelf slides into the case and over the wires (**E**).

Flush-Fit Drawer

The Cadillac of drawers, a flush-fit drawer has the look and feel of fine craftsmanship. It's just as well—this type of drawer is more challenging to fit than any other. A flush-fit drawer involves many aspects of general drawer making, so it's a good exercise in mastering the art of a well-made and well-fitted drawer.

A fail-safe method for determining the correct height or width for the drawer parts is to measure directly from the opening. Hold a drawer front or side up to the finished opening and mark the exact height; then cut to your mark **(A)**. This approach leaves you enough material so that you can plane the drawer down for the correct fit into the opening once you've assembled it.

Usually, assembling a dovetailed drawer doesn't require the use of clamps. After tapping the joints together, and while the glue is still wet, check the drawer for square.

If the drawer is out of square, give the longer of the two diagonals a sound rap by tapping the rear of the drawer on a hard surface **(B)**. When the drawer is square, set it aside on a flat surface until the glue dries.

After the glue has dried, use a smooth plane to level the top and bottom edges of the drawer. Periodically check that you're planing the drawer flat by checking it against a flat surface, such as your benchtop. To prevent tearing out the fibers, turn the plane around the corners as you work **(C)**. Plane more off on taller drawers to allow for wood movement.

(Continued on p. 222.)

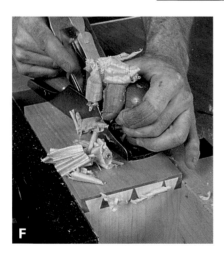

Next, set your plane for a very fine cut and shave the drawer sides down until the pins and tails are level. Clamp the drawer front in a bench vise and support the side on a wide board. Work in from each end to avoid breaking off any fibers **(D)**. Check your progress with a straightedge and stop often to test-fit the drawer in the case opening. Keep shaving until the drawer slides in easily without any side-to-side play. Finish by sanding the sides lightly with 220-grit sandpaper wrapped around a felt block.

With the drawer stops in place, install the drawer into the case and mark the amount the front protrudes by scribing around the drawer **(E)**.

Back at the bench, plane lightly across the face of the drawer to your marks **(F)**. Now that you've fitted the drawer, add your favorite pull hardware.

Finally, rabbet a plywood drawer bottom and slide it into the grooves in the drawer **(G)**.

[TIP] On large drawers, glue the plywood for drawer bottoms into the grooves. It significantly increases the strength of the drawer and helps stiffen the corner joints.

Finish up by driving screws or nails through the bottom and into the back of the drawer. If possible, use ⅜-in. or thicker plywood on anything but very small drawers. Thin ¼-in. plywood has a chintzy sound and feel.

Another option is to install a solid-wood bottom (*without glue!*) and let it extend past the back of the drawer to function as a drawer stop.

Half-Overlay Drawer

At the opposite end of the spectrum from flush-fit drawers are half-overlay drawers, often referred to as half inset. Because half-overlay drawers are so easy to fit into a drawer opening, this type of construction is perfect for utility drawers, kitchen drawers, and anytime you have multiple drawers and want to get the job done fast. A portion of the drawer front conceals the opening in the cabinet, so you can have as much as ⅜ in. of space between the opening and the back of the drawer front, allowing you to make a front with a "sloppy" fit. Half-overlay drawers are often used with metal ball-bearing slides, which further eases the installation.

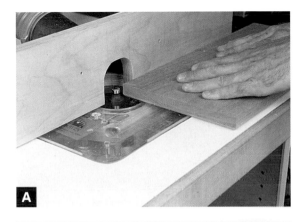

> See *"Installing Commercial Slides"* on p. 226.

See *"Installing Commercial Slides"* on p. 226.

You can cut the drawer joints before or after you create the overlay in the drawer front. The order of construction isn't critical. To make the half overlay, start by rounding over the edges of the drawer front on the router table using a ¼-in. roundover bit **(A)**.

Next, set up the table saw with an auxiliary fence and a dado blade and cut a ⅜-in.-deep by ⅜-in.-wide rabbet on all four sides of the front **(B)**.

A typical bank of half-overlay drawers shows gently rounded edges **(C)**. You can space adjacent drawers relatively far apart by incorporating the drawers into a face frame made from wide stiles and rails. This saves you from having to fit the drawer fronts to exacting reveals.

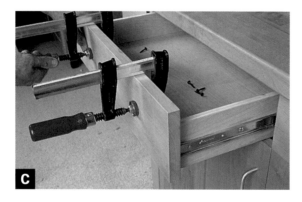

Full-Overlay Drawer

Found on Euro-style cabinets, a full-overlay drawer is one of the easiest drawers to make, but not necessarily the simplest to fit. The drawer front lays completely over the face frame of the cabinet, concealing the drawer opening.

Unlike other drawer types, the final fit of a full-overlay drawer often depends on its neighboring adjacent drawers. The idea is to have a 1/8-in. or less gap between all the drawers (and any overlay doors, too). The result is a seamless, contemporary look and feel. Achieving this small reveal between drawers is a challenge, but it's straight-forward if you follow the right steps.

You can build the drawer as a complete unit, extending the front beyond the sides. I prefer a simpler method, that of building a drawer box and then attaching a false front to the box that overlays the face of the cabinet. Because the front overlays the box, you can use sturdy box joints or through dovetails for a long-lasting drawer, without seeing the joints from the front of the drawer.

Once you've constructed the drawer box, drill and countersink the back side of the front for screws **(A)**.

Install the drawer box flush to the front of the case and use double-sided (carpet) tape to adhere the false front to the box **(B)**.

Gently pull out the drawer and immediately clamp the front to the box **(C)**. Then drive two screws from inside the drawer box and into the front.

Slide the drawer back into the case and check the fit **(D)**. If the reveal is even, add more screws to secure the front permanently to the box. If the gap needs work, remove the drawer front and plane its edges or reposition the front by using screws in different holes. When the front fits correctly, add two more screws.

Divided Drawer

One of the simplest ways of dividing a drawer or other box-type opening is to join the dividers themselves with half-lap joints cut on the table saw. If you cut the dividers a hair short of their intended resting spot and add strips of felt to each end, you can press-fit the dividers in place. Start by finish-planing the divider material **(A)**. Then cut the stock $1/32$ in. smaller than the drawer or case opening. Lay out the joints with a square, making the notches equal to the thickness of the planed stock **(B)**.

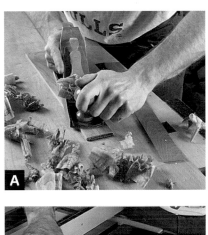
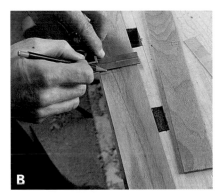

Saw the first notch on the table saw by making a couple of passes using the miter gauge **(C)**. Check the fit. The joint should *almost* fit but be too tight to put together fully **(D)**. Repeat the procedure to cut the notch in the second piece.

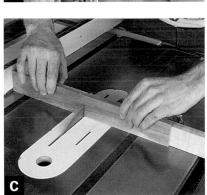
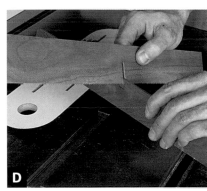

Sand the dividers for the final fit with 220-grit paper wrapped around a felt block **(E)**. Self-stick felt applied to the ends of each finished divider holds them in tension against the drawer or case opening **(F)**.

Installing Commercial Slides

Side-mounted slides remain popular with many cabinetmakers and kitchen designers. Affordable and easy to install, they come in left and right pairs for each drawer, and each slide consists of two parts: a runner, which is screwed to the drawer side, and a housing for that runner, which attaches to the inside of the case.

When installing the runners on the drawer, use a jig to align the runner accurately. At this point, install only two or three screws in the elongated holes—enough to hold the runner in place **(A)**. How high on the side should you position the runner? You should aim for aligning the runner with the height of your drawer pull or handle. For example, if you plan to mount the handle centered on the drawer front, then center the runner on the side. This gives you the best action and feel.

Use a plywood spacer in the case opening to align the slide housing in the cabinet. The shim ensures that the slides on both sides of the case are level with each other and that they're square and parallel to the case **(B)**. After hanging and fitting the drawer to the correct depth of the cabinet, add the remaining screws **(C)**.

Installing Under-Mount Slides

When the thought of looking at metal hardware on the side of your carefully crafted drawer gives you the heebie-jeebies, use an under-mount side.

Mount the case and drawer slides as one member into the case. Then drill a hole in the bottom edge of each drawer side, near the front of the drawer **(A)**. Slip the drawer into the case and lower the drawer so the holes you've drilled engage pins at the front of the slides **(B)**. When you pull out the drawer, you won't see any hardware at all **(C)**.

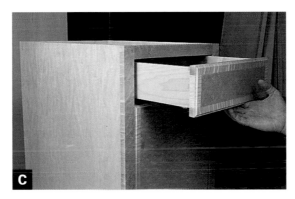

A

B

Shopmade Pulls

Making your own pulls or handles is a very satis-fying aspect of furniture making and is tons of fun. There's no limit to the designs you can incorporate into your work, and it personalizes your furniture in a way that commercial hardware can't. The pulls shown here are just a sampling of what you can make if you let your imagination roam free. And all these designs will work great as door pulls, too.

▶ **For more on doors, see pp. 230-245.**

Here's a chance to use those prized leftover scraps of wood you've been saving since the last millennium. This pull is as simple as it gets, and that's probably why I like it so much. Use a live-edged piece of wood—burled or highly figured woods are my favorites—to make each pull unique. Sculpt the shape of the pull on the band-saw however you wish; just be sure to keep the mounting face flat. Try beveling the ends for a dramatic effect **(A)**.

Drill and countersink the inside of the drawer front for screws and drill pilot holes in the back of the pull. Spread some glue on the pull and secure it to the drawer with screws driven through the back of the drawer front **(B)**.

Protruding-Strip Pull

To make a very simple but very effective pull, apply a strip to the top edge of the drawer front. If you select your stock carefully for color and grain, you can fool the eye into thinking that the pull was carved into the front, instead of being simply glued in place. The best method is to shape the strip before gluing it to the drawer.

Cove the underside on the router table using a coving bit. Make the cut in successively deeper passes **(A)**. Then round over the top and bottom of the leading edge **(B)**.

Glue and clamp the strip to the drawer front **(C)**. When the glue has dried, clean up any small misalignments with a goose-neck scraper and planes.

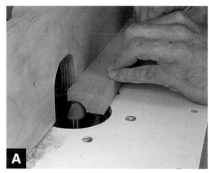
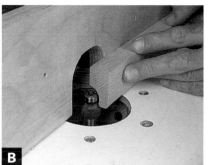

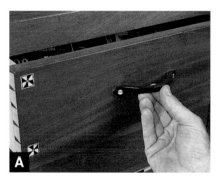

Curved Pull

Made from any dense, close-grained hardwood such as maple, rosewood, or ebony, a curved pull has a sophisticated look **(A)**. The faux screws shown here add to the charm, although their main function is to conceal the screws that secure the pull to the drawer.

Lay out the pull profile on the stock using two plywood templates, one for the side of the pull **(B)** and one for the top **(C)**. Cut out the shape on the bandsaw.

Use a drum or spindle sander to help fair the curves and remove the saw marks; then counter-bore, countersink, and drill a shank hole at a slight angle through the pull for screws **(D)**. Plug the hole with a dowel made from a contrasting wood; but before you glue in the dowel, saw a kerf in one end with a handsaw. Install the dowel and tap a wedge into the kerf made from contrasting wood to mimic the slotted head of a screw.

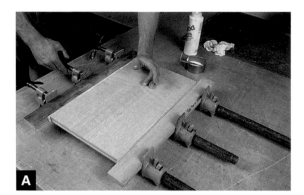

Flat Panel

The most basic of all doors is a simple flat panel. Although you can make a panel from solid wood, there's a high probability that the door will warp if it's of any considerable width or length. A better choice is a man-made material, such as MDF, because of its inherent stability. But MDF needs a surface covering of veneer or paint to conceal its bland appearance. Veneered hardwood plywood is another choice, but like MDF, you'll need to conceal the raw edges. For edging on doors, I prefer thin solid-wood banding over veneer edge-banding. If you make your banding from the same species as the plywood veneer, with similar color and grain patterns, it will blend inconspicuously with the panel. Make the banding about 1/8 in. thick, which provides enough material for easing over the sharp edges without exposing the plywood core.

Dimension the panel to account for the combined thickness of the edging; then glue and clamp the two edges that will become the vertical surfaces on the door. Make sure to cut the banding slightly thicker and longer than the panel **(A)**. Once the glue has dried, rout the excess with a laminate bit or trim it flush with a handplane.

Add the two horizontal bandings, making a butt joint at the corners **(B)**.

You can ease over the edges of the banding with a plane or rout a small 1/8-in. roundover **(C)**. Once the door is installed, the corner joints will be invisible from the top of the door.

Raised Frame and Panel

For solid-wood doors of any size, frame-and-panel construction solves the problem of warping and natural wood movement. The frame, made from stiles and rails that are on the narrow side, is relatively stable and thus not prone to warp. Inside the frame is a wide panel captured in grooves cut in the frame. The panel "floats" inside the frame so it can move freely as it expands and contracts, without stressing the framework around it (A).

Cut the frame joints, then groove the stiles and rails for the panel. Dimension your panel to the exact size of the inside perimeter of the frame plus the full depth of its grooves.

You can raise panels on the router table using a panel-raising bit or use a panel raiser on the shaper. (For more on raised panels, see *Taunton's Complete Illustrated Guide to Shaping Wood*, by Lonnie Bird, The Taunton Press.) Making a full-depth cut in one pass will overload the cutter and the machine, plus it can be dangerous. Instead, make the cut in two or three passes. A subfence temporarily clamped to the shaper fence lets you make a shallow cut on the first pass (B). To make the final, full-depth cut, remove the subfence (C).

> ⚠️ **WARNING** Always unplug the machine when making bit changes on a router or shaper.

(Continued on p. 232.)

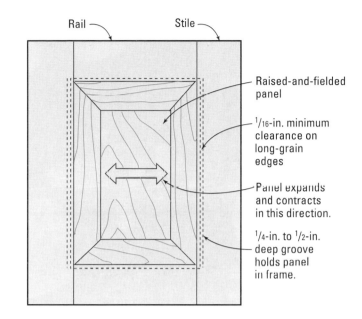

Rail — Stile —

Raised-and-fielded panel

$^{1}/_{16}$-in. minimum clearance on long-grain edges

Panel expands and contracts in this direction.

$^{1}/_{4}$-in. to $^{1}/_{2}$-in. deep groove holds panel in frame.

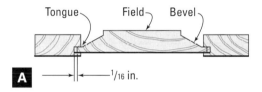

Tongue — Field — Bevel —

A — $^{1}/_{16}$ in.

B

C

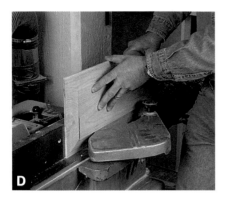

Before assembling the door, there are three important steps to take. First, joint ¹/₁₆ in. to ¹/₈ in. off each long-grain edge of the panel. This allows room for the panel to expand in the groove of the frame **(D)**. (For more on calculating expansion and contraction of solid-wood panels, see *Understanding Wood,* by R. Bruce Hoadley, The Taunton Press.)

Next, if the finished door will be colored, prefinish the same long-grain edges of the panel with the stain you'll use to color the door **(E)**. That way, when the panel shrinks during the dry season, it won't expose the lighter colored lip of the panel.

Last, to keep the panel from rattling in the frame, pin the panels from the back in the center or use spacers between the panel and the grooves. One method is to use little rubber balls (sold as Space Balls® through many woodworking mail-order catalogs) that fit into ¹/₄-in.-wide grooves and compress when the panel expands **(F)**.

Align your clamps carefully over the joints and glue up the frame and panel. Make sure no glue migrates from the joints to the edges of the panel, or the panel will bind in the frame and eventually crack. Furniture maker Edward Schoen's glue-up table has notches that automatically center pipe clamps for easy assembly **(G)**.

A variation on the frame-and-panel style is a flat panel fitted in a frame. You can significantly increase the overall strength of the door if you make the panel from veneered plywood or MDF—or any stable sheet stock—and glue it into the grooves of the frame. To dress up the perimeter of the panel, you can miter decorative molding inside the frame and glue and nail it to the panel **(H)**.

Arch-Top Frame and Panel

Introducing a simple arch at the top of a door is easier than you might think, as long as you follow the construction sequence step by step. The first step is to make a full-size drawing of the door, including the curve of the top rail. One warning: Don't aim for a small radius on the rail, because the shoulders will have weak short grain and can snap off if the angle is too severe. A curve with a radius of 10 in. or larger is ideal. (For more complex curves, see *Taunton's Complete Illustrated Guide to Shaping Wood*, by Lonnie Bird, The Taunton Press.)

Choose your door stock carefully. Whenever possible, use straight-grained material for the stiles. For the curved rail to look its best, select a board with curving grain and cut the rail stock to follow the curve. Cut the frame joints first while the stock is still square; then transfer the curve of the rail on your drawing onto the rail stock by setting a large compass to the correct radius **(A)**.

Bandsaw the curve in the rail, staying to the waste side of your layout line **(B)**. Then clean up the sawn surface with a spokeshave or a spindle sander **(C)**. For the smoothest surface, sand downhill to the grain.

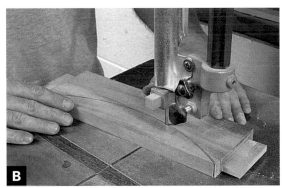

Groove the frame members on the router table with a ¼-in. ball-bearing slotting cutter. Use the fence for the straight pieces; then remove the fence and ride the curved rail against the bearing. Use a starting pin and a guard (not shown) to make the cut safely **(D)**.

(Continued on p. 234.)

E

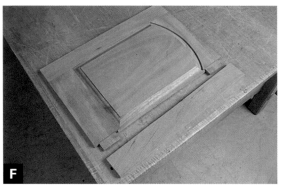

F

Use the same layout method to mark the curve at the top of the panel, increasing the radius for the panel by the depth of the groove you cut in the rail. Now bandsaw the curve and smooth the surface as before; then raise the panel on the router table using a bearing-guided panel-raising bit and a starting pin (E). Make several passes, raising the height of the bit in increments until the panel fits the grooves in the frame. The panel should slide easily into the stiles and rails without rattling (F).

[TIP] Sanding in the right direction can result in much smoother surfaces. Like planing wood, the key is to sand so that the fibers of the wood are pointing away from you. Whenever possible, follow the "downhill" sanding technique, flipping over the workpiece when necessary.

Board and Batten

A board-and-batten door has a rugged, rustic appeal. If you pay attention to the details, it can be quite elegant, too. This type of door is made from boards laid edge to edge and held together by splines and by stout battens at the back. Start by milling individual boards to length. Your boards can be random in width or you can make them all the same for a more symmetrical effect. You can chamfer the edges of the boards where they meet, rout beads, or simply leave the edges square.

Use a slotting cutter in the router table to mill $1/4$-in.-wide by $3/8$-in.-deep grooves in the edges of the boards **(A)**. Be careful not to cut grooves in the outer edges of the two outside boards.

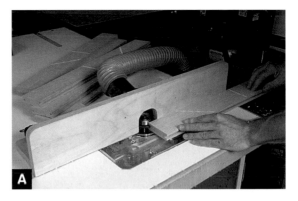

Rip some spline material to fit the combined depth of the two grooves. To prevent the splines from falling out of the door, spot glue one spline into each board, except for a single outer board **(B)**.

Fit all the splines and boards together, dry-clamp them, and check the panel for square. Don't glue the boards together or they'll split or curl as they move against the battens. Then attach the battens onto the backside of the panel with screws through countersunk holes **(C)**. I like to use trim-head screws for their low profile. You can add plugs to cover the screws if you wish, but I think the little holes make a nice detail.

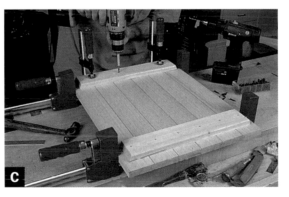

> ⚠️ **WARNING** Cut against the rotation of the router bit when slotting. Failure to do so can cause the router to grab the workpiece and pull your hands in.

(Continued on p. 236.)

Add a diagonal brace between the battens. The brace stiffens the construction and prevents the door from racking. Getting the brace to fit tightly between the battens can be tricky. The best approach is to clamp the brace stock across the battens and knife two lines at each end of the brace where it meets the inside edge of the batten (D). Then square your marks onto the face of the brace and cut a miter on each end.

Attach the brace in the same manner as the battens by screwing it into the back of the door (E). The front of the finished door (F) does not reveal the bracing and screws.

Dividing Up a Door

Here's a simple approach to making divided or glass-light doors based on a little router jig **(A)**. Construct and assemble a door as you would a standard frame; then level the joints if necessary with a plane and trim the door to fit its intended cabinet.

Once you've trimmed the door, rout a ³/₈-in.-wide rabbet into the inner edge on the back side of the frame. The actual rabbet depth isn't critical. I usually make the rabbet about half as deep as the frame's thickness. This leaves plenty of room for the glass and a wood strip or some caulk to hold the glass in the frame. Make sure to lay a sacrificial sheet under the door or raise the door on blocks to avoid routing into your benchtop. An oversize baseplate on the router serves as a stable platform for riding the frame, making it easier to cut the rabbet to a uniform depth **(B)**.

Square the rounded corners of the rabbet with a chisel. For accuracy, extend the straight edges of the rabbet onto the frame with a ruler; then chisel to your marks. Work slowly up to your marks by taking thin slices, using a mallet to chop the end-grain shoulders and paring the long-grain shoulders by hand **(C)**.

After finishing the rabbet, measure the thickness of the remaining ledge below the rabbet and mill the muntin strips to the same thickness by ⁵/₈ in. wide. Cut each strip to the correct length by holding it in position over the rabbets and marking where the ends meet the frame. Then use a dado blade to rabbet the ends of the muntins by half the muntins' thickness and to mill dadoes where adjacent muntins overlap. Remember to flip one of the muntins over when cutting the

(Continued on p. 238.)

With this glass-light jig, you can rout ³/₈-in.-long by ⁵/₈-in.-wide pockets in a rabbeted frame for ⁵/₈-in.-wide glass muntins. Sandpaper under the jig lets you hold it in position without clamps.

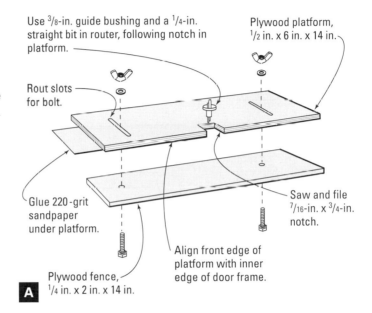

Use ³/₈-in. guide bushing and a ¹/₄-in. straight bit in router, following notch in platform.

Plywood platform, ¹/₂ in. x 6 in. x 14 in.

Rout slots for bolt.

Glue 220-grit sandpaper under platform.

Saw and file ⁷/₁₆-in. x ³/₄-in. notch.

Align front edge of platform with inner edge of door frame.

A Plywood fence, ¹/₄ in. x 2 in. x 14 in.

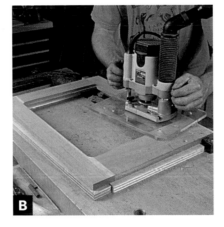 **B**

 **C**

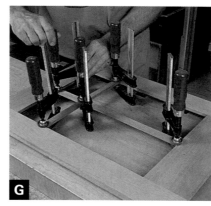

intersecting dadoes so the rabbeted ends in both muntins will face the same direction **(D)**. Make test cuts in scrap until the two muntins fit together with their surfaces flush.

Fit the muntins together and lay them into the rabbeted frame; mark where they rest on the rabbets. Then cut ⅝-in.-wide pockets in the rabbets for the muntins using the router jig, aligning the jig to your marks. If necessary, you can square up the rounded corners of the pockets with a chisel or simply round the ends of the tongues on the muntins. Remember, the joint won't be seen once the glass retainer strips are in place **(E)**.

Spread glue on the tongues of the muntins and in the pockets in the frame; press the assembly into the pockets **(F)**. A few clamps will pull the joints together and keep everything tight until the glue sets **(G)**.

Have a glass shop cut the glass ⅛ in. smaller than the rabbeted opening, and lay the glass in the rabbets. You can use caulk to hold the glass in the frame or miter wood strips to fit into the rabbet. Tack the strips temporarily into the frame to check the fit **(H)**. Then apply a finish to the door before permanently installing the glass. From the front, you won't see any of the overlapping joinery **(I)**.

Surface-Mounted Hinges

One of the easiest hinges to install is the surface-mounted hinge. There are many varieties, including hinges for inset or half-overlay doors and hinges that close by themselves via springs concealed in the barrels. Usually, a surface-mounted hinge is used when a decorative effect is desired, such as the butterfly hinge shown here **(A)**.

Fit and position the door into the case; then lay the hinges into position, making sure the center-line of the hinge barrels are centered between the door and the case. Drill pilot holes for screws with a self-centering drill bit. To facilitate driving the screws, wax the threads with a little paraffin or beeswax **(B)**. Then install the screws and you're done.

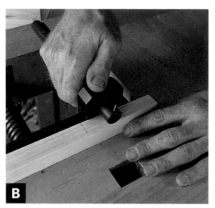

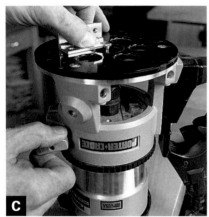

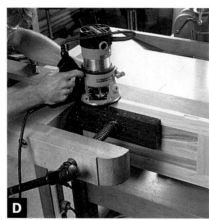

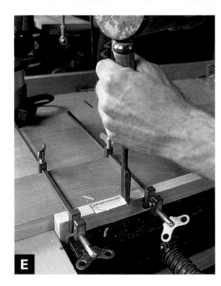

Butt Hinges

With a butt hinge, you'll need to mortise the leaves into both the door and the case. Whenever possible, lay out and cut the mortises in the case side before assembling the cabinet. Then fit the door and use a marking knife to transfer the mortise location to the door **(A)**.

Here's the process for accurately laying out and cutting the mortises for the leaves: First, determine the correct depth of the hinge into the door and the case. Next, lay out the length of each hinge by squaring lines across the work with a pencil and a square. Then use a marking gauge to mark the long-grain shoulder **(B)**.

Install a $^1/_4$-in. straight bit in the router and adjust the bit height to the thickness of the hinge leaf. The simplest way to do this is to lay the leaf directly on the baseplate of the router **(C)**. Make a test cut in scrap to check the depth before routing the real thing.

Rout freehand inside your layout lines, staying about $^1/_{16}$ in. from the marks **(D)**. Then clean up the shoulders by hand with a sharp chisel. Back up the delicate long-grain shoulder by clamping a block behind the door stile **(E)**.

Install the hinges by placing each hinge into its respective mortise and using a self-centering drill bit to drill accurate pilot holes for screws. At this point, drill only one hole for each leaf **(F)**. Hang the door on a single screw through each leaf and check the fit. If you need to make adjustments, back off the first set of screws, shift the door into position, and drill and install the second set of screws. Once the fit is perfect, install all the screws.

Knife Hinges

Knife hinges are one of the most elegant and inconspicuous types of hinges; and installed correctly, their action is delightfully smooth **(A)**. The best hinges have separate blades. You mortise the pin blade into the case; the pinless blade is mortised into the door. There are two types of knife hinges: straight hinges for overlay doors and offset hinges for inset doors **(B)**. Make sure you buy right-hand offset hinges for doors hinged on the right side of the case and left-hand offset hinges for the opposite side.

Cut the hinge mortises in the case before assembly and fit the door to the case before cutting the door mortises. Correct layout of the mortises is crucial for a good fit. Mark the outlines of each hinge with a sharp pencil or knife; then rout freehand to the exact thickness of the blade, staying within the marked lines. Use a $1/4$-in. straight bit and clamp a scrap block level with the door to prevent the router from tipping **(C)**.

Pare the case mortises to the exact size of the hinge, but leave the door mortises a hair short for now **(D)**.

Install the pin blades into the case, press the door blades onto the pin blades, and slide the door between the blades. Install a single screw in each door blade and check the fit of the door. Make adjustments by lengthening one or both door mortises with a chisel. When the door hangs evenly, drive in the final screws **(E)**.

A

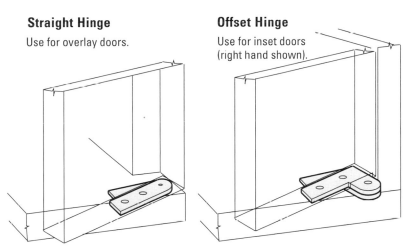

Straight Hinge
Use for overlay doors.

Offset Hinge
Use for inset doors
(right hand shown).

Hinge Layout

Lay out the pin leaf on the cabinet's top and bottom, flush to the sides of the case. For clearance, lay out the pinless blade on the door so it overhangs the door's edge by $1/32$ in.

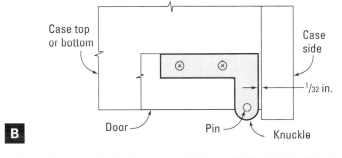

Case top or bottom

Case side

$1/32$ in.

Door

Pin

Knuckle

B

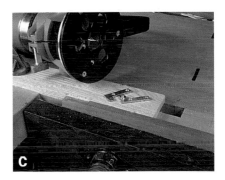

C

D

E

Overlay **Half Overlay** **Inset**

Baseplate

Cabinet

Door Cup

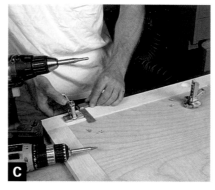

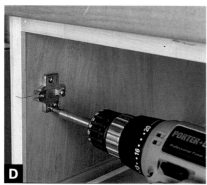

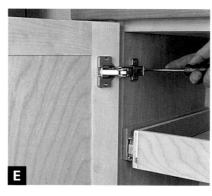

Euro-Style Hinges

Cup hinges, also called Euro hinges, are part of the gear used in the 32mm cabinetry system in Europe. They're appropriate for doors that get everyday use, like kitchen cabinets. Each hinge consists of a cup, which is mortised and screwed into the back of the door, and a base-plate, which screws into the case side. Once the door is hung, you can adjust the door up and down, in and out, and side to side.

There are three styles of cup hinges: overlay, half overlay, and inset. All the hinges are available in different degrees of opening (A).

Installation is easy. Mark a centerline on the door stile for the height of each hinge. Refer to the manufacturer's directions for the correct setback, or distance from the edge of the door to the center of the hinge mortise, and set up a fence on the drill press to establish that distance. Use a 35mm hinge-boring bit to drill the holes for the cup (a $1^3/8$-in. Forstner bit works in a pinch). Set the depth stop on your drill press accordingly to drill the correct depth (B).

Install the hinges into the door by drilling pilot holes for the screws. For accuracy, use a square to align the hinge to the edge of the door; then drill the holes (C).

Measure the height and center-to-center distances of the installed hinges on the door and transfer these measurements to the case to locate the baseplates. Install the baseplates on the cabinet with screws (D). Then slide the hinges over the baseplates and secure the door (E).

[TIP] **When you have a number of doors to install, it helps to transfer the correct layout dimensions to a piece of ¼-in. plywood and use that to mark the hinge locations. That way, all the hinge locations are uniform and layout is quick.**

Continuous Hinges

A continuous hinge, or piano hinge, is one of the strongest pieces of gear you can use to connect a door to a frame, making it well suited for heavy doors. For relatively small piano hinges, you can surface mount the leaves directly to the door edge and the case frame. But bigger hinges—those with $5/8$-in.-wide leaves or larger—require setting into the door to avoid ending up with an unsightly gap between the case and the door.

Instead of cutting a mortise, you cut a rabbet in the door. To determine the correct rabbet depth, position the hinge in the closed position with the leaves parallel to each other and measure the thickness of one leaf plus the barrel. Then cut the rabbet to that depth **(A)**. You can mill the rabbet on the table saw or with a router and straight bit.

Drill pilot holes for the screws and mount the hinge on the door frame by securing one leaf in the rabbet. Hang the door by surface mounting the opposite leaf onto the case **(B)**.

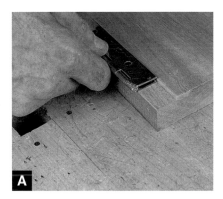

No-Mortise Hinges

A type of butt hinge, the no-mortise hinge is great for hanging doors quickly and without fuss, and it works with frame or frameless cabinets. The best part is that there's no mortise to cut in either the door or the case, which makes the job of hinging much easier.

To locate the holes for the screws, turn the hinge over and snug up the barrel against the face of the door stile; then drill pilot holes through the leaf and into the stile **(A)**. Now turn the hinge over and install it right-side up on the door.

With the door fitted and positioned temporarily in the case opening, mark the location of the hinge onto the front of the case. Use the center sections of the hinge barrel to eyeball the marks **(B)**.

Remove the door and use a spare hinge to drill pilot holes in the cabinet. You can accurately position the hinge without measuring by holding the barrel tight to the frame and aligning the center barrel sections to your marks on the case **(C)**. Then replace the door with the hinge leaves open and drive the screws to attach the door to the cabinet **(D)**.

Escutcheons

An inset escutcheon protects the keyhole-shaped opening for a lock, and it dresses up an otherwise plain door front or drawer. It's important that you install the escutcheon before fitting a lock mortise. The first step is to drill a hole to accept the escutcheon's circular head. Use a brad-point bit or a Forstner bit for this operation, drilling to the same depth as the escutcheon (**A**). Then drill a second, smaller hole through the first hole for the key, sized to the lock you'll install.

Next, place the escutcheon onto the workpiece. If your escutcheon is tapered, place the smaller side down. Insert a dowel the same size as the keyhole through the hole and through the escutcheon to aid in positioning the escutcheon. Then scribe around the lower half of the escutcheon (**B**).

At this point, you'll need to cut out the rest of the keyhole with a coping saw.

Then use chisels and small gouges of the appropriate sweep to cut a recess into the workpiece, chiseling up to your scribed lines. Chisel to the same depth as the large hole (**C**).

To install the escutcheon, mix some sanding dust with epoxy, line the recess with the mix, and tap the escutcheon into the recess (**D**). If you're installing an escutcheon that's been colored or coated with a finish, gently tap the escutcheon until it sits flush with the surface and wipe off any glue residue. For new, bright-brass escutcheons, level the surface with a file once the adhesive has cured; then smooth the metal and the wood with successively finer grits of sandpaper wrapped around a felt block (**E**).

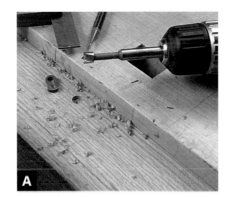

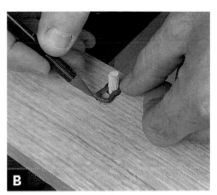

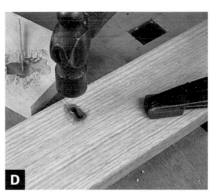

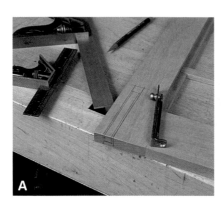

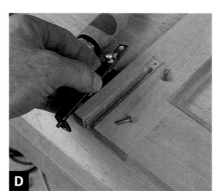

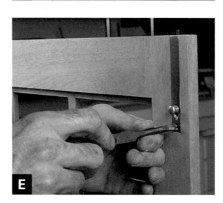

Door Bolts

When two doors meet, you can lock them together with a mortise lock but you'll need to provide a catch on one of the doors so both doors stay secure.

➤ See *"Mortised Locks"* on p. 248.

A door bolt fits the bill and works with inset doors. Installed on the back of one door, the bolt holds that door and prevents the adjoining door from being opened until the mortise lock is released. I like to install the bolt on the left door, so the door on the right becomes the primary, or "keyed," door. The catch works best if installed at the top of the door, with a corresponding hole in the top frame for the sliding bolt. This way, the hole for the bolt won't accumulate debris.

The key to successful installation is to accurately lay out for the three mortises that are needed to fit the catch. Draw the outline of the catch on the back and edge of the door; then draw the inner mortise for the bolt mechanism **(A)**. Rout the inner, deep mortise freehand, staying inside your layout lines. It doesn't matter if the walls of the mortise are rough. The aim is simply to provide free space for the sliding bolt to operate **(B)**.

Next, rout the two shallow mortises, one on the back of the stile and one on the top edge. Stay inside your layout lines and use a chisel to pare up to the walls of the mortise **(C)**. The mortise depth should equal the thickness of the catch's plate **(D)**.

Install the catch into the mortises and secure it with two screws: one at the top and one at the lower part of the catch **(E)**. Hang the door; then transfer the bolt location to the case frame by tapping the bolt into the frame, which will leave a telltale mark. Finally, drill a hole on your mark for the bolt.

Cylinder Locks

Perfect for utility drawers or doors—or wherever you need a sturdy, simple-to-install lock—the cylinder, or cam, lock can be mounted by drilling a single hole through the workpiece **(A)**. A cam lever engages the back of the cabinet's frame or a wooden block attached inside the cabinet.

It's easier if you drill and install the lock before hanging the door. Choose a lock matched to the thickness of your work and use the supplied template to lay out the hole location **(B)**. Then drill a ³/₄-in.-diameter hole through the face of the door **(C)**.

Install the decorative ring and the cylinder through the front of the door; then add the cam lever and the parts that secure the lock from behind **(D)**.

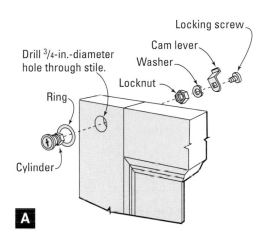

Locking screw
Cam lever
Drill ³/₄-in.-diameter hole through stile.
Washer
Locknut
Ring
Cylinder

A

B

C

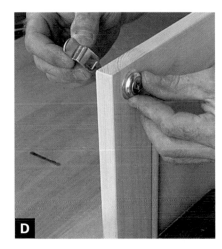

D

With its sliding bolt, this half-mortise lock will secure flush-mounted drawers or doors.

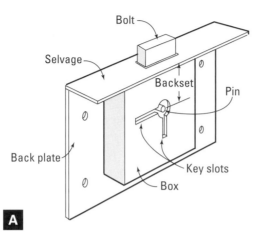

A

B

C

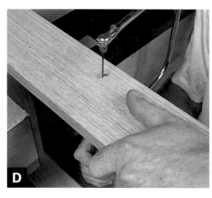

D

Mortised Locks

Half-mortise locks, so named because they require only a pocket or half mortise for fitting, work equally well on doors or drawers **(A)**. Once fitted, the lock is discreet, since all you see is a key hole or escutcheon. Half-mortise locks come in a variety of styles. In all cases, though, installation of the lock body is the same.

The lock shown here is used for flush-mounted drawers and doors; a key turns a bolt into a mortise that you cut in the case. If you use this lock on a door, be sure to specify whether the lock is for a left-hand or right-hand door. Start by laying out the keyhole location on the front of the door or drawer. Measure the backset on the lock and transfer this measurement onto the work. Drill a hole through the workpiece the same size as the hole in the lock. *Note:* If you're going to install an inset escutcheon, do it now before installing the lock.

A half-mortise lock requires three mortises. Cut the first mortise by positioning the lock on the back of the workpiece and scribing around the box. Use a router and a small straight bit to remove the waste inside your scribed lines; then finish up by chiseling the shoulders to the layout lines **(B)**.

Turning the lock around, hold it with the back plate against the work and the selvage flush with the top edge; then scribe and cut the second mortise for the back plate. Next, transfer the selvage measurements to the edge of the work and chisel the third mortise. The lock should fit securely in all three mortises **(C)**.

Finish up by laying out the wedged-shaped, lower half of the keyhole on the face of the work and saw out the opening with a coping saw **(D)**. Install the lock with screws driven into the back side of the door or drawer.

Bullet Catches

Hidden at the bottom or top of a door, the small bullet catch works on inset doors, where there's a frame above or below the door. The catch consists of two parts: a bullet-shaped cylinder, which contains a small, spring-loaded ball, and a strike plate, into which the ball catches. Tension from the ball holds the door in position when it's closed.

Install the bullet in a stepped hole in the bottom of the door. First, drill a shallow $5/16$-in.-diameter hole for the flange; then drill a deeper $1/4$-in.-diameter hole for the cylinder. Tap the bullet into the hole, adding a drop of cyanoacrylate adhesive (one brand is Super Glue) to secure it **(A)**. The flange should be flush with the surface of the door.

Hang the door and mark the cabinet for the strike plate by transferring the center point of the bullet. Install the strike with small pins onto the surface of the frame **(B)**.

Double-Ball Catches

A double-ball catch is easy to install and allows for adjustment after the door is hung. Secure the ball part of the catch to the case, either on the side, top, or bottom. If necessary, you can shim the catch into the correct position relative to the door by mounting it onto a block screwed to the case. This is a good technique to use whenever off-the-shelf hardware doesn't fit into what you've built **(A)**.

Transfer the center measurement of the catch in the case to the back of the door and install the finger, or strike, onto the door **(B)**. Check the fit. If the catch grabs the door too tightly or too loosely, you can adjust the tension of the balls by turning small screws located on the top and bottom of the catch **(C)**.

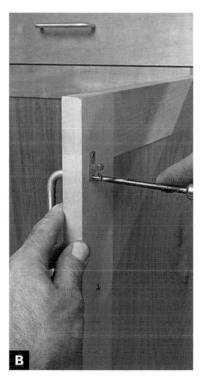

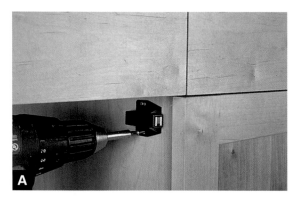

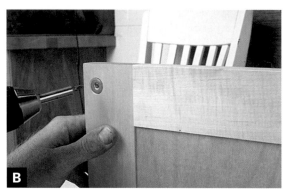

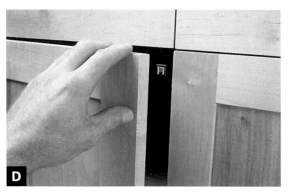

Touch Latches

When you want the sleek lines of a door without hardware—including no handles or pulls—a touch latch is the answer. There are two parts to the latch, a magnetized push-arm mechanism and a steel contact washer. First screw the arm mechanism inside the cabinet, either on the top or on the case side. When locating the mechanism, be sure to allow clearance for the arm to move inward about ⅛ in. without the door contacting the face of the cabinet. Position the screws in the elongated holes first, so you can adjust the final fit of the hardware before installing the remaining screws **(A)**.

Once the push arm is in place, measure its exact center and transfer this measurement to the back of the door; next, install the metal washer on the door. I like to drill a shallow mortise for the plate with a Forstner bit to give the hardware a neater appearance **(B)**. The magnet in the cabinet contacts the washer and pulls on it, keeping the door closed.

To open the door, simply push inward about ⅛ in. **(C)**. The push-arm springs forward and pushes the door out of the cabinet about ½ in., allowing you to grasp the edge of the door with your fingers **(D)**.

Adjustable Magnet Catches

One of my favorite catches is the inexpensive plastic catch that houses an adjustable magnet. Although the style may not suit the finest of cabinets, its greatest attribute is the ability to adjust the magnet into or away from the face of the case by simply turning the magnet with a wide, flat screwdriver. This arrangement lets you fine-tune the fit of the door to the case after it's hung—a great benefit.

To install the catch on paired doors in a frame-style cabinet, glue a spacer block underneath the top of the case and drill a 3/8-in.-diameter hole into it for the stub tenon on each catch **(A)**. Install the catch by squeezing the ribbed tenon into the hole with a clamp **(B)**.

Drill a small hole in the back of the door for the metal pin and disk that attracts the magnet and, as you did for the catch, install the disk with a clamp **(C)**.

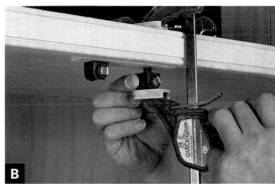

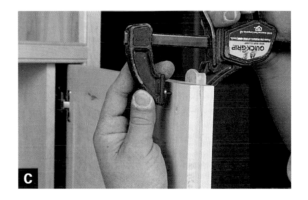

A

Sizing the Toekick

A comfortable size for a kick space is when x = 2$\frac{1}{2}$ in. and y = 4$\frac{1}{2}$ in. You can adjust these measurements up or down by 1 in. to suit your furniture while still leaving room for stray feet.

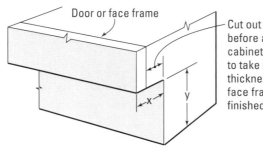

Door or face frame

Cut out kick space before assembling cabinet, but be sure to take into account thickness of door or face frame to calculate finished depth of kick space.

x
y

Finished Toekick

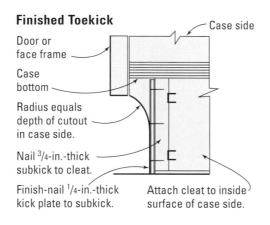

Door or face frame

Case bottom

Radius equals depth of cutout in case side.

Nail $\frac{3}{4}$-in.-thick subkick to cleat.

Finish-nail $\frac{1}{4}$-in.-thick kick plate to subkick.

Case side

Attach cleat to inside surface of case side.

Unfinished Toekick

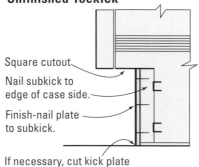

Square cutout

Nail subkick to edge of case side.

Finish-nail plate to subkick.

If necessary, cut kick plate extra-wide and scribe to contour of floor.

B

Integral Base with Toekick

You have two options when incorporating a kick space under a cabinet: Construct the base as a separate assembly and then secure it to the case, or make the base an integral part of the cabinet.

► See *"Applied Base with Toekick"* on p. 255.

For cabinets with finished sides—where you'll see the side of the case when it's installed—you'll need to construct the case sides so they conceal the ends of the kick plate once it's installed.

Once you've cut the case joints, but before assembling the cabinet, use a template to trace the outline of the kick radius onto the side of the case **(A)**. Size the template to take into account the thickness of the subkick and finished kick plate, plus any face frame material or doors **(B)**. For economy, the example shown here uses a two-part sandwich for the toekick: $\frac{1}{4}$-in. plywood over particleboard or utility plywood.

Use a jigsaw to cut the profile on the corner of the case side **(C)**. Cut on the waste side of your layout line; then clean up and smooth the surface on a spindle sander or with a half-round mill file and sandpaper.

If the case side is plywood, you can cover the raw edge by adding a strip of commercial edge-banding. The thin banding will conform to the curve of the kick with heat and pressure from an iron **(D)**.

Mark the inside of the case side, taking into account the combined thickness of the subkick and the kick plate, and then glue and staple a plywood nailing cleat to the case **(E)**.

Attach the subkick—which can be made from any $3/4$-in.-thick material, such as plywood or particleboard—to the cleat **(F)**. Then attach your finished kick material over the subkick with small brads or finish nails so it's flush with the edge of the case side. Thin $1/4$-in. hardwood plywood is a great material for the kick plate, since it's backed up by the thicker subkick **(G)**.

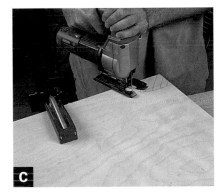

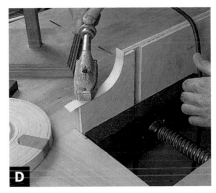

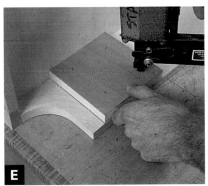

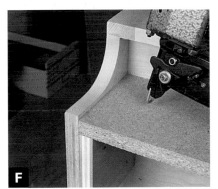

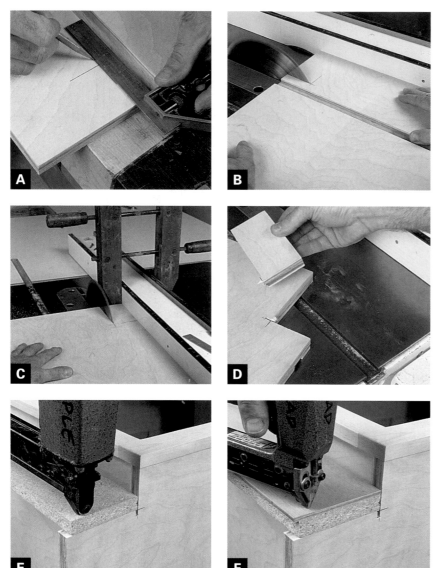

Inside Toekick

When you're faced with an unfinished case side (one that will be covered up by adjoining cases or built into the corner wall of a room), building the kick space is much simpler. Start by laying out the depth and height of the kick on both sides of the case side **(A)**. Remember to take into account the thickness of the subkick and kick plate plus any frame or door material.

On the table saw, set the rip fence to the height of the kick, allowing for the blade's thickness, and raise the blade to full height. Be sure to keep your hands clear of the blade and use a blade guard. Position the inside surface of the case so it's facing up on the saw table and make a cross-cut to establish the height of the kick, cutting up to your layout line. Stop when you reach the line; then turn off the saw and let the blade spin to a stop before backing the workpiece out from the blade **(B)**.

With the blade still raised, adjust the fence to the depth of the kick. Clamp a stop block to the fence to limit the cut about 1/4 in. shy of your lay-out line. Turn the case side over so the outside surface is facing up and push the workpiece into the blade and up to the stop **(C)**. Turn off the saw as before, remove the workpiece, and pry away the waste **(D)**. A sharp chisel will remove any leftover material.

On an unfinished case side, instead of positioning the subkick on the inside of the case, you secure it directly over the edge of the side **(E)**. Then cover the subkick with your finished plywood kick **(F)**.

> ⚠️ **WARNING** Safe practice on a table saw calls for raising the blade slightly above the work surface—unless a specific operation calls for a higher blade angle.

Applied Base with Toekick

An applied base with a kick space is often easier to construct than an integral base. And it's particularly handy when you're installing a built-in cabinet, because it makes leveling the case a cinch. To make an applied kick for a freestanding case, build the kick base and cabinet as separate assemblies; then join them together with screws **(A)**.

To extend the toekick around the corners on a case with finished sides, factor in the overhang of the case on the front and both sides when determining the width and length of the base, as shown. Don't forget to allow for the finished toekick material. Then build the base from strips of ³/₄-in. plywood ripped to the correct width to raise the case to the necessary height. Glue and nail the parts together, making sure the interior strips are square to the assembly **(B)**. Always align the interior strips in the base so they fall directly under any partitions in the case for support. Strips every 2 ft. are sufficient to carry the weight of even large cases.

After the basic frame of the base is assembled, add nailing cleats inside the frame, aligning them flush with the top edges of the base **(C)**. Then lay the cabinet on its back and attach the base assembly by driving screws through countersunk holes in the cleats and into the case bottom **(D)**.

Complete the base by applying a finished kick plate made from ¹/₄-in. hardwood plywood onto the front and sides of the base. For a seamless look at the corners, miter adjacent kick plates and use glue and brads or finish nails to attach them to the base **(E)**.

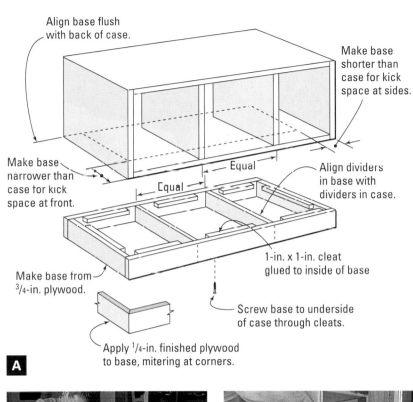

Align base flush with back of case.

Make base shorter than case for kick space at sides.

Make base narrower than case for kick space at front.

Equal

Equal

Align dividers in base with dividers in case.

1-in. x 1-in. cleat glued to inside of base

Make base from ³/₄-in. plywood.

Screw base to underside of case through cleats.

Apply ¹/₄-in. finished plywood to base, mitering at corners.

A

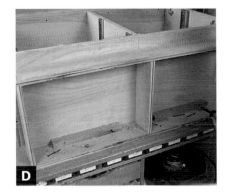

B

C

D

E

A

Scrolled and Mitered Feet

The mitered foot design shown here is very simple in form and is reminiscent of the bare-bones approach used by Shaker furniture makers of the past **(A)**. Construction is uncomplicated **(B)**.

Use the jigsaw or bandsaw to cut a scrolled profile on the case sides before assembling the cabinet. For the front scrollwork, it's easiest to glue the mitered feet and rail to the case after the joints are cut but while the stock is still square **(C)**. Once the glue has dried, trace the profile on the assembly and use the jigsaw to cut to your outline **(D)**. Clean up and smooth the sawn contours with a round-bottomed spokeshave or a sanding drum chucked in a portable drill.

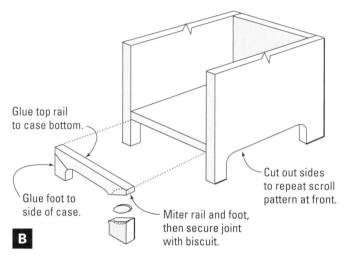

Glue top rail to case bottom.

Glue foot to side of case.

Miter rail and foot, then secure joint with biscuit.

Cut out sides to repeat scroll pattern at front.

B

C

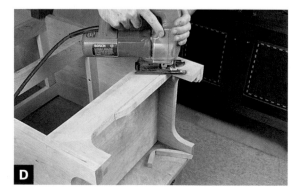

D

Removable Plywood Back

Using plywood for a case back has the advantage of stability, allowing you to use a wide panel without the concern for wood movement. And screwing the back into rabbets in the case lets you remove it for applying a finish. Before you assemble the cabinet, rabbet the sides ³/₈ in. deep and make the rabbet width equal to the thickness of the back panel. Use a stacked dado blade and attach an auxiliary fence to the rip fence so you can bury the blade **(A)**.

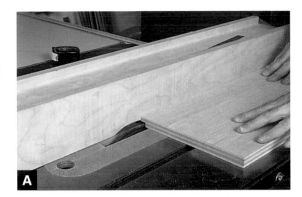

Once you've assembled the case, countersink the back for screws and secure the back without glue into the rabbets and into the top and bottom of the case. Temporarily clamp across the case to keep the sides tight to the back. Then toenail the screws at a slight angle for good purchase into the rabbets **(B)**.

When it comes time for applying a finish, remove the back and lay it horizontally for more control over the finishing process. Finishing the insides of the cabinet without the back in place is much easier, too, since you can reach the very back surfaces without running into abrupt corners **(C)**.

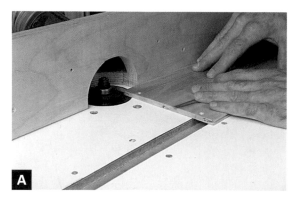

A

Grooved-and-Splined Back

A splined back panel is made from several separate boards fitted edge to edge and then let into rabbets in the case. Grooves along the edges of the boards accept wood splines, which stiffen the assembly and conceal gaps between adjacent boards. Start by routing a narrow groove along the edges of each backboard. You can use a thin $\frac{1}{16}$-in. slotting cutter to rout grooves of any width by simply adjusting the bit height after each pass **(A)**.

Rip some splines to fit the grooves. The width of the splines should equal the combined depth of two grooves. Fit the backboards together, slipping the splines between the boards without using glue **(B)**.

Install the boards as a discreet panel into rabbets in the back of the case, screwing them in place through countersunk holes. Make sure to leave a small gap between each board for expansion **(C)**.

B

C

Frame-and-Panel Back

For a back that looks as good as the front of the cabinet, you can glue a frame-and-panel back into rabbets milled in the case. This is a ton of work, so it's worthwhile only if the piece is really high end or it will be freestanding and seen from the back.

Mill the rabbets slightly deeper than the frame is thick; then assemble the case. The key to a tight-fitting joint is to build the frame slightly larger than the rabbet opening in the case and then plane a very slight back-bevel on the edge of the frame until it just fits the case **(A)**.

Grab your bar clamps, because you're going to need all of them to attach the back to the case. Brush glue into the rabbets; then drop the back into them and clamp the sides, top, and bottom of the case to pull the joints tight. Cauls between the case and the clamps help distribute the clamping pressure **(B)**.

You'll have some cleanup work to do once the glue has dried. Use a handplane to level the slightly raised rabbeted edges of the case flush to the back panel **(C)**.

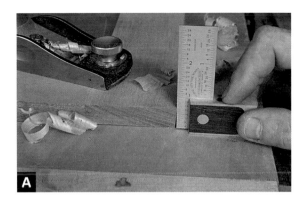

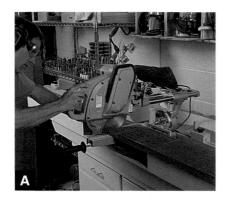

Wide Solid-Wood Top

Constructing a wide, solid-wood top is straight-forward if you follow a few basic steps. The same procedure can be used for making all sorts of wide panels, from case sides, tops, and bottoms to shelves and other horizontal surfaces. Begin by crosscutting rough stock oversize in length by 4 in. or so **(A)**.

Flatten one face of each board on the jointer **(B)**. Then thickness plane the opposite face **(C)** and continue planing equally on both sides until you've reached the desired thickness. Joint one edge on each board **(D)**; then rip the opposite edge on the table saw and joint that edge, too.

Here's a technique that saves time and effort: Before you glue the boards together, handplane the show surfaces to remove any machine marks. This way, all you'll need to do is flush up the joints after glue-up, instead of planing or sanding the entire surface **(E)**. Arrange the boards for the best possible grain pattern across the joints and mark a V to help you orient the boards during glue-up **(F)**.

To keep the boards flat and aligned with each other during gluing, clamp stout battens across the ends. Wax paper under the battens prevent them from sticking to the glue. First, apply light pressure across the joints with bar clamps. Then clamp the battens to the ends and go back and fully tighten the bar clamps **(G)**. Once the glue has dried, rip both long edges to remove any marks or dings and to ensure that the edges are parallel **(H)**.

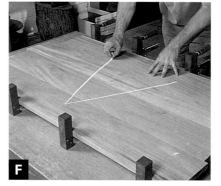

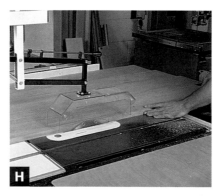

Drop-In Table Leaves

Look in common woodworking catalogs and you'll come across *table extension slides*. These clever wood or metal pieces of gear attach to the underside of a tabletop and let you separate the top into two halves. Dropping a table leaf into the gap between the two halves provides you with extra table surface. Table pins or biscuits in the top and leaves serve to line up the parts and keep the surface flat. The pins, available in brass, wood, and plastic, are essentially dowels with rounded ends. Biscuits work just as well when glued on one side only—so that the exposed biscuit can fit into the slot in a leaf. Whether using the table pins or biscuits, the first order of business is to build the table frame as two separate halves, being careful to check the free rails for square as you glue up the frame **(A)**.

Next, secure a half top to each frame with tabletop clips. Be sure to brace the free ends of the aprons with plywood gussets **(B)**. Glue the table pins or biscuits in only one table half **(C)**. Push the two halves together and screw the extension slides to the underside. Pull out each slide by about ¼ in. to ensure the two tabletop halves will fit tightly once they're closed **(D)**.

Now make your leaf, or leaves, in a similar manner to the two halves. You can attach aprons to the leaf for a seamless look once it's installed, or keep the leaf flat. Just remember that an apron makes storing the leaf more problematic. Make sure to brace the aprons with corner blocks and slot both ends of the leaf, including the aprons. Glue the pins or biscuits in only one end **(E)**.

To add a leaf, spread the table apart and lay the leaf over the extended wood rails, aligning the pins or biscuits into their respective slots **(F)**. Now push the table halves together **(G)**.

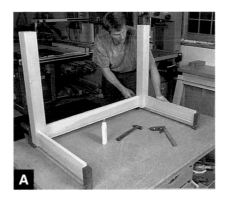

A

B

C

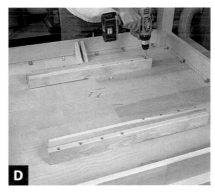

D

E

F

G

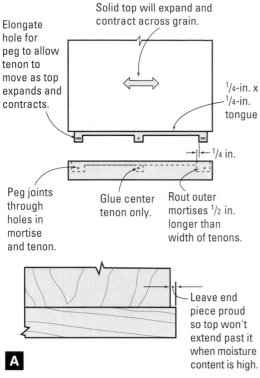

Solid top will expand and contract across grain.

Elongate hole for peg to allow tenon to move as top expands and contracts.

¹/₄-in. x ¹/₄-in. tongue

¹/₄ in.

Peg joints through holes in mortise and tenon.

Glue center tenon only.

Rout outer mortises ¹/₂ in. longer than width of tenons.

Leave end piece proud so top won't extend past it when moisture content is high.

A

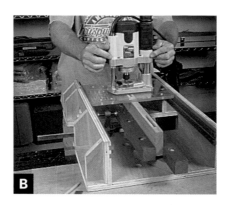

B

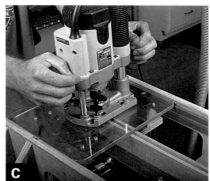

C

D

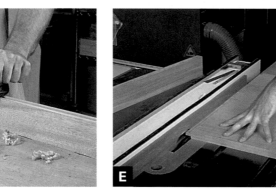

E

F

G

Breadboard Ends

Breadboard ends add a nice touch to a top, concealing its end-grain edges and offering an air of distinction. It also serves to hold a wide solid-wood surface flat. When constructing a breadboard end, the trick is to attach it in such a manner as to allow the solid top to expand and contract. If you glue the end piece entirely across the top, the top will eventually split due to wood movement. The traditional approach is to cut tenons on the end of the top; then mill mortises into the breadboard end. By gluing only the center tenon, the top is free to expand and contract **(A)**. Start by cutting the end piece about 1 in. longer than the width of the top and then mill three mortises in the end, about 1 in. deep by 3 in. to 4 in. wide **(B)**. After cutting the mortises, rout or saw a ¹/₄-in.-deep groove between them **(C)**.

To ensure a tight fit of the breadboard to the top, plane a few shavings from the center of the piece. This "springs" the breadboard so the ends—which won't be glued—remain tight to the top **(D)**.

On the table saw, use a stacked dado blade to mill a 1-in.-long tongue on the tabletop. Make the tongue in two passes on each side of the top. For the first pass, use double-sided tape to attach a subfence to the rip fence and push the panel across the blade **(E)**. Then remove the subfence and cut the tongue to full length by running the panel against the rip fence **(F)**. This way there's no need to move the rip fence, reducing the chance for error.

Next, lay out the three tenons on the tongue, so that the two outer tenons are about ¹/₂ in. narrower than their respective mortises are long. Then lay out the ¹/₄-in.-deep tongue for the groove you milled in the breadboard. Cut the tenons and the tongue with a jigsaw, following your layout lines **(G)**. Saw the outer shoulders with a backsaw **(H)**. To ease the transition between the breadboard end and the top, plane a slight chamfer on the inner edges of the end and along the shoulders of the top **(I)**.

Temporarily fit the breadboard to the top and crosscut it to length. If you suspect the top will expand, depending on its current moisture content, it's best to cut the end about $1/8$ in. or so longer than the top is wide. Once you cut the end to length, clamp it to the tabletop and drill for $1/4$-in. pegs from the underside of the top, through the center of each tenon **(J)**. Then remove the breadboard and elongate the two outer peg holes with a coping saw **(K)**.

[TIP] **A piece of masking tape wrapped around the drill bit makes a quick depth stop. Leave a flap hanging off to serve as a conspicuous flag.**

Brush glue on the center mortise and tenon only **(L)**; then attach the breadboard with a single clamp **(M)**. Drive the pegs through the tenons and into the top from the underside, adding a drop of glue at the end of the peg to keep it from falling out **(N)**. For now, the finished breadboard end, with its nicely chamfered edges, protrudes slightly past the tabletop **(O)**. As the top expands, the ends will align flush. With a change in seasons, the ends once again protrude. This is a better-looking solution than having the top extend past the breadboard ends.

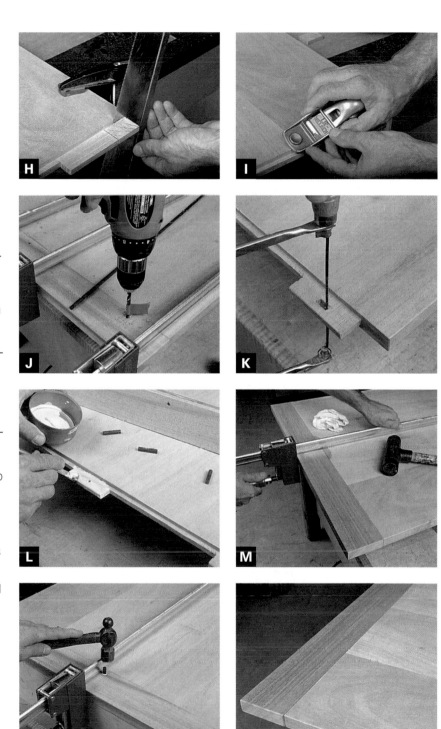

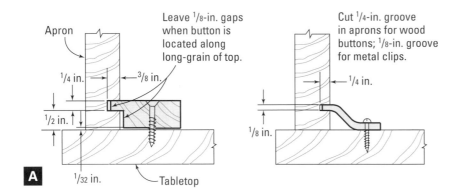

Apron

Leave ¹/₈-in. gaps when button is located along long-grain of top.

Cut ¹/₄-in. groove in aprons for wood buttons; ¹/₈-in. groove for metal clips.

¹/₄ in.　　³/₈ in.

¹/₄ in.

¹/₂ in.

¹/₈ in.

A　　¹/₃₂ in.　　Tabletop

Wood Buttons

An effective and simple method for attaching a tabletop to a frame is to use wood "buttons" (**A**). I always make a batch of buttons and save the extras for later use. Start by cutting a series of ¹/₂-in.-wide notches in a long length of ³/₄-in. by 1-in.-wide stock on the table saw (**B**). Space the notches about 1 in. apart.

On the miter saw, crosscut individual buttons by aligning the blade with the left shoulder of each notch (**C**). Taking into account the ¹/₈-in. saw kerf, crosscutting in this manner produces a ³/₈-in. tongue on each button. Finish the buttons by countersinking and boring a pilot hole through each button for a screw.

Once you've made the buttons, groove the inside of the aprons before assembling the frame. Use a ¹/₄-in.-wide dado blade and adjust the height to cut a groove ³/₈ in. deep. Set your rip fence so the resulting groove will be offset about ¹/₃₂ in. with the button's tongue, as shown in the drawing. An arrow drawn on a strip of masking tape indicates the correct edge to run against the fence (**D**).

> ⚠ **WARNING** Don't gauge cross-cuts directly from the rip fence. The work can bind and kick back. For safety, clamp a block to the rip fence; then use it to gauge the correct distance of the stock to the blade.

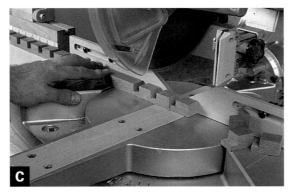

B

C

D

Assemble the base; then place your tabletop up-side down and center the base over its surface. Position the buttons into the grooves in the aprons, keeping some near the corners to re-inforce the joints. Make sure to leave a gap be-tween each button and apron when they fall on a long-grain surface. Position adjacent buttons tight to the aprons **(E)**. Drive a screw through each button and into the underside of the top **(F)**. The gaps on the long-grain areas allow the top to expand and contract freely, while the buttons hold the top tight to the aprons.

[TIP] **Mistakes happen. You glued up your table frame, but forgot to groove all the aprons for tabletop fasteners. For an easy fix, use a biscuit jointer to cut slots inside the aprons. A standard biscuit cut-ter will cut a slot the correct width for metal tabletop clips.**

Splines and Glue

On veneered or plywood tabletops—where wood movement is not an issue—you can glue an apron directly to the underside of the top. To stiffen the connection and ensure exact alignment, College of the Redwoods student and furniture maker Konrad Leo Horsch used short plywood splines fitted in both the curved aprons and the top of his Lady's Writing Desk.

Rout grooves in the underside of the top and into the top edges of the aprons; then glue the splines into the aprons every 3 in. or so **(A)**.

Assemble the top to the base with glue, using plenty of clamps to draw the joints tight. The result is a perfect fit of base to top with no visible connections **(B)**.

Wood Cleats

An effective and elegant way to attach a tabletop is to secure wood cleats to the top of the frame and then screw through the cleats and into the underside of the top. Half notches cut in the tops of the legs and aprons and in the cleats let you lock them flush with the top of the frame. Countersunk screws hold them fast **(A)**. The cleats that run along the center of the top can be drilled with an ordinary hole for a screw; cleats along the perimeter of the frame need to have slotted screw holes to allow the top to expand and contract.

With the tabletop upside down, center the base over it and drive screws through the cleats and into the top **(B)**.

Metal Tabletop Fasteners

Also called Z-clips because of their shape, metal tabletop fasteners are installed in a similar fashion as are wood buttons.

Cut all your apron joinery first; then cut a $1/8$-in. by $1/2$-in.-deep groove in each rail on its inside face, using a standard sawblade **(A)**.

With the tabletop upside down on the bench, center the base over it and carefully arrange the clips. Like wood buttons, be sure to leave room between each clip and the rail when it's positioned across the grain **(B)**. Predrill for screws and use pan-head screws to secure the clips to the tabletop **(C)**.

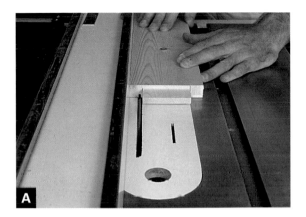

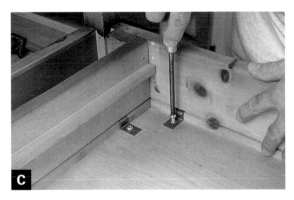

A

Deep Screw Holes

Securing a tabletop with screws is a legitimate approach, as long as you follow a few simple guidelines. First, make sure your screws pass through no more than 1 in. of rail or apron width. On rails wider than 1 in., simply counterbore to the correct depth with a Forstner bit **(A)**. Then drill a clearance hole through the rail for the screw. Keeping the screw area of the rail rather thin ensures that the screw won't loosen over time as the rail swells or shrinks as a result of wood movement.

Another wood-movement issue is when you're screwing into a solid-wood tops. You must allow the top to move or you risk cracking the top or pulling apart the frame joints. The easiest way to accommodate the top's natural movement is to slot the screw holes in the rails **(B)**. On the top side of each rail, angle a drill bit back and forth to enlarge the hole. Make sure to orient the slot in the direction that the top will move **(C)**.

Lay the top upside down and center the base over it. Then drive the screws into pilot holes drilled into the top **(D)**.

Tabletop

Rail

Keep this area 1 in. thick or less to minimize the effects of wood movement in the apron or rail.

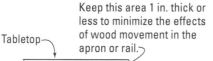

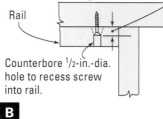

Counterbore ½-in.-dia. hole to recess screw into rail.

When screwing a rail that runs with the long grain of a top, slot the top of the hole to allow screw to move.

B

C

D

Pocket Holes

When using a pocket hole, you angle the screw slightly, allowing it to start much closer to the surface of the top. There are many excellent commercial pocket-hole jigs that you can use or you can make your own from a hard, dense piece of wood. The idea is to use an angled guide block to drill a 1/2-in. counterbore into the apron and finish up by extending a shank hole through the apron. The oversize counterbore gives the screw room to move as the top expands and contracts with variations in seasonal moisture content.

Start by sawing a wedge of scrap material to a 20-degree angle on the bandsaw or table saw. Then clamp a 1 1/2-in. by 2-in. square of hardwood to the wedge and to the drill press table. Use a 1/2-in. Forstner bit to drill an angled hole through the center of the block, allowing the bit to exit on one side (A).

After drilling, cut one end off the block so the pocket hole is the correct distance from the end of the block (B). Then clamp the block to the inside face of the apron and flush with its top edge. Using the same bit you used on the drill press, drill through the block and into the face of the apron. Use a piece of masking tape to gauge the correct depth (C).

Remove the block and extend the hole through the apron, starting with a jobber's bit or any extra-long drill bit (D). Then finish by drilling through the apron from the top edge with a 1/4-in. bit (E). The oversize hole will allow the screw to move as the top expands and contracts. Secure the top to the apron with a #6 pan-head screw, using a washer under the head (F).

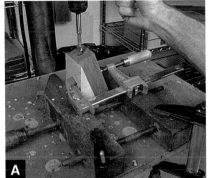

A

B

C

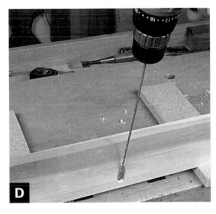

D

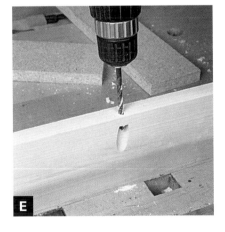

E

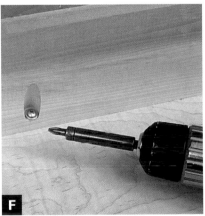

F

Sharpening

Planes

➤ Preparing the Back of a New Blade (p. 271)

➤ Sharpening a Plane Blade (p. 272)

➤ Honing without a Jig (p. 273)

➤ Preparing Chip Breakers (p. 274)

Chisels

➤ Paring and Mortise Chisels (p. 275)

Scrapers

➤ Card Scraper (p. 276)

➤ Curved Scraper (p. 277)

Spokeshaves

➤ Concave Spokeshave Blade (p. 278)

➤ Flat Spokeshave Blade (p. 279)

Handsaws

➤ Jointing and Setting the Teeth (p. 280)

➤ Checking and Adjusting the Set (p. 281)

➤ Sharpening a Ripsaw (p. 282)

➤ Sharpening a Crosscut Saw (p. 283)

Preparing the Back of a New Blade

Before using a new blade, check the back. It may need to be honed to remove mill marks left from the factory and to ensure that it is completely flat (A). If the surface is not flat and polished, it will be impossible to get a truly sharp edge on the blade. Honing the back is a quick job as long as you spend enough time with the coarse-grit stones. You should only have to do this to a blade once.

Lay the back of the blade on a 220-grit stone, and with firm pressure, run it back and forth over the surface (B). It's not necessary to dress the entire back, just the area at the end of the blade near the bevel. Once the scratch pattern from the 220-grit stone is uniform (C), move to the 1000-grit stone, then to the 4000-grit stone and finally to the 8000-grit stone. Make sure that you have removed all the scratches from one grit before moving to the next one. The blade will look progressively more polished with each stone (D, E). Take special care on the finest grit (F). It cuts more slowly, so don't hurry. When you are finished, the back of the blade, especially the area near the end of the blade, should be smooth and flat (G).

Additional polishing—with diamond paste, for example—may be a good idea when you intend to use the plane to produce a finished surface on wood. But in most cases, the surface left by an 8000-grit stone will be fine.

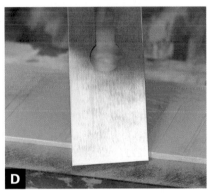

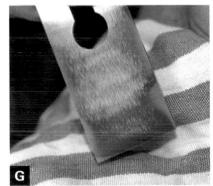

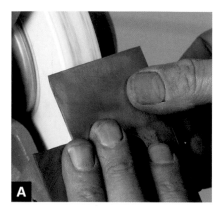

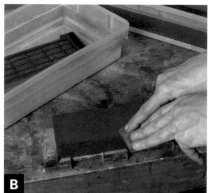

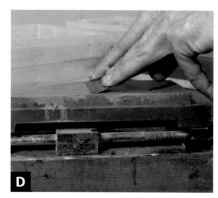

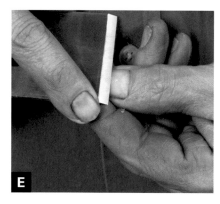

Sharpening a Plane Blade

Using a slow-speed (1725 rpm) grinder equipped with white aluminum oxide wheels, grind a primary bevel of roughly 25 degrees on the plane blade **(A)**. Then hone the blade on a 1200-grit waterstone **(B)**. To establish the proper angle for honing, slowly rock the bevel angle on the stone until you feel its tip and heel stabilize on the stone. Then move the blade over the stone, keeping your forearms and wrists locked to avoid rocking the blade. Work the right and left edges of the blade a bit more than the center. This will help keep the corners of the blade from digging in as you plane. It's not necessary or desirable to hone past the point where you've created a ⅟₃₂-in.-wide flat at the leading edge of the bevel.

Now switch to a 6000-grit waterstone. Use a Nagura stone to create a fine slurry on the water-stone, then polish the back of the blade **(C)**. When the back is shiny, turn the blade over and register its bevel on the stone as you did before. Then tip the blade forward about 5 degrees and lock your forearms and wrists. Working in a small circular motion, hone the tip of the bevel to create a polished "microbevel" **(D)**. As before, work the right and left edges a bit more.

The blade is sharp when you can slice little curls off your thumbnail **(E)**. Note how the polished microbevel and heel are shinier than the rest of the bevel, which is duller from the coarse grinding-wheel scratches.

Honing without a Jig

Although honing jigs are very useful, it's also possible to produce an excellent edge without one **(A)**. Both grinding and honing can be done freehand. It just takes some practice.

To hone the blade, stand comfortably before your sharpening bench, one foot in front of the other. Grip the blade firmly with both hands **(B)**. Locate the bevel so it's flat on the surface of the stone. You can find this point by raising and lowering the blade slightly until you feel the entire bevel come into contact with the stone (you can raise the blade slightly if you want to hone only a secondary bevel). Next, lock your arms and move the blade across the stone by rocking your entire body forward **(C)** and then back. Take care not to change the angle of the blade on the stone as you work—that's the really hard part of working without a jig. It will take some practice to avoid putting a rounded bevel on the blade. Begin on the 220-grit stone and work your way up through the grits—1000, 4000, and finally the 8000. Then back the blade off as you normally would to remove the wire edge.

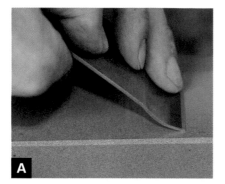
A

B

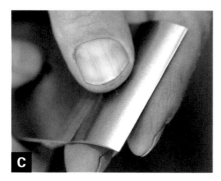
C

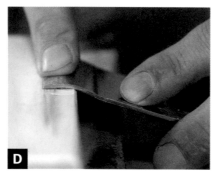
D

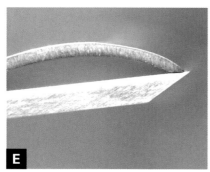
E

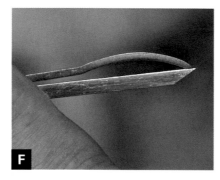
F

Preparing Chip Breakers

A new chip breaker, or back iron as it's also called, needs attention before a plane will work at its best. This is another one of those preliminary jobs that will not need repeating. Even a used tool will benefit from honing and setting up the chip breaker correctly.

The curved top of the chip breaker, from the front edge to a point about ¼ in. or so back, should be honed smooth. Start with the 220-grit stone **(A)** to remove any deep scratches or to reshape the front of the breaker into a smooth curve. Hold the chip breaker on the stone, and draw it toward you while rotating it up toward the vertical. Keep an eye on the tip. Repeat on the 1000-, 4000-, and 8000-grit stones.

After honing, buff the edge smooth with an abrasive hand block **(B)**, a fine diamond hone, or a cloth buffing wheel if you have one. The face should be smooth **(C)**.

The surface that contacts the blade also must be smooth and flat. It should meet the blade across the entire edge without gaps so wood chips will not become wedged between it and the blade. Before you start, blacken the flat on the edge of the breaker with a felt marker so you can check your progress as you go. You will be able to see exactly what part of the breaker is in contact with the stone and whether you are inadvertently tipping the blade as you work. Hold the flat edge of the chip breaker firmly on the stone, and hone it by stroking sideways down the length of the stone **(D)**. Use 220-, 1000-, and 4000-grit stones. It's not necessary to go all the way up to an 8000-grit stone.

When fitted to the blade, the chip breaker should be in firm contact along the entire front edge **(E)**. Hold it up to the light to check for gaps **(F)**. A honed chip breaker that fits well will noticeably improve the performance of a plane.

Paring and Mortise Chisels

The first step in sharpening any chisel is to pre-pare the back, just as you would a plane iron (A). Make sure to keep the chisel flat as you work it over the stone. If the back is very rough, start with a 220-grit stone, and work up through 1000, 4000, and 8000 grits until all scratches are removed and the back near the cutting edge is shiny (B). Next, grind the bevel. If you're unsure what the bevel angle is, check it with a gauge before grinding (C). It is easiest to keep a chisel square by using a jig that clamps the edges of the chisel. This honing guide has been modified by adding two pins (D) so it can be used more conveniently with the tool rest of a grinder. Set the chisel to the correct angle and grind (E). If you're using a high-speed grinder, don't grind to the very edge of the bevel. Instead, leave a small flat. It will help you avoid burning the edge, but it's not necessary when using a slow-speed grinder like this Tormek®. After grinding, set the chisel in the jig for a 1-degree or 2-degree sec-ondary bevel and hone (F), then back off the blade on the 8000-grit stone. If you record the distance the chisel must project from the honing guide to obtain a specific angle with a line on a piece of wood, you will be able to quickly set the next chisel to the same distance. Test for sharp-ness on end grain.

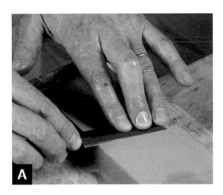

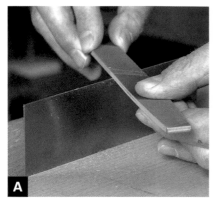

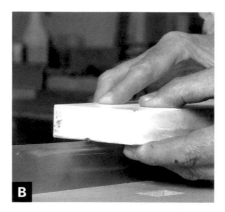

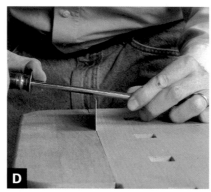

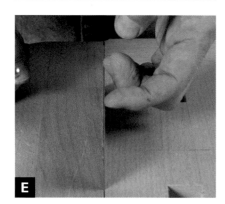

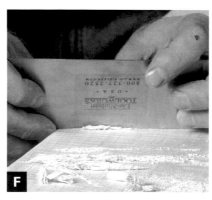

Card Scraper

The first step in sharpening a card scraper is to file the edge square. Hold the scraper in a vise, and use a fine file, such as a mill bastard **(A)**. Take light strokes. Hone the filed edge first with a 1000-grit stone and then with a 4000-grit stone, either by keeping the hand scraper in the vise and holding the stone **(B)** or by taking the scraper to a bench-mounted stone. Be careful to keep the scraper square to the stone. Then hone the flat sides of the scraper on a 1000-grit stone to remove any burr caused by filing **(C)**. Now you are ready to roll a burr with a your burnisher. To create a burr, hold the scraper upright in the vise. Begin by holding the burnisher at 90 degrees to the blade, then increase the angle with successive passes **(D)**. Use firm pressure. Work the edge until you can feel a distinct hook all the way across the edge **(E)**. Be careful not to cut yourself on the upright scraper! A properly sharpened scraper will produce shavings, not dust **(F)**.

Curved Scraper

A curved scraper is sharpened exactly the same way as a straight one. Start by honing the sides flat (**A**). Holding the scraper in a vise, file (**B**) and stone (**C**) as much of the curved edge as you plan to use. Be careful to keep the file and stone square to the scraper. Then burnish (**D**). The scraper is ready to use (**E**).

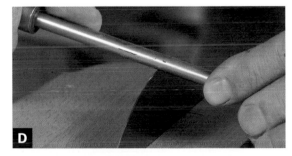

A

B

C

D

E

F

G

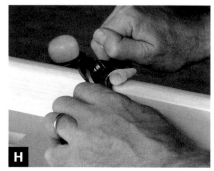

H

Concave Spokeshave Blade

Use slipstones or a large-diameter dowel wrapped with abrasive paper **(A)**. Cut pieces of paper large enough to wrap around the dowel, spray the back of the paper with adhesive **(B)** and roll the paper tightly to the dowel **(C)**. Roll a different grit paper on each end of the dowel (you'll need two dowels and four grits of paper). After preparing the back of the blade **(D)**, clamp the blade upright in a vise **(E)** and hone the bevel **(F)**. It helps to roll the dowel across the edge with each forward stroke. The finished blade should have a smooth radius **(G)** and cut cleanly **(H)**.

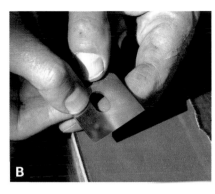

Flat Spokeshave Blade

Flat blades can be sharpened on waterstones or oilstones or on different grits of sandpaper as they are here. Start by gluing pieces of silicon-carbide paper to a piece of plate glass with spray adhesive. I'm using four grits: 220, 600, 1000, and 2000. Hone the back of the blade first **(A)** until the surface is smooth and polished **(B)**. Smaller spokeshave blades are short and don't fit in most jigs, but the Stanley jig will work for some of them **(C)**. Bevel angle is determined by the amount of blade that extends beyond the edge of the jig **(D)**. Another option is to bolt the blade to a small block of wood, then clamp the assembly in the honing guide or hone the bevel freehand. After preparing the back, hone the bevel on progressively finer grits of paper **(E)** until you are satisfied with the edge **(F)**. Then back off the blade on your finest grit to remove the wire edge **(G)**, and try the spokeshave on a scrap of wood **(H)**.

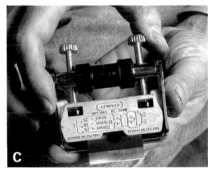

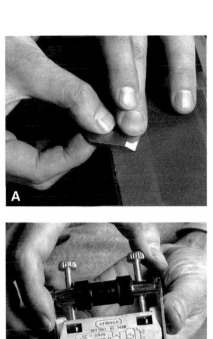

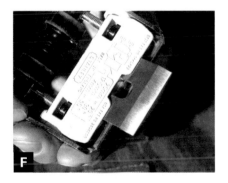

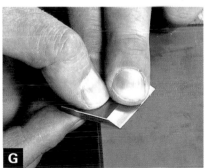

Jointing and Setting the Teeth

Over time, sawteeth may become uneven in height **(A)** and will need jointing to make them even again. Do this by using a smooth mill file held in a block of wood **(B)**. The block should keep the file at 90 degrees to the sawblade. Working the length of the sawblade evenly, file until the tops of the teeth are even. The flat spots on top of the teeth are likely to vary from tooth to tooth because they were not even to start with. Don't worry about that; teeth will be brought to a uniform shape as you file. Periodically, you also must reset the teeth. To do so, set every other tooth, then turn the saw around in the vise and set the remaining teeth **(C, D)**. Be careful to use the same hand pressure each time to keep the set as even as possible. Set the dial on the saw set to correspond to the number of teeth on the saw, then test it on the teeth nearest the handle first since they are used less. Use gentle pressure with the set.

Checking and Adjusting the Set

After filing, check the amount of set on both sides. An easy way to do this is with a square and a feeler gauge **(A)**. Rest the handle of the square on the teeth, then check the distance between the sawblade and the handle. Use a feeler gauge equal to the amount of set you are looking for. The set on this dovetail saw is 0.002 in., and the set should be even on both sides of the blade. If you find you've given the saw too much set, you can adjust it by clamping the teeth lightly in a small, smooth-jawed vise **(B)**. This is useful to know if you make a mistake, but it's not a normal part of setting a saw. Clamp one area of the blade, and apply gentle pressure. Loosen the vise and clamp the next section, taking care to use the same amount of pressure each time.

When you're finished, make a test cut with the saw. If the cut does not follow a straight pencil line, the set is uneven. The set is too heavy on the side of the saw that the kerf bends toward. You can correct too much set, or an uneven set, by lightly honing the heavy side with a fine sharpening stone, such as a fine India slipstone. Take only a few strokes, and hone from the back of the saw to the tip. Test again.

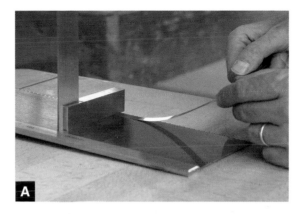

A

B

C

D

E

Sharpening a Ripsaw

After setting, blacken the tops of the teeth with a marker to make it easier to see what you are doing as you file **(A)**. Because the teeth are filed at 90 degrees to the sawblade, a ripsaw is the easiest kind of saw to sharpen. Start by putting the saw in a vise **(B)** so the teeth are as close as possible to the jaws. This will help to prevent the blade from vibrating and the file from chattering. You'll get better results if you make sure the saw is horizontal. Start filing the teeth closest to the handle, and work toward the front of the saw (this is a good habit because the back teeth usually get less use, so get your rhythm going here where it doesn't matter as much). On a ripsaw, the front of the sawtooth may be at 90 degrees or lean back slightly. This is called the rake angle. On this saw, it is 8 degrees. Cant the file at that angle, keeping an eye on the top of the file to maintain a consistent angle. You will be filing the front of one tooth and the back of the adjacent one at the same time.

Take the same number of strokes on each tooth. Keep the file horizontal **(C)**, at right angles to the blade **(D)** and at the proper rake angle. File only enough to remove the black mark on each tooth **(E)**. You can file all the teeth on a ripsaw from the same side, but since the file cuts the tooth leaning away from you with less chatter, it's a good practice to file every other tooth, then turn the saw around in the vise and repeat the filing process. Once again for the sake of consistency, start at the handle end and work toward the tip of the saw.

Sharpening a Crosscut Saw

Placing the crosscut saw in a vise, joint and set it as necessary. Blacken the teeth with a marker **(A)**, and reset the saw low in the vise, making sure it is horizontal. Beginning at the rear of the saw, file every other tooth with the same number of strokes and the same amount of pressure. The only difficulty in filing a crosscut saw is in maintaining the proper angles between the file and the teeth as you move down the length of the blade. In this case, the rake angle, the amount the tooth leans back, is 15 degrees. On a crosscut saw, the face of each tooth is angled off perpendicular, so the handle of the file is angled back toward the handle of the saw. Here, the angle also is 15 degrees **(B)**. This is the fleam angle. Stand comfortably and, keeping an eye on the top of the file, be careful to hold the file at a consistent angle in the stroke as you move down the saw.

It is helpful to use a guide of some sort to help maintain the right angle. A protractor, or a line, on the bench behind the saw, is one way **(C)**. File every other tooth (just the ones bent away from you), then flip the saw around and repeat from the other side. Test the saw on a scrap of wood **(D)**. If it does not follow a straight pencil line, the set is uneven. If the set is too heavy or uneven, correct it as you would on a ripsaw and test again.

Finishing

Surface Preparation

➤ Flattening and Smoothing with a Random Orbit Sander (p. 285)

➤ Hand-Sanding (p. 286)

➤ Smoothing an Edge Roundover (p. 287)

➤ Fairing and Sanding a Curve by Hand (p. 287)

Fixing Defects

➤ Mending Broken Wood (p. 288)

➤ Steaming a Dent (p. 288)

➤ Filling Gaps with Putty (p. 289)

➤ Filling Gaps with Epoxy (p. 289)

➤ Filling Cracks and Knots with Epoxy (p. 290)

➤ Filling Cracks and Splits with Cyanoacrylate Glue (p. 290)

Coloring Wood

➤ Applying Water-Based Stains and Dyes (p. 291)

➤ Applying Oil-Based Pigment Stains (p. 292)

Applying Finish

➤ Preparing the Brush (p. 293)

➤ The Basic Brushstroke (p. 293)

➤ Brushing Shellac and Lacquer (p. 294)

➤ Spraying Flat Surfaces (p. 295)

➤ Spraying Complicated Items (p. 296)

➤ Spraying Vertical Surfaces (p. 296)

➤ Applying Wiping Varnish (p. 297)

➤ Applying Pure Oil Finishes (p. 298)

➤ Brushing Varnish (p. 299)

➤ French Polishing (p. 300)

➤ Padding Shellac (p. 302)

➤ Brushing Water-Based Finish (p. 303)

➤ Spraying Water-Based Finish (p. 304)

Rubbing Out Finishes

➤ Rubbing to Satin (p. 305)

➤ Rubbing to Gloss (p. 306)

Flattening and Smoothing with a Random Orbit Sander

Although not as effective as a belt sander, a random orbit sander can be used to flatten a panel. Theoretically it doesn't matter which direction you move the tool because the large circular scratches from the spinning pad are cancelled out by the shorter "looping" scratches produced by the eccentric orbit **(A)**. However, using the same cross-hatching technique described for belt sanding helps ensure a more consistent surface. Most random orbit sanders have either a 5-in.-dia. pad or a 6-in.-dia. pad. I prefer a 6-in.-dia. pad because of its larger surface area.

After scraping any glue residue from the panel, outfit the sander with 100-grit paper or finer. Start by moving the sander at one angle **(B)**, then switch to the opposite **(C)**. After you reach your final grit, sand with that same grit by hand **(D)** to remove the cross-grain scratches.

One drawback to a random orbit sander is that its round pad won't reach well into corners and intersections. (For those purposes, try a vibrator sander.)

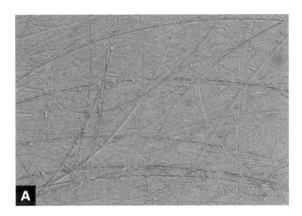

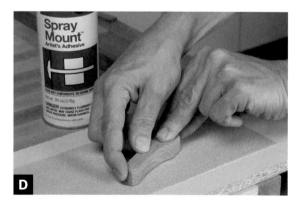

Hand-Sanding

Tear a sheet of 9-in.-by-11-in. sandpaper into quarters, and wrap it around a rubber or cork-faced sanding block. Moving back and forth along the grain using moderate pressure, sand from one end of the workpiece to the other (**A**). To maximize your effort, sand at a slight bias of about 7 to10 degrees to the grain, which cuts the wood fibers more effectively than sanding directly parallel to the grain. With each stroke, overlap the previous one by about half (**B**). Periodically remove the sawdust from your paper by swiping it across a gray synthetic abrasive pad or a piece of stiff-fiber carpet. Pay attention to the "bite" of the sandpaper as you work. Don't try to overuse the paper; when it starts slipping, toss it out.

When sanding small chamfers, use your left thumb and right forefinger to register the sanding block flat on the face of the chamfer (**C**). Position your left-hand forefinger under the bottom edge to steady the block. Afterward, ease the edges of the chamfer using 220-grit sandpaper on a sanding block.

Sanding small parts can be challenging because it's almost impossible to sand parts flat without rounding them over if you bring the sandpaper or tool to the piece. It's also extremely difficult to hold small parts, so it's best that you bring the part to the paper. The best way to sand small parts flat is to make a sanding board. Take a piece of sandpaper and glue it to a piece of melamine or plywood with contact adhesive. Then move the part back and forth on the sanding board to sand it (**D**).

[TIP] It doesn't make much difference if you sand past 220 grit. However, if you plan on using a water-based finish product, sanding to 320 will minimize grain-raising.

Smoothing an Edge Roundover

The edge created by a roundover router bit is one of the most common profiles you'll encounter in furniture. To sand this profile, begin by fairing what's left of the original square edge into the roundover portion. When sanding the end grain, which is dense and tough, start with sandpaper wrapped around a cork-faced sanding block (**A**). Hold the part securely and sand from the flat section of the edge onto the roundover, rolling the block around the profile so it's parallel to the grain at the end of the stroke. Next, smooth the roundover using a contour sanding block (**B**). To remove the cross-grain scratches this creates, follow up by sanding the roundover shoe-shine style, using a piece of sandpaper folded into thirds for strength (**C**). When you're sanding the long grain edges, a rubber contour sander takes care of all the operations above at once because the side grain isn't as tough as end grain (**D**).

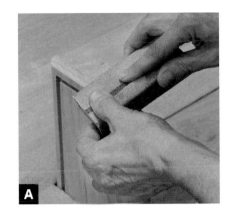
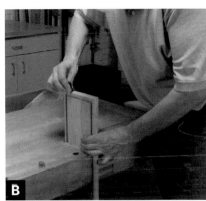
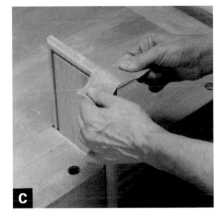

Fairing and Sanding a Curve by Hand

To remove the irregularities from a curve, begin by fairing it with a smoothing file. Hold the file with both hands at an angle to the edge, using the half-round side for concave curves (**A**) and the flat side for convex curves. Gauge the smoothness of the surface using your fingers and your eyes (**B**). The best surface comes from using a custom sanding block made by tracing the profile of the curve onto a piece of scrap (**C**). The sanding block need only be several inches long, but it should be slightly thicker than the edge to be sanded. Use double-sided tape or other adhesive to attach a piece of cork to the sanding block so the sandpaper will conform better to the profile (**D**).

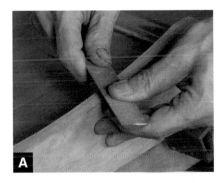

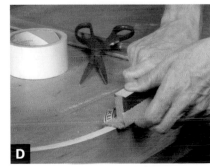

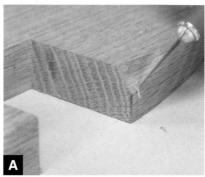

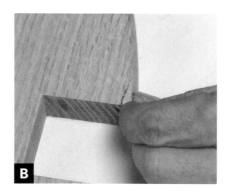

Mending Broken Wood

If a piece of wood breaks off during machining, glue it back on immediately to avoid losing it. If the piece has totally broken free, use an X-Acto knife to remove any small slivers that may keep the piece from properly reseating **(A)**. To reattach it, I use medium- or thick-viscosity cyanoacrylate glue, after smearing paste wax on my fingers to resist the glue when I press the part back into place **(B)**. Sand the repair smooth before the glue cures completely **(C)**. The resulting glue-and-sawdust mixture will create a form of "putty" that fills any gaps.

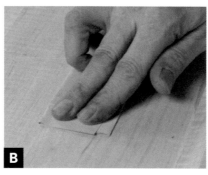

Steaming a Dent

An investigatory swipe with solvent before staining revealed a small dent in this curly maple top. To repair a dent like this, begin by wiping it with distilled water to swell the wood fibers. Then place a cloth wetted with distilled water over the dent and lay a hot iron set for "cotton" on top for about 30 seconds **(A)**. Check the dent periodically and steam again if necessary until it won't swell any further. Finish up by sanding the area smooth, gently feathering outward into the adjacent area **(B)**.

Filling Gaps with Putty

This gap was caused by an error in machining the rail for this frame-and-panel door. I would normally patch a gap this size by using solid wood. However, this gap is in short grain, and it would be nearly impossible to crosscut such a thin sliver of wood without breaking it. Instead, I applied latex putty after masking off the area to each side of the gap **(A)**. After the putty hardened, I removed the tape, which left a narrow ridge of putty as high as the tape was thick **(B)**. I finished up by leveling the surface, using sandpaper wrapped around a rigid block **(C)**.

If a gap is deep, as on this mitered table corner, it's better to use polyester resin filler, which shrinks very little. It's available in wood tones, or you can tint the base filler using dry pigments. Make sure to mask off the areas adjacent to the repair **(D)**.

Filling Gaps with Epoxy

Colorless five-minute epoxy is a great gap filler because it's fast-curing and easily tinted. When you add black and brown pigment, the epoxy will match the wenge edge inlay in this ash tabletop. To repair a gap next to the inlay, I first excavated the residual glue from the gap, using an X-Acto knife **(A)**. After masking off the ash, I mixed some dry pigment into just one part of the epoxy **(B)**. I then mixed the two parts together and applied the epoxy to the gap, leaving it a bit higher than the surrounding wood **(C)**. Though the epoxy starts to cure in five minutes, it's not hard enough to sand until several hours after application.

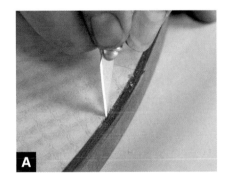
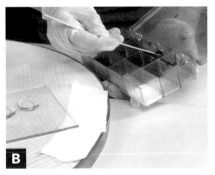

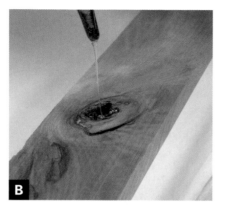

Filling Cracks and Knots with Epoxy

Epoxy serves as a great filler for large cracks and knots such as those on this walnut board. The epoxy will flow and settle better if you heat the knot first, using a heat gun on a low setting **(A)**. To apply the epoxy, simply dribble it into the knothole with a stick of wood or a small artist's palette knife **(B)**.

If you like, you can reinforce the board by driving slivers of wood into the splits after taping one side of the board and filling the holes with epoxy. It's best to rive the slivers from a scrap board using a chisel **(C)**. Because riven wood is split along the grain, it will conform to the shape of the crack better without breaking. Tap the slivers in lightly with a hammer **(D)**. After the epoxy has cured, saw off the ends of the slivers and sand the filled area.

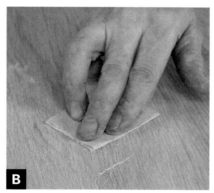
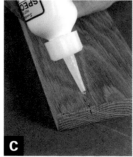

Filling Cracks and Splits with Cyanoacrylate Glue

Cyanoacrylate glue is available in various viscosities, ranging from watery to molasseslike. Use the thin-viscosity glue to fill small stress cracks like the one on this white oak top **(A)**. Afterward, simply sand the area with 150-grit sandpaper, which compresses sanding dust into the glue, making the crack virtually disappear **(B)**.

For larger cracks, like the one on the end of this white oak board, use the thicker-viscosity glue **(C)**. After applying the glue to the crack, sand the area to mix sanding dust into the glue, creating a paste that fills the crack **(D)**. A quick spritz with CA glue activator hardens the paste immediately. A second application may be necessary for large splits.

Applying Water-Based Stains and Dyes

Before staining wood like this coarse-grained oak, prepare the surface by sanding it through 220 grit. Then raise the grain by wetting it with distilled water **(A)**. After the water dries, resand the surface with 320-grit paper.

When staining casework like this nightstand, begin with the interior. This familiarizes you with the working quality of the stain and allows you to adjust the color if necessary before staining the more critical outside. Use a foam brush to work the stain into corners, but use a rag wherever possible, as it's faster and you'll avoid lap marks **(B)**. Work from the bottom up to avoid dripping the stain onto bare wood, and do the top last **(C)**.

If you need to darken the color slightly, apply a second coat of the stain. To darken or change the color dramatically, apply a stronger dye concentration or different color. It will be easier to judge the effect if you do this after the first coat has dried **(D)**.

[VARIATION] When applying dyes to a complicated piece, a plant mister works particularly well.

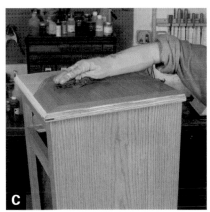

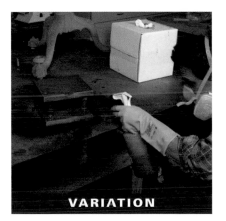

VARIATION

Applying Oil-Based Pigment Stains

To apply oil-based wiping stain, begin by stirring the contents thoroughly. Make sure you scrape all the pigment off the bottom of the can using the flat end of a stick and that you incorporate it into the liquid. Using a brush, rag, or pad, apply the stain to the wood in whichever direction you want (**A**). Within five minutes, wipe away the excess stain with a clean absorbent cloth, turning the cloth frequently to expose clean sections as you work. Wipe off the stain in any direction you wish. After you've removed as much of the excess stain as you can, lightly wipe parallel to the grain to minimize any application marks. Because pigment stains contain binder, you should now have a good read on what the wood will look like with a clear finish. If the stained surface is then too dark, wipe it down with mineral spirits or naphtha. If you need to lighten it further or if the stain has gotten tacky, use a synthetic abrasive pad soaked with the appropriate solvent for the stain (**B**). If the stain is the wrong color or not dark enough, simply apply a different stain (**C**).

Preparing the Brush

Brushing problems, such as debris in the finish and loose hairs, can be avoided by preparing the brush before you use it. The best preventive maintenance starts with storing brushes in drawers to protect them from sawdust and other airborne particles (A). Before you use a brush, flick the bristle ends back and forth to displace dust (B). Remove any loose hairs if they're visible. Dunk the brush all the way up to the metal ferrule in the solvent used for thinning and cleaning the finish. Scrape the excess solvent off the brush by dragging it across the lip of the container, and then blot up the excess with a clean, dry cotton rag (C). This solvent dip conditions the bristles, makes the initial coats go on more smoothly, and makes the brush easier to clean later.

The Basic Brushstroke

The basic brushstroke for tops or other flat, horizontal surfaces allows you to flow on a finish. Condition the bristles of the brush as described in the preceding essay, then dip the bristles to about half of their total length into a container filled with the finish. Gently squeeze off the excess against the sides of the container (A). Starting about 3 in. in from the edge (B), pull the brush lightly toward the edge and lift up at the end (C).

Come back to where you started, and brush to the opposite end to complete the pass (D). Duplicate the procedure, overlapping your strokes from ¼ in. to ½ in. to complete (E). Try to work quickly to allow yourself enough time to "tip off" the finish afterward. This is done by holding the brush perpendicular to the board and lightly dragging it across the surface. Varnishes allow you a good deal of open time to come back and tip off, while fast-drying lacquers and shellac make it more difficult.

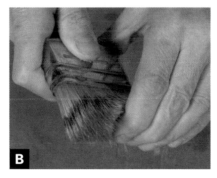
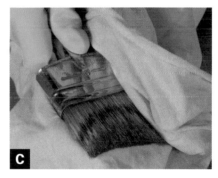

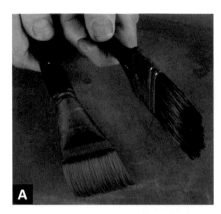

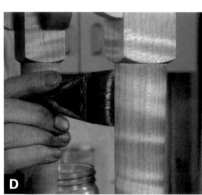

Brushing Shellac and Lacquer

To lay down fast-drying finishes like lacquer and shellac, I like to use a technique that deposits a thinner, more quickly drying coat. When applying shellac, I use a 1-lb.-cut mixture. For lacquer, I use brushing lacquer thinned one-to-one with lacquer thinner. The best brushes for this technique are artist's brushes that don't have much bristle content, so they hold less finish **(A)**. This means a smaller chance of depositing thicker amounts of finish when you start your brushstroke. Rather than flowing on a coat the width of the brush, you can work sections at a time.

Working a 4-in-by-4-in. section, begin near an edge and drag the brush off the edge of the workpiece **(B)**. Reload the brush, and work another section and then whisk back and forth quickly between the two sections to blend them together. These brushes are well suited to complicated or small areas, as you can flick whisper-thin layers of shellac or lacquer onto edges **(C)**. When brushing round or turned items, you can use a light "flicking" stroke in a round-and-round fashion to prevent drips **(D)**.

Spraying Flat Surfaces

The basic spray technique for tops and other flat surfaces is called a crosshatch, box-coat, or double-pass spray. Spray all four edges first, holding the gun perpendicular to the edge, then bring the gun up to a 45-degree angle to the surface, and spray once to get extra finish on top of the edges **(A)**. Working at a 90-degree angle to grain, start your first pass at the edge closest to you. With the gun off the edge, pull the trigger so finish is coming out before it hits the edge **(B)**. and move it across the surface, holding it perpendicular to the top and at the correct distance. (Your gun manual should provide guidelines.) Keep the trigger depressed until after you've passed the opposite edge of the workpiece, and then repeat the pass, overlapping the first one by half **(C)**. Continue until you reach the end, then rotate the workpiece 90 degrees and repeat **(D)**. (It helps to work on a turntable.) Crosshatching ensures even coverage of finish.

[TIP] **You can wipe away a drip immediately with your finger as long as you don't risk damaging a delicate toner or glaze underneath. Respray the affected area afterward.**

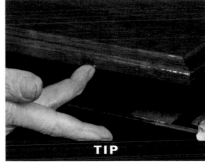

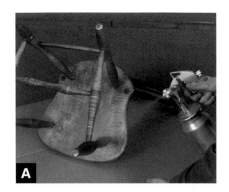

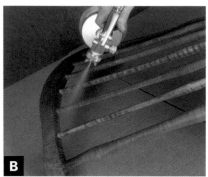

Spraying Complicated Items

Spraying complicated, three-dimensional projects like chairs requires that you work from the least visible parts first to the most visible. For a chair, turn it over to have better access to the stretchers, and then begin by spraying the bottom of the seat **(A)**. Don't forget the bottom of the crest rail or similar unseen areas that need finish **(B)**. Spray the back and crest, and the edges of the seat, but leave the top of the seat for last. To get finish into the top back of the seat where the spindles are connected, come in from the front of the seat and spray right through the spindles **(C)**. Then quickly rotate the chair 180 degrees by spinning your turntable, and spray the back of the seat top **(D)**.

Spraying Vertical Surfaces

To efficiently spray a large vertical side like the one on this entertainment center, it helps to use a remote pressure-feed spray rig. Start at the bottom of one side and spray upward **(A)**. With a pressure-feed rig, just orient the gun 90 degrees to the side, which will lay down a horizontal pattern. If you use a gravity-feed or suction gun, you can turn the air cap to orient the pattern horizontally. Overlap each previous pass by half, as when spraying horizontal surfaces **(B)**, but make only a single pass to avoid drips. Placing items on a turntable allows you to easily spin them to spray both sides. For face frames, start from the bottom and work up. If possible, adjust the width of the gun's fan pattern to match the width of the frame members **(C)**.

Applying Wiping Varnish

Before applying varnish by wiping, first determine the solids content of the product you'll be using. If the solids content exceeds 30 percent—as is the case with most modern varnishes—thin the varnish one-to-one with mineral spirits **(A)**. Alternatively, you can use naphtha as the thinner, which will speed up the dry time.

Flood the first coat on and wipe it off after a few minutes **(B)**. This coat should be dry enough so you can apply a second coat in two to four hours. I usually apply subsequent coats using a folded nontextured paper towel like Viva™. Using a flip-top bottle, I dispense the varnish onto about an inch of the leading edge of the paper towel and wipe it on the workpiece **(C)**. Rather than applying the finish and wiping it away like an oil, wipe a coat of varnish on thin, then leave it to dry. You can typically apply two or three coats per day. Sanding between coats isn't necessary.

After applying three or four coats, you can lightly sand the varnish to smooth the surface. This is one of the key steps to a high-quality finish. Using 600-grit paper, sand the surface using a light touch **(D)**. Finish up by smoothing it with 0000 steel wool. You can stop here for a natural, low-luster sheen, or apply additional coats for more luster and depth.

Applying Pure Oil Finishes

Before applying the first coat of a pure oil finish like boiled linseed oil, warm it for faster penetration. Begin by heating the oil to 150° F. in a double boiler **(A)**. Flood the first coat on liberally, replenishing any dry spots as they appear **(B)**. Allow the oil to sit for 15 to 30 minutes, and then remove all the excess from the surface with a rag.

Let the first coat dry overnight, then apply a second unheated coat, exactly the same as the first, except that you can use a piece of 600-grit wet/dry sandpaper to wet-sand the second coat into the wood **(C)**. This creates a slurry of oil and sanding dust that will make the surface smoother by helping to fill the pores. Afterward, wipe the surface clean with a rag, leaving a thin film of oil. You can apply as many additional coats as you like. Each one will increase the depth and luster of the wood. After applying the final coat, you can wax the dried finish or burnish it with a clean, dry rag to increase luster.

[**VARIATION**] **Thinning pure tung oil one-to-one with mineral spirits will make it dry faster. Preheating the oil isn't necessary in this case.**

VARIATION

Brushing Varnish

When brushing on varnish, apply a sealer coat first. You can use a varnish sanding sealer or simply thin the first coat of varnish one-to-one with naphtha. I often use shellac instead because it dries enough to scuff-sand in 30 minutes **(A)**. After scuff- sanding, use a tack cloth to remove all the sanding debris **(B)**.

Next, brush on a coat of unthinned varnish using the "flow-on" technique.

▶ See *"Brushing Shellac and Lacquer"* on p. 294.

Tip off the varnish to level it out afterward **(C)**. Apply a minimum of two coats—more if you want a thicker build. You do not have to sand after every coat as long as the coats are applied within a day of each other. However, you may want to scuff-sand between coats to flatten out brushstrokes or remove bits of debris. You can use wet/dry sandpaper lubricated with mineral spirits, or dry sandpaper, as shown here. Some varnishes gum up sandpaper, but you can remove the gummy "corns" by swiping the sandpaper on a piece of synthetic abrasive pad **(D)**.

To brush vertical surfaces, apply the varnish by first brushing from side to side. Then smooth it out by tipping it off, moving from top to bottom **(E)**.

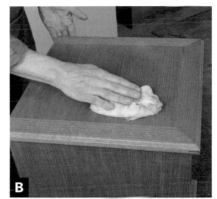

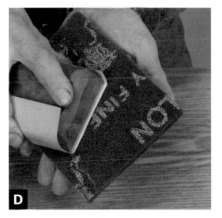

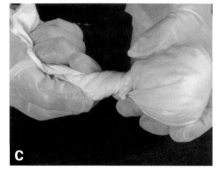

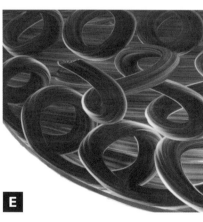

French Polishing

Begin by applying a coat of boiled linseed oil to the surface, rubbing it in with a clean cotton rag **(A)**. When you're working with open-pored woods, the next step is to fill the pores. To do this, sprinkle some rottenstone over the surface and work it into the grain using a circular motion. (You can use 4F pumice on unstained wood.) As the rottenstone mixes with the oil on the surface, it should become dark and less chalky looking **(B)**. If it stays chalky looking, add more oil. Examine the surface in backlighting to make sure all the grain is filled, then wipe it with a clean cloth to remove the excess. Apply more oil and rottenstone the next day, and then let the piece sit for at least three days.

Next, apply a coat of shellac using a two-part pad made by wrapping a 14-in.-square of 80 thread-per-inch unbleached muslin around a golf ball–sized wad of cotton or wool **(C)**. Pour an ounce of denatured alcohol into the core and twist the ends of the muslin over, leaving no seams or wrinkles on the bottom. Flatten the pad by pressing it down gently down on a clean surface. Then open the cover again and "charge" the core with 1 oz. of dewaxed 1-lb.-cut shellac. Wipe the shellac onto the workpiece in straight strokes, moving from one edge to the other three times. When the shellac dries out, recharge the core with more.

When the shellac starts becoming too tacky to wipe, apply a few drops of baby oil to the bottom of the pad to lubricate it **(D)**. Then start rubbing in circles and figure eights. Make 6-in. to 8-in.-wide curlycues at the perimeter and rub the center area, moving in a figure-eight pattern **(E)**. (Note that the rubbing pattern shown in the photo was made using white polishing compound simply to show the process.) After 15 to 20 minutes, the surface should start to shine. Your goal here is to "body" the shellac enough to completely fill the grain. This bodying process will go faster if you switch to a 2-lb.-cut shellac. When the grain appears filled and the surface is covered with a "lens" of shellac, stop and let the finish dry overnight.

The next day, sand the shellac lightly with P600-grit sandpaper lubricated with mineral spirits or naphtha **(F)**. Afterward, smooth the surface further with 0000 steel wool or gray abrasive pads. Then remove the sanding residue and continue the bodying process using 2-lb.-cut shellac, lubricating the pad with baby oil and moving it in curlycues and figure eights to build the shellac evenly. When the pad starts to dry out, instead of charging it with more shellac, simply bear down harder using 30 to 40 lbs. of pressure **(G)**. (You can test your pressure using a bathroom scale.) You're finished with the bodying process when the pores are no longer visible after an overnight drying. This process may take three days for open-pored woods, while close-pored woods might require only a day.

After the surface dries for a day or so, you're ready to clear the residual oil from it. To do this, wipe the surface with a clean, soft cloth dampened with naphtha. Then, in preparation for bringing up the final brilliant shine, first pour 1 oz. of denatured alcohol into a clean absorbent cotton cloth **(H)**. Work the cloth between your hands to distribute the alcohol until it feels as moist as a dog's nose. Then gently sweep the rag across the finished surface, working more quickly as the alcohol dries out, until you're buffing it as though shining shoes with a brush **(I)**. As the rag loads up with oil, change its position to present fresh material to the workpiece.

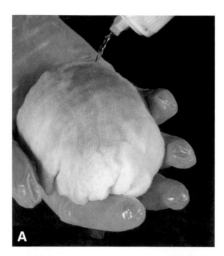

Padding Shellac

Padding shellac is a technique, not a product. The procedure differs from French polishing in that no lubricating oil is used. Also, the application pad is made and used differently.

Make an applicator pad by wadding up a lint-free absorbent cloth so there are no seams or wrinkles on the bottom. Squirt about 1 oz. of denatured alcohol into the pad, squeezing the cloth to distribute the alcohol throughout and to wring out the excess. Next, squirt 1 to 2 oz. of 2-lb.-cut shellac onto the bottom **(A)**. Apply the first coat to the workpiece, flooding the surface, then wiping off the excess **(B)**. After 30 minutes, scuff-sand with P600-grit sandpaper and remove the dust.

To apply the next coat, load the pad with shellac again. Beginning at the edge nearest you, swoop down onto one end of the workpiece, dragging the pad fully across it **(C)**, then swooping up off the opposite end, like an airplane landing and immediately taking off again **(D)**. Next, reverse the stroke you just made, making a swooping pass over the same area but from the opposite direction. Continue across the full width of the workpiece in this same fashion, always moving in the direction of the grain. After you've covered the entire workpiece, it should be dry enough to repeat the process again from the beginning. Afterward, finish the edges of the workpiece in the same manner.

As the pad starts to dry out, reload it with more shellac. A dry pad can leave streaks or fibers in the sticky shellac. After the surface dries, rub out any application marks using fine sandpaper followed by 0000 steel wool. Build the finish to any thickness you wish.

Padding is best suited to flat surfaces. When finishing corners and tight areas where the pad can't easily reach, begin by applying several coats of shellac with a brush to create an initial build.

Brushing Water-Based Finish

If you wish, you can use dewaxed shellac as a sealer under water-based finish. On this cherry table it will eliminate grain raising and seal in any residual sodium hydroxide used as a chemical stain (A). If you don't wish to use shellac, instead sponge the wood with distilled water after sanding it to 220 grit to raise the grain. After the wood feels dry to the touch, resand it with 320-grit paper.

Dip a synthetic bristle brush into water to condition it, then wring out the excess. Strain the finish through a fine or medium strainer into a cup, and dip the brush halfway up the bristles into the finish. Press the bristles against the side of the cup to remove excess finish (B). Apply the finish in smooth, wet strokes with the tip of the brush (C). Try to flow the finish off the tip of the brush without pressing down too hard on the bristles. While the finish is still wet, level it off by lightly dragging the tip of the bristles fully across the surface while holding the brush vertically. To brush edges, corners, and nonflat areas, lightly load just the very tip of the brush for more precise control (D). Work in a warm room with plenty of air circulation to help the finish dry properly, but don't blow air across the finish as you're brushing it.

After the first coat dries, it may feel rough. If the wood is unstained, you can scuff-sand it at this point. With stained wood, though, you may want to apply an additional coat before scuff-sanding to avoid cutting through the stain. On complicated areas use a cushioned abrasive pad (E). Two coats suffice for the base of this table, but three were applied to the top, which will see a bit more wear.

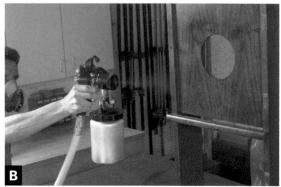

Spraying Water-Based Finish

To set up for spraying a water-based finish, first strain the finish into the gun cup, then adjust the gun for low fluid delivery. To get the feel of the operation, begin by spraying on a nonshow surface on your project, such as the underside of a table or the inside of a cabinet **(A)**. Move the gun in a slow, steady motion, maintaining a consistent distance from the workpiece. After completing a section, check the surface for drips or runs, particularly on perpendicular surfaces. If you see them, you're applying too heavy a coat, and you'll need to adjust the gun's fluid delivery, move it faster across the workpiece, or back it up a bit as you spray. Once the gun is adjusted properly and you get the feel for how fast to move the gun, spray the outside of your project **(B)**. Use a nail board for finishing the doors.

The first coat should be hard enough to sand in about an hour. However, if your workpiece was stained, it's better to apply two coats of finish before sanding to minimize the chance of cutting through the stain. Use 400-grit or finer sandpaper **(C)**. Remove the sanding dust by wiping the surface with a damp rag, then with a tack cloth suited for water-based finishes. Apply the final coats lightly, about an hour or two apart **(D)**. I wanted a flat finish for this clock, so I applied two coats of gloss topped by a coat of flat to avoid a hazy look on the dark wood from three coats of flat finish.

Rubbing to Satin

The perfectly flat and silky finish often seen on high-end furniture is likely a rubbed satin finish. This is best done on evaporative finishes, but you can do it on reactive finishes as long as your final coat is at least 2 to 3 mils thick when dry.

Start by wet sanding to level the finish. Use rubbing oil, which is messier than soapy water but makes the sandpaper cut faster and last longer. Start with 400-grit (P600-800) paper wrapped around a cork block, and continue up to 600 grit (P1200) **(A)**. Here, I sand right up to the edges where the raised profiled edge starts, and switch to a gray synthetic pad for the molded edge. Wipe away the slurry and make sure the surface has an even pattern of scratches with no low spots **(B)**. If just a few isolated imperfections remain, it may be prudent to live with them rather than risk cutting through the finish with continued sanding.

If you would like the steel wool to cut a little less aggressively, you can use a steel wool lubricant called wool lube or wool wax, which is a thick, syrupy soap. Do not use this product on shellac or water-based finishes because its alkalinity may harm them. For these finishes use rubbing oil. After dribbling some on the surface, use a cork block wrapped with steel wool to rub the surface, moving in the direction of the grain to create a "brushed-metal" effect **(C)**. Go over the whole surface from one edge to the other at least six times. Rub the molded edges by hand **(D)**.

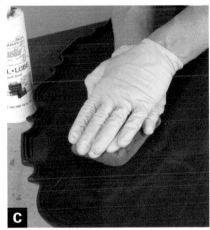

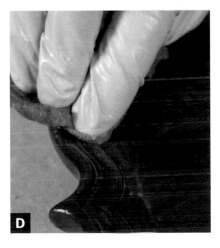

Rubbing to Gloss

Start by sanding with 320-grit (P600) paper lubricated with soapy water made by adding a capful of dishwashing detergent to a quart of water. Wrap a quarter-sheet of sandpaper around a cork block and wet sand the finish to remove brush marks and other defects **(A)**. The surface should have a dull sheen after you wipe away the slurry. On narrow pieces like frames, sand by hand to avoid cutting through the edges **(B)**.

Continue wet-sanding to 1000 grit (P2000). Traditionally, abrasive powders have been used after wet sanding to bring the surface sheen up higher. Use 4F pumice first, which removes the scratches left by the fine sandpaper. Rub the pumice with a damp rag in circular motion **(C)**. To bring the finish up to gloss, rub with rottenstone next. The pumice and rottenstone will leave a slight residue in the open pores of woods like mahogany, so in those cases, finish up by applying dark wax **(D)**. If you want a slightly less glossy surface, rub with 0000 steel wool after applying the wax.

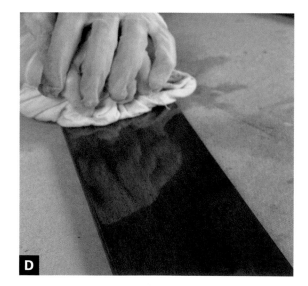

Index

Other Books in the Series:

HARDCOVER

**The Complete Illustrated
Guide to Joinery**
Gary Rogowski
ISBN 1-56158-401-0
Product #070535
$39.95 U.S.
$54.95 Canada

**The Complete Illustrated
Guide to Furniture and
Cabinet Construction**
Andy Rae
ISBN 1-56158-402-9
Product #070534
$39.95 U.S.
$54.95 Canada

**The Complete Illustrated
Guide to Shaping Wood**
Lonnie Bird
ISBN 1-56158-400-2
Product #070533
$39.95 U.S.
$54.95 Canada

**Taunton's Complete Illustrated
Guide to Finishing**
Jeff Jewitt
ISBN 1-56158-592-0
Product #070712
$39.95 U.S.
$54.95 Canada

**Taunton's Complete Illustrated
Guide to Sharpening**
Tom Lie-Nielsen
ISBN 1-56158-657-9
Product #070737
$39.95 U.S.
$54.95 Canada

**Taunton's Complete Illustrated
Guide to Using
Woodworking Tools**
Lonnie Bird
ISBN 1-56158-597-1
Product #070729
$39.95 U.S.
$54.95 Canada

**Taunton's Complete Illustrated
Guide to Turning**
Richard Raffan
ISBN 1-56158-672-2
Product #070757
$39.95 U.S.
$54.95 Canada

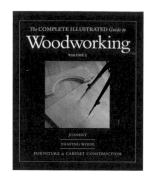

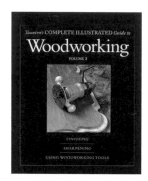

THE COMPLETE ILLUSTRATED GUIDES SLIPCASE SET VOLUME 1

**The Complete Illustrated
Guide to Joinery**

**The Complete Illustrated
Guide to Furniture and
Cabinet Construction**

**The Complete Illustrated
Guide to Shaping Wood**
ISBN 1-56158-602-1
Product #070665
$120.00 U.S.
$170.00 Canada

TAUNTON'S COMPLETE ILLUSTRATED GUIDES SLIPCASE SET VOLUME 2

**Taunton's Complete Illustrated
Guide to Using Woodworking
Tools**

**Taunton's Complete Illustrated
Guide to Sharpening**

**Taunton's Complete Illustrated
Guide to Finishing**
ISBN 1-56158-745-1
Product #070817
$120.00 U.S.
$170.00 Canada

PAPERBACK

**Taunton's Complete Illustrated
Guide to
Period Furniture Details**

Lonnie Bird
ISBN 1-56158-590-4
Product #070708
$27.00 U.S.
$38.00 Canada

**Taunton's Complete Illustrated
Guide to Choosing and
Installing Hardware**

Bob Settich
ISBN 1-56158-561-0
Product #070647
$29.95 U.S.
$42.00 Canada

**Taunton's Complete Illustrated
Guide to Box Making**
Doug Stowe
ISBN 1-56158-593-9
Product #070721
$24.95 U.S.
$34.95 Canada